# <u>In</u>clusive
# Systemic
# Economic
# Injustice

## Corruption, Exclusion, & Oppression in My Hometown:
### How White and Black Public Officials Injure Black Communities, Today

## Brian K. Rice
*The Community Engineer*

WE MUST TRIUMP DESPITE GREAT ODDS. OUR FUTURE, FAMILIES, AND OUR COMMUNITY MUST HAVE THE BEST OF US. OUR RIGHTS ARE WORTH FIGHTING FOR. OUR FUTURE IS WORTH FIGHTING FOR. OUR COMMUNITY IS WORTH FIGHTING FOR.

BRIAN K. RICE

**Inclusive - Systemic Economic Injustice**
Corruption, Exclusion & Oppression in My Hometown:
The transition from White to Black public officials and overt to
inclusive discrimination in Black communities post-2020.
By Brian K. Rice, The Community Engineer
www.briankrice.com

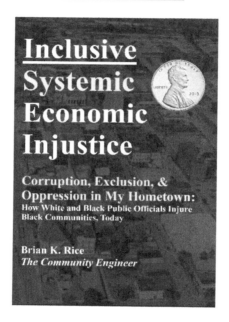

# Copyright page

The Brian K. Rice papers, paper 1: A Federal Based Case Study on Economic Deprivation of Rights in Black Communities

## Inclusive - Systemic Economic Injustice

Corruption, Exclusion & Oppression in My Hometown: How White and Black Public Officials Injure Black Communities, Today

Published by:
Brian K. Rice
Birmingham, AL
www.briankrice.com
Inclusive Systemic Economic Injustice
Book Title Credits
© Copyright October 1 26 2024 by Brian K. Rice
Edition 1
ISBN: 9798862814521
Imprint: Independently published
Written by Brian K. Rice

Printed in the United States of America.

I would like to dedicate this book to those who have been deprived of their rights by their elected officials.

I am grateful for the support of the men and women who helped me during my isolated times while preparing this book. I would like to express my gratitude to three groups of people from different faiths. I would like to thank the men of the Nation of Islam who have shared their knowledge and encouraged me along the way. I would like to thank those of the Christian faith who have encouraged me with biblical text who did not falter and looked the other way. Lastly, I would like to thank the one lone soldier who has stepped away from his original belief in faith who has also encouraged me and guided me to stand for the deprived in our community.

I would also like to thank my parents for instilling the principles that have guided me throughout my life. Although I am grateful for having the ability to prepare this book, I am also angry that we live in a world where evil backed by public servants can crush a persons dream for building a better future for themselves, their family, their future family and their community. I hope that my experiences can help others to stand up for their rights, family, and community.

Lastly, I want to express my gratitude to the friends and former friends who have shown me their true colors. This journey has not been an easy one, and I sincerely do not wish it upon anyone. Therefore, I have done what I can to share my story with the larger community to help others stand up for their rights and their community.

Table of Contents

# ABOUT THE AUTHOR AND HIS WHY.

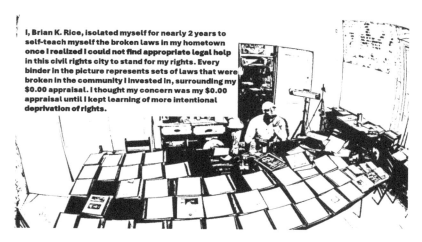

I, Brian K. Rice, isolated myself for nearly 2 years to self-teach myself the broken laws in my hometown once I realized I could not find appropriate legal help in this civil rights city to stand for my rights. Every binder in the picture represents sets of laws that were broken in the community I invested in, surrounding my $0.00 appraisal. I thought my concern was my $0.00 appraisal until I kept learning of more intentional deprivation of rights.

I, Brian K. Rice, isolated myself for nearly 2 years, determined to learn the facts and depth of broken laws in my hometown once I realized I could not find appropriate legal help in this city, known for its civil rights movement, to stand for my rights. Every binder in the picture represents sets of laws that were broken, surrounding my $0.00 appraisal. I thought my concern was my $0.00 appraisal until I learned of more intentional deprivation of rights for the community and city in which I invested in.

I was born and raised in Birmingham, AL, a full generation after the Civil Rights Movement and today, it is exactly 60 years since the fire hoses and 44 years since the first black mayor.

I dreamed of making it big in baseball like many kids. An academic scholarship took me to my beloved Historically Black College and University (HBCU) on the hill of Alabama A&M University (AAMU). The men of the Nu Epsilon Chapter of Omega Psi Phi Fraternity, Inc. on the hill prepared me with an intense focus on key principles I used daily. AAMU prepared me for the world. I have traveled throughout the U.S. and other countries through engineering, but there was always something that bothered me in my travels: the conditions of the deprived black communities.

Outside of traveling for work regularly, I made Knoxville, TN; Milwaukee, WI; Richmond, VA; Charlotte, NC; and Houston, TX, home for a considerable period of time before moving back to Birmingham.

I loved living in Charlotte, NC, more than any other city. I was selected to be a member of the statewide E.A. Morris Fellowship for Emerging Leaders, the organization funded by mostly Republicans, trained the next generation of leaders where some were likely Democrat leaders, but the majority were likely Republican leaders. The E.A. Morris Fellowship was an awesome experience. My confidence increased tenfold during this period of time as we discussed various aspects of politics, non-profits and our big project that we had to present at the end of the year-long program. I prepared this huge proposal for the Governor of North Carolina around economic development, small business development and workforce development.

I joined the Charlotte Junior Chamber of Commerce during the 2008 – 2009 recession period. This group was a great training ground for economic development, and we repeated the Jaycees Creed in every meeting. The words within the creed state, "That government should be of laws rather than of men," are instrumental in my federal lawsuit against the City of Birmingham for their actions that caused more deprivation in my hometown in already deprived communities.

"We Believe: That faith in God gives meaning and purpose to human life; That the brotherhood of man transcends the sovereignty of nations; That economic justice can best be won by free men through free enterprise; That government should be of laws rather than of men; That earth's great treasure lies in human personality; And that service to humanity is the best work of life."

The Urban League of Central Carolinas embraced me the moment I arrived in Charlotte, NC, and I learned the great work of the National Urban League. I became a student of their past and their present.

There are a few additional key aspects in Charlotte that prepared me for Birmingham:

(1) I came across a Birmingham, AL, 2010 AL.com article titled 'The Killing Years' that displayed 140 males and around 130 black people arrested for murder. The picture of all these men has constantly reminded me why we must create better opportunities in our communities. The Killing Years picture is one of my whys for moving back to Birmingham and finding a way to create more constructive spaces. I had no idea of the amount of people and the color of people who would attempt to stop me.

(2) I went to Caribou Coffee in the Dilworth Neighborhood one day, and I wore a shirt that said, "Birmingham, the Magic City." A white gentleman approached me and said, "Birmingham, the Tragic City." This individual was a student at Birmingham Southern during the 1960s Civil Rights movement, and he said he and his friends made that statement when they came back years later and looked over the city from Red Mountain. The man told me I must read 'Slavery by Another Name' by Douglas Blackmon and Carry Me Home by Diane McWhorter. I read Slavery by Another Name immediately, and I saw the darkness of how Birmingham and Alabama made their wealth through the early 1900s through an immoral process of arresting black men primarily for any made-up charge whenever they needed mine workers, timber workers, road workers, railroad workers and so on. This tactic allowed Birmingham to sell the country's cheapest steel, making them a direct economic threat to Pittsburgh and U.S. Steel. U.S. Steel bought out every entity they could in the region, and they continued the torture of black laborers through convict leasing for nearly 2 more decades to increase their profits. Reading 'Slavery by Another Name' made me wonder and research other economic aspects of the black community in my hometown going back to 1817.

My mother asked me what I wanted for Christmas a few months earlier. I said I didn't know at first, and then I said can you buy me some history books on Birmingham. My mother went to Reed's Bookstore, Birmingham's most famous historic bookstore. The store appears to be jumbled together with rare books, but it is in order.

Nearly 15 years later, I visit Reed's Bookstore the Birmingham Public Library archives, and more regularly searching for facts that confirm the black experience in the Birmingham area for the past 200-plus years. I became a self-made archivist with an intense focus on the economic conditions of black Birmingham. This passion has been my greatest tool to stand against the systems of injustice in my hometown. I can recite articles and books with ease. The only issue is that most people around me don't know their history, which is by design, and they repeat the unfortunate aspects.

I read old city council reports, Birmingham Chamber of Commerce reports, Alabama Power reports, microfilm and many other mediums as a fun pastime that takes my mind off of the active fight in front of me. I have always been intrigued by the fact that Birmingham has had 4 plus decades of Black mayors surrounded by decaying and deprived black communities.

Each experience from AAMU to Omega Psi Phi to Engineering to the Charlotte Jr Chamber of Commerce and my intense passion for studying local black economic conditions has prepared me for my stance against systemic economic injustice in my hometown.

I often think of 'The Bridge Builder' by Ms. Will Allen Dromgoole, where the author reminds us that just because you made it over the obstacle doesn't mean the person behind you will. It is for you to build the bridge for those coming after you. The systems of economic injustice are crushing human possibility, and I have chosen to fight for my rights and the rights of those coming behind me. Deprivation is widespread in our communities across the country.

The engineering principles I learned at AAMU and in the workforce for over 20 years have prepared me to look at communities and the existing problems, like any system that needs improvement. I am often called the Community Engineer for how I approach the concerns I see.

I, Brian K. Rice, stand for our economic rights because, without economic rights, our families and communities will remain malnourished, unhealthy, and imbalanced.

## Part 1 of the Introduction: My Close Friend, the FBI, and the Perfection of Racism:

This book is divided into two critical components. The first focuses on small business conditions that deprive black businesses of opportunities created by black leaders. The second addresses real estate injustice in my hometown.

All statements that require the courts to confirm during the judicial process of being innocent until proven guilty are alleged. As the author, I have done my absolute best to back every statement with actual sources for the facts that involve matters of public interest and matters of public concern that fall under our 1st amendment rights, especially for public figures, public servants and those who volunteered to be public servants. As the reader, you may determine for yourself the truth of what is causing our communities more deprivation.

Why did I name the book Inclusive Systemic Economic Injustice? It is because I realized that black communities in many cities across the country are not just faced with traditional forms of racism, discrimination, oppression, redlining, and inside deals violating their rights from others. Black leaders have joined in the oppression since securing political access and corporate jobs since integration. Many are oppressing their former communities at devastating levels. Many know they are being oppressed by their own in addition to an already stacked system. Many feel powerless to do anything about it. To whom can the intentionally deprived turn to for help when their own in leadership are crushing them?

I came back to Birmingham, and it took me a while to recognize who and what entities are intentionally breaking laws to deprive our communities.

When I realized one of my closest friends in life was on the other side of the federal evidence I've sent to state and federal agencies regarding real concerns about white-collar crimes and economic suppression in my hometown, I knew I had a choice; that choice was to walk away and act like it is not happening even though it is unlawfully crushing me and my community economically or it is for me to stand up. It is not easy to stand even when the circumstances are minor. I have witnessed too much deprivation of rights inside the black community, breeding more deprivation and self-destruction. I chose to stand up and put community over friendship. I then said to myself that Jim Crow isn't the same Jim in Birmingham, AL, and across many cities in America. My friend and others who carry the DNA of the oppressed American Descendants of Slavery have taken up the mantle and chosen the traits of their former oppressors to suppress their own. I don't know of other times this former best friend was in the middle of rigging resources, but one day, I asked the following question before mentioning any lawsuit for what he was involved in that would take place nearly 2 years later.

I said, "What happened? Why was Downtown Ensley left out? He responded and said he was there when they were discussing Ensley. He then said he was the one who likely prepared the paperwork that his CEO signed off on. Moments later, the best friend said, "I plead ignorance if this ever comes up in court." He stood up and walked off, and at that point, I knew he chose fraud over friendship. I had never researched his previous actions until that evening, and I saw his connections as a pawn on the table willing to turn a blind eye to his friend and his community. I have debated whether I will write a former best friend in the lawsuit, even though he has chosen fraud over me. I expect a discovery phase in court, and I plan to subpoena him at a minimum to see if he will continue to choose fraudulent concealment over truth. I am convinced he knows many details of the fraud as a pawn on the chess board that injured my community. If the DOJ decides to connect him to white-collar crimes as I move forward legally with the civil action, then it is up to them, but I cannot watch our community continue to be robbed of needed resources when we are in dire need of so much to turn the tide.

I have no hate for my former best friend. I have no hate for the black mayor who has taken multiple actions to make sure I remain oppressed. I have no hate for the many black leaders in the city who exiled and blackballed me for standing up for my economic rights while never saying anything about those who committed the undeniable fraud and unlawful activity. **I hate the system they represent. The system is built on injustice that constantly injures my community. It is the system that I have an issue with, and to fight the system injuring me and my community in this situation, unfortunately, I have to sue my friend, multiple former associates, along with co-conspirators in federal court.**

While searching for information to stand for economic rights in Birmingham, I came across the following words, "Operation Stolen Dreams." "Operation Stolen Dreams" have always stuck with me because many dreams of the deprived have been stolen by deceit from those with resources and in power.

The federal government "launched a multi-agency initiative that initially led to a total of 485 arrests" "in less than 4 months" in 2010. The federal government was focused on fraud schemes that injured many Americans tied to mortgage fraud. The "Losses from various fraud schemes were estimated to exceed $2 billion." Attorney General Eric Holder stated, "Mortgage fraud ruins lives, destroys families, and devastates whole communities," as he announced the results of "Operation Stolen Dreams."

I have asked myself: How can black families provide and alter any of the unfortunate conditions in their communities if their businesses are receiving less than 1/3 of 1% of local contracts while white businesses and others are receiving over 99% of contracts in a nearly 70% majority black city in critical areas where they have capacity to compete. In conjunction with this book, I am sharing the full unreleased City of Birmingham racial disparity study on my personal website, www.briankrice.com, completed in 2022 and hidden from the public by a majority Black government through 2023.

The numbers of the disparity study are extremely low for the black professionals seeking to secure contracts in a majority-black city. I thought my economic injustice setbacks in one underserved community were my only fight for progress until I discovered more examples crushing the greater black community in the City of

Birmingham. Entire communities are economically starved, and everyone in authority keeps it secret to keep the majority unaware of their inaction to serve the people of the government that voted for them. I can't look the other way.

Here is one example: Just imagine learning your majority black local government will not share the most recent small business disparity study because the numbers are so bad against their community while they pretend in the eyes of the public that they are inclusive. I call this the appearance of progress. The appearance of progress is one of the greatest forms of deceit. The appearance of progress has distracted the local community for several decades, and those distracted go along with life as normal while facing overwhelming deprivation.

*In the 2022 disparity study covering the years of 2015 – 2019 in the area of Professional Services contracts, African Americans received $146,950 out of $16,974,896 (0.87%) in a nearly 68 - 73% plus black city over the most recent 5-year study completed in 2022. In the same disparity study, the numbers get much worse than 0.87% in contracts.*

*Just imagine being in a 68 - 73% plus majority black city, led by a black mayor for 44 years and a majority black city council for 38 years and $60,133,191 was spent by the same city and black entrepreneurs only received just barely $184,404 which is 0.31% of all goods supplied to the city over the last 5 years.*

The numbers of 2020 and 2021 were left out of the 2022 study, ensuring the recent numbers are already dated, making it harder to bring up during any active lawsuit lingering from the past 1 or 2 years. Since this is the case, let's work with our most recent data.

Unfortunately, racial disparity study is not the worst part of what I've discovered in my hometown that constantly abuses the word "Inclusion." We have city leaders running known inside real estate deals and oppressing the already deprived communities.

*Imagine you could assume the City of Birmingham's highest economic development position. Imagine you were allowed to write out your private economic plans as if misuse of office laws and public corruption don't exist, boosting your $84 million development. Imagine you resign and then walk back into city hall as the president of your new company less than one year later. Imagine, you are approved for your development request based on your city economic development director plans you wrote the previous yea on the inside. All city design review committee members, city councilors, attorneys, and the city's mayor proudly support you while ignoring "revolving door" ethics laws.*

The City of Birmingham's former economic development director did that in 2020 and 2021. I personally sent official documents to the State regulatory agency for abuse of office, and they chose conscious disregard to abuse of power and misuse of office from public officials and employees. I hoped they would hold the former employee accountable before ever thinking of writing this book. I now write to share the concealed truth with the people of the government.

*Imagine you are still operating as the city's economic development director and creating additional plans to benefit you and your company for personal gain. Imagine your plans involve $600 million plus in developments benefiting the company you just left just a few days earlier, and everyone in local leadership chooses to turn a blind eye to your known ethics violations.*

The local acts of the above statement involve a double public employee, Josh Carpenter, who was simultaneously a municipal and state employee. All in leadership turned a blind eye and acted with deliberate indifference and conscious disregard under the color of law of known inside dealing. I included my actual letter to the Department of Justice and FBI in the chapter titled "Actual Letters to the FBI."

I also explained the concerns with Birmingham Promise and the misuse of black kids as the cover to run a complicated campaign scheme. It's unfortunate, but more unfortunate is the number of public leaders turning a blind eye to known violations. Please read the chapter titled "Actual Letter to the FBI" for details that I believe the people of the government should be aware of involving their tax dollars.

Public servants performing inside deals on public tax dollars are major matters of public interest and concern that invoke our 1st Amendment rights in the U.S. Constitution. I share the following with the hope that the people of the government will be informed.

This is dangerous with public tax dollars and public responsibility. When abuse of office is allowed, it breeds more abuse. Over time, people will not know what the law is versus the pattern of practices or customs. If the legislative branch, executive branch, and judicial branch allow for this then there are no checks and balances in government and "we have a government of men and not of laws." This statement is restated in the Alabama 1901 Constitution under Section 43 along with many other state constitutions across the country.

When I was in my 20s as a member of the Charlotte Junior Chamber of Commerce, commonly referred to as the Jaycees, we opened our meetings with the Jaycees creed.

*"We Believe: That faith in God gives meaning and purpose to human life. That the brotherhood of man transcends the sovereignty of nations. That economic justice can best be won by free men through free enterprise. That government should be of laws rather than of men. That earth's great treasure lies in human personality. And that service to humanity is the best work of life!"*

I am completely disappointed in local leaders who blame the deprived, oppressed and excluded while they ignore their inaction to uphold the unequal system baked with barriers to entry.

I will dive deeper into this book with real examples dealing with local housing discrimination, economic sacrifice zones, commercial real estate, affirmative action, manipulation of federal resources, manipulation of state resources, reverse redlining, redlining and more.

## PART 2 OF THE INTRODUCTION: REAL ESTATE INJUSTICE:

Between 2019 and 2023, friends and associates would send me national articles where black investors and homeowners nationwide faced unfair appraisals and banking situations regularly. I collected them, and over time, I realized that very little was shared related to commercial buildings that black Americans owned, where the concerns are more damaging to communities.

The black supermajority Farish Street Historic District in Jackson, MS, is one of the most depressing examples of economic deprivation I have seen in the country. I saw it for the first time a few years ago, and I was stunned at block after block of vacant, blighted, underdeveloped buildings. I started thinking about intentional economic deprivation. This area was the bottom of the bottoms, but what is sadder is that this area was almost identical to many other places where black Americans are the super majority owners of commercial buildings. I drove around the area at night when I first saw the conditions. I was eager to go to sleep for the first time so I could wake up and jog the district during the day. I never finished my jog because I stopped in amazement at the economic deprivation where the surrounding developments were developing in every direction except the black direction.

Pictures below are from Farish Street Historic District in Downtown Jackson, MS in 2023. There is block after block after block of undeveloped and completely vacant buildings.

(see pics on next page)

Farish St, Jackson, MS (Black Historic District)

Farish St, Jackson, MS (Black Historic District)

Farish St, Jackson, MS (Black Historic District)

Brian K. Rice on Farish St, Jackson, MS (Black Historic District) (2023)

I researched when Jackson had elected their first black mayor, and there was nearly a 25-year consecutive stretch. Just 3 to 4 hours away in Birmingham, we have had a 44-year straight run of black mayors, and we have several super majority black-owned commercial districts that look like replicas of deprivation, and the local leaders are silent about the actual conditions.

At first, all I could think of was Downtown Ensley in Birmingham, AL, where I invested and have been met with roadblocks from over a dozen local, state and federal entities who all turned a blind eye to my 5th and 14th Amendment of the U.S. Constitution property rights. I then began to think of all the cities I visited across the country with unfortunate but similar economic conditions for black Americans who resided there.

I thought of Valdosta, GA and how they built a bridge directly in the middle and on top of the black business district that is also immediately adjacent to railroad tracks. It is a true example of economic deprivation.

Valdosta, GA 2023 (Black Historic area)

I thought about the news stories that were shared with me:

*NY Times: "Home Appraised with a Black Owner: $472,000. With a white Owner: $750,000." Black Maryland couple, August 18th, 2022, by Debra Kamin*

I thought about the Brookings Institute studies that were completed in 2022:

*Brookings.edu: "How racial bias appraisals affect the devaluation of homes in majority black neighborhoods" by Jonathan Rothwell and Andre M. Perry December 5th, 2022.*

*"The cost of devaluation across the 113 metro areas in the U.S. with at least one majority black neighborhood is approximately $162 billion."*

I thought about more appraisal stories as recent as 2023:

*NPR, March 9th, 2023: "Black couple settles lawsuit claiming their home appraisal was lowballed due to bias."*

*"The couple decided to "white wash" the house. They removed family photos and art work, books, hair products and anything else that might indicate that a black family lived there. They also asked a white friend to be present at the house and greet the appraiser as if she were the homeowner and to display some of her family*

*photos in the house. The Austins were not at home during the appraisal."*

I thought about home bias civil enforcement programs led by the Department of Justice:

Now, when you pause for a second, and look back over history, black contractors were crushed for the next 30 years and counting. The local newspapers repeat the same few names today as growth never happened properly.

I thought of the Wylam business district just minutes from Downtown Ensley in Birmingham. Wylam looks like a movie set where the theme could easily be economic deprivation.

Wylam Business District, Birmingham, AL (more deprivation)

Wylam Business District, Birmingham, AL (more deprivation)

I thought of Chattanooga, TN, not far from Downtown, where the theme of economic deprivation continued.

Chattanooga, TN

Chattanooga, TN (Boarded up buildings with words of encouragement painted on them versus restored buildings)

I saw the example from Chattanooga repeated in almost every underdeveloped Black commercial district I have visited. Across the country, it is common to see buildings with painted words, memories and dreams of what could be on the boarded-up windows because there are no resources to redevelop the spaces.

I thought of Lockland, OH, immediately adjacent to Wyoming, OH, only separated by a single rail track and a traffic light. In Wyoming, you see a thriving economic model next to a model of underdeveloped buildings.

Lockland, OH looking towards Wyoming, OH just over the tracks.

Lockland, OH

I thought about Fern St. in Knoxville, TN.

Fern St, Knoxville, TN (more of the same deprivation)

I thought about the Over the Rhine area in Cincinnati, OH. In the Over the Rhine area in 2022, I saw the sprinkles of the new gentrifiers surrounded by underdeveloped buildings full of black Americans.

Cincinnati, OH (Over the Rhine area with massive, underdeveloped buildings in 2022)

I thought about Africatown, built around heavy polluting industries in the Mobile, AL area that directly attack the residents daily, injuring the "Life" part of the U.S. Constitution. I thought of Cancer Alley in Louisiana. I thought of Collegeville, North Birmingham, Harriman Park areas in Birmingham, surrounded by polluting industries.

Africa Town, AL picture of adjacent industrial plant. Africa Town is the home of the last ship to arrive in the U.S.

I thought about Downtown Prichard, AL, and how the Federal Opportunity Zone stops just before reaching the area, just like Downtown Ensley.

Prichard, AL 2023 showing blocks of demolished buildings.

Prichard, AL, black residents are showing pride through murals in their underdeveloped commercial district.

Prichard, AL, black residents are showing pride through murals in their underdeveloped commercial district.

Prichard, AL, black residents are surrounded by a vastly underdeveloped commercial district.

Prichard, AL, black residents place sign on buildings in picture above that says, "Stop Killing Each Other."

Imagine the entire commercial district full of healthy businesses and programs where the resources allow. Just imagine how many jobs could be provided. Imagine a new vision of entrepreneurs and professionals for those who have chosen another life. Imagine the youth spaces that could be created inside several buildings to divert negative thoughts before they appear. As long as there is severe economic starvation, the buildings will remain.

The conditions of America's poorest and most deprived areas never leave my mind. These images show the reality of economic injustice, benign neglect, municipal disinvestment, and 10-year IRS Federal Opportunity Zone tax fraud. The picture below is just one snapshot of Downtown Ensley.

I thought about the $21.25 million land and building sale in the area of Birmingham that is in the most affluent area on paper and has the highest poverty on paper at the same time.

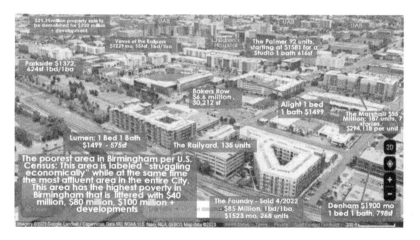

No matter how you crunch the numbers:

Okay, let's say my math is way off using data points comparing the largest sales and the poorest values so let me use the data prepared directly by the City of Birmingham in their master plan which covers a similar area with additional census tracts. In 2019, Ensley price per acre is $29,879 and all Downtown Birmingham in the city center is $321,950 and in the Birmingham Improvement District (BID) district which hyper focuses even more into center city listed at $763,832 per acre is falsely ranked with a "known false report to influence legislation" as more distressed and poorer than $29,879 per acre. No matter how you crunch the data $29,879 or $5355 is not greater than $763,832 or $321,950 or $8,400,000 per acre unless the government of the people and the elected officials continue a current imbalance in federal resources for truly impoverished census tracts.

In Birmingham in Census Tract 45, we have land of about 2.5 acres on the conservative side that sold for $21.25 million for the purpose of tearing down all structures on the lot to build a $200+ million development in December 2021. Everything is within this census tract which includes the state's largest employer with over $4 Billion in annual revenue and its entire footprint with the largest funded University in the state of Alabama the 2nd poorest area in the State of Alabama. Let's take 21.25 million and divide it by 2.5 acres which means the associated parcels are worth $8.4 million an acre roughly and it's listed as the poorest of all poorest areas in Birmingham, AL. Now, Let's compare this area to the truly poorest census tract in Birmingham, AL where the Collegeville neighborhood sits which is a EPA designated Superfund site because it is the most polluted area in Birmingham. Let's look at 3055 35th Ave N, Birmingham, AL 35207, the same zip code I grew up in. This parcel is 4.65 acres and Jefferson County lists the market value at $24,900. Now, let's take the $24,900 and divide it by 4.65 acres and you would reach a calculation of $5,355 per acre roughly. Now, since I've been a victim of unfair comps where systemic injustice allows for abuse then in this case the truly poorest area in the city at $5355 per acre is listed as the 2nd poorest area in Birmingham behind land sold at $8,400,000 per acre. $8,400,000 cannot be poorer than $5,355 unless we turn a blind eye to inalienable rights of "life, liberty and property". Even if my calculations were off by tens of thousands of dollars for the poorest area and a several million for the most affluent area by using more comps, the most affluent area still should not be listed as the poorest area in the face of the truly impoverished.

Back to real poverty and truly distressed areas:

I thought about how my 8 commercial buildings were appraised at $0.00 through undeniable appraisal fraud and cover-ups at the state and federal levels. I created this picture below called **"The Trash and The Penny."** Everything on the ground that I have not picked up and placed in the trash bag has a recycling value of more than a penny. Based on economic fraud, everything on the ground is appraised more than the 8 buildings I own of nearly 33,000 sf. You can see 5 of the 8 buildings in the background where there are several tenants where 100 % of the rental income was omitted in my appraisal. 100% of the comps are unbelievable, causing my buildings to be appraised at $0.00 for the buildings. No public entity will hold the unethical appraisers or bank accountable. No local real estate or banking professionals will speak against those who created the fraud. It is easier to attack me, blame me, and attempt to justify the undeniable fraud.

I thought my problem was just the $0.00 appraisal until I started getting attacked by black public leaders, black real estate professionals, black bankers, black lawyers and more for speaking up about undeniable redlining conditions. These local black leaders have won in this intentionally deprived environment, and they look down on others for not being in their same class. Many have placed themselves on pedestals while ignoring widespread economic deprivation all around the neighborhoods they grew up in or, at a minimum, had family members and friends to grow up in.

I continually ask myself what is happening in my hometown when I started seeing laws broken to enrich those they wanted to enrich and deprive the already deprived. I kept asking why are there many black leaders sitting at the table of opportunity conditioned to break the law in their corporate and public official roles to enrich others and then choose to break the law to crush their own.

Before starting this journey, I had no idea they were breaking laws until I started studying them. Racketeering was taking place all around me. I could never have imagined the hate I would receive for standing up for my constitutional property rights after my buildings were unlawfully appraised for less than a single penny by the most popular black leaders in my hometown. I never imagined being intentionally deprived by many of my former friends and associates. I don't wish anyone to experience what I have experienced in my hometown.

I went from being accepted in almost any circle of influence to being blackballed and exiled for standing up for my undeniable economic rights. Many have tried to convince me to let it go. How can I let go of "unequal protection of the law" or "due process of the law" if I am a citizen in this country who has property rights that have been trampled? The trampling of my property rights has stopped me from developing my properties and providing for my life.

Yes, I could walk away and get it out of the "mud," as some will say, but why do African Americans have to walk away from their rights?

Why can't I and my neighbors across the country have equal protection of the law? My buildings would have been restored with equal protection and due process of the law. With equal rights, our communities can thrive. With equal rights, our cities can be full of healthy and balanced communities.

I don't want to live knowing that I have rights, and I turned a blind eye to them. I don't want to live knowing my neighbors have rights grossly denied, and I turn a blind eye to them.

If I accept the $0.00 appraisal, the bank, appraisal company, and public entities are emboldened to take more of our rights. The next person will face the same trampling of rights. I want equal rights and a $0.00 appraisal written by CBRE, Inc. (the largest appraisal company in the U.S.) and backed by Synovus Bank, the Alabama State Appraisal Board, the Federal Reserve Board of Governors, the Federal Appraisal Subcommittee, and the Alabama Department of Public Examiners, is NOT equal protection of the law.

I originally thought I was dealing with a single appraisal problem until public entity after public entity acted with conscious disregard for my property rights. I eventually learned even more devastating news about the community I invested in, where a black mayor and white economic development director had led efforts to exclude the area from federal-backed resources for 10 years covering 2018 to 2028 that also deprived my community of federal-backed resources. Everyone I have filed a complaint with has turned a blind eye to modern-day redlining under the color of law.

I've reported the acts along with my fraudulent $0.00 appraisal to multiple state and federal agencies and unfortunately the repeated acts of conscious disregard and turning a blind eye at different levels of government made me realize the following: **"Systemic injustice manifests when the ideals of the U.S. Constitution and laws of this country and the ideals of human rights are consciously disregarded at one or several layers of government."** For many of us, systemic injustice is injuring us at the local, state and federal levels of government.

I now know why there is blight everywhere in our communities. The blighted, underdeveloped buildings are widespread in America's black neighborhoods, and they sit at the bottom of America's economy. The deprivation of rights has been obvious in every city I have ever visited with a descent black population.

*I now say,* **"With due process of the law and equal protection of the law, we can build healthy and balanced communities. With Economic Justice, our communities can thrive."** *Suppose public leaders take those key principles away, which are the foundation of the 5th and 14th Amendments of the U.S. Constitution. In that case, intentional oppression, suppression, and deprivation will destroy American communities and those who live there."*

I am convinced I will never look down on intentionally deprived communities. I will never look down on an intentionally deprived black community anywhere in this country as most know their rights have been ignored, and their conditions were created by others before them who chose to deprive the same people for generations. The devastating results of generational trauma compounds like interest; it destroys normal human processes and breeds toxic energy.

I wish my journey weren't full of roadblocks from the public agencies I sought help from. I wish the following words from the 5th Amendment, "No person shall be… deprived of life, liberty, or property, without due process of law," were the guidelines of the public agencies I went to for help. I've been dismissed at every level of government thus far. I wish the words of the 14th Amendment, "No state shall make or enforce any law which shall abridge the privileges or immunities of citizens of the United States; nor shall any state deprive any person of life, liberty, or property, without due process of law; nor deny to any person within its jurisdiction the equal protection of the laws," were not dismissed as unimportant.

I'm now aware of what the 5th and 14th Amendment of the U.S. Constitution says and what it truly means to me as a citizen. I've seen state and federal violation after violation, depriving these communities and businesses my entire life. I was too unaware of rights to realize what those rights were. When I grew older, I started to adopt the same language of those historically deprived around me when I would say, "It's the System" or "They" are doing this to us. I've since stepped inside one of my hometown's most targeted and shunned majority black communities. Over time, I have realized the entire community has been and is still targeted with serial violations under the color of law.

It is not easy to stand in a complicated legal system when you have been historically stripped of resources, and others like you. It is hard to find others to stand with you when people are conditioned to the suppressed environment. It is not easy or safe to stand against great odds, but our communities, livelihood, families, and future are worth fighting for. To secure rights, the most devalued must stand against the giants of corporations, wealthy private individuals, gatekeepers, and those public servants who administer services who are there to protect our rights.

## My Hometown

I hope what I have shared will help you fight for equal rights. I hope what I have shared will cause federal actions to correct the intentional economic deprivation of rights in my hometown and similar communities across the country. Reparations are based on the root word "Repair". Reparations require more than an apology; we need resources to help us repair the intentionally deprived and destructed environment. The intentional injuries to our communities are longstanding practices or customs committed under the color of law regardless of the race of the public servant. Our communities have been intentionally injured more than other communities. I'm convinced that systemic injustice manifests when the ideals of the U.S. Constitution, the laws of this country, and the ideals of human rights are consciously disregarded at one or several layers of government. For many of us, systemic injustice is injuring us at the local, State and Federal levels of government. When a system destroys our economy and intentionally imbalances our families and communities, deprivation and destruction will grow from the forced trauma. When families and communities are imbalanced under systemic color of law violations, who can we turn to as we have human rights violations and U.S. Constitutional violations?

I'm convinced, with equal rights, our communities can thrive. With equal rights, our cities can be full of healthy and balanced communities.

My why

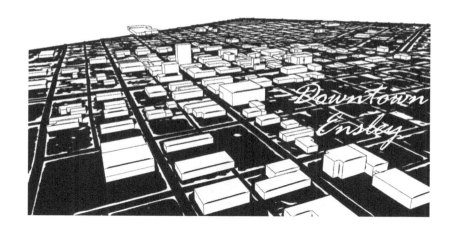

The Trash and the Penny

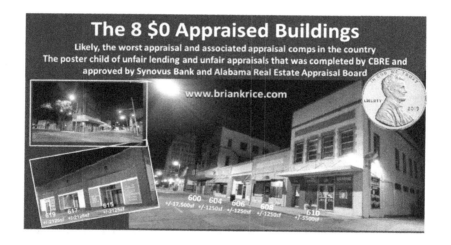

## The 8 $0 Appraised Buildings
Likely, the worst appraisal and associated appraisal comps in the country
The poster child of unfair lending and unfair appraisals that was completed by CBRE and
approved by Synovus Bank and Alabama Real Estate Appraisal Board

www.briankrice.com

## CHAPTER 1: THE SILENT CRIES OF 40+ YEARS OF BLACK ENTREPRENEURS IN BIRMINGHAM

In 1980, Richard Arrington Jr., Birmingham's first black mayor, was quoted as saying the following in 'Back to Birmingham' by Jimmie Lewis Franklin about the black middle class.

*"Many focus on their own success, without remembering the 'hell holes, cotton fields and ghettos.'"*

It is dangerous and it is deception at its finest when leaders boast of a few successful entrepreneurs while widespread deprivation exists in the same city.

If we ignore these realities with a nearly 70% black city for another 40 years under local black majority political leadership and white corporate leadership (1979-2021), then we are repeating history but covertly. If we continue covert deprivation, then we are repeating the efforts of local white political and corporate leadership (1871-1979) when they overtly deprived the black community.

If widespread deprivation continues in its current form, bring more body bags in an already top 3 city for homicides. If we ignore the realities of deprivation in our communities, prepare for the perfect storm of gentrification, where enough of the property and people's value are killed. The 2017 book How to Kill a City by P. E. Moskowitz will remain the recipe to deprive communities until the major investors are ready to conquer.

If we continue to ignore these realities while we sit on the sidelines, watching the widespread deprivation of the rights of the already deprived. Our sideline efforts slowly nourish deprivation and create a guaranteed future for toxic energy and cheap land. Death by homicide and poverty is nourished even more.

Deprivation and the toxic energy that grew out of the deprivation had many mentors when the black business community continually cried for help and access to resources for 4 plus decades under their black elected officials.

Obstruction of commerce for black businesses in Birmingham has remained a reality for too many and for too long, as expressed in the following articles:

**Source: The Birmingham News April 7th, 1980, article "Few blacks own firms" by Phil Neel**

*In 1958 less than 1% of the businesses in Downtown Birmingham were owned by blacks.*

**Source: The Birmingham Post Herald July 25th, 1969, article Getting Financial Aid is 'Brick Wall' to Black Businessman by Barbara Casson**

*1st interviewed person: "My firm is doing well now. If the market were more open I could do better, but why borrow money for a market that is not open. I don't have time to fight these problems. **The fighting will have to be done by someone else.**"*

*2nd interviewed person: "My father has been in groceries since 1927 and I decided since his business had helped me get an education, that's where I ought to be," "I went to a white banker for a loan. He told me I ought to teach school instead. He would give me a loan for a new car but not for a grocery business."*

**Source: The Birmingham Post Herald July 13th, 1982, article by Terry Horne**

*"Minority contractors put out of the ball game."*

*"Only a few years back, their firm was cited as a big fish, one of the large black firms taking advantage of the city's requirement that 15 percent of all municipal construction contracts go to minority firms." "Times have changed. A year and a half ago, the city's minority participation program sank into legal morasss, brought when the Associated General Contractors of Alabama, a group of white commercial builders, sued. And [the former general contractor] is back at his old job working as a construction superintendent for a black contractor." It's only been a little more*

*than six months since the U.S. Supreme Court nailed shut the door on Birmingham's affirmative action program for minority contractors."*

**Source: The Birmingham News July 24th, 1988, article "City is rocky soil for black business" by Bob Blalock, Jeff Hansen, and Ingrid Kindred**

*In 1982, Birmingham rank last of 48 U.S. cities for "worst metro for black business."*

*1997-2002 M/WBE business enterprise in Birmingham MSA accounted for 0.77% of public contracting dollars (the number is lower for black businesses in 73.5% black city) (Source: City of Birmingham 2007 Disparity Study)*

**Source: The Birmingham News July 24th, 1988, article "City is rocky soil for black business" by Bob Blalock, Jeff Hansen, and Ingrid Kindred**

*"In Birmingham, a city almost 60 percent black, with a black mayor and a majority black City Council, many blacks are waking up to a reality that the American dream of owning a successful business is just that a dream."*

*Tim Clay, executive director of the federally supported Minority Business Development Center: "It's really as bad as it seems." "If you look at the number of black businesses and black people, there should be more black business."*

*"Desegregation created a wretching need for change in the business strategies pursued by black firms." "Black consumers went to shop at white businesses, but integration... did not compel whites to patronize black business establishments."*

*"Some blacks think that because Birmingham held little opportunity for black entrepreneurs, many of the best and brightest left 20 and 30 years ago." (Written 1988 describing the period of white Jim Crow)*

*Henry P. Johnson said he has not found many successful black business men eager to share the secrets of their success with young entrepreneurs. "When I came here, I couldn't get help. black people are really selfish here." "They (thriving black businesses) want to be successful, but they don't want you to be successful."*

*Real estate developer Jackie Davison: "If you can find five people in this town who said there was someone who helped them get ahead, it would be shocking. There's no mentoring."*

*Owens says, "We've accepted that people discriminate."*

**Source: The Birmingham News July 25th, 1988, article "Blacks say it's tough to get business loans" by Jeff Hansen and Bob Blalock**

*"Reginald Swanson, opened a general dental practice in 1981. He got a loan to start his practice in 1981, never missed a payment and sowed profits ... into real estate investments." "Yet when he went to get another bank loan... he was refused by five Birmingham banks."*

*"Henry Thompson, a lawyer, said some black health professionals in Birmingham have felt they could have been much further along professionally if they could have gotten the help from banks (as their white classmates in medical or dental school)."*

*"Banks are redlining the minority areas."*

**Source: Minority-owned businesses on the rise in Birmingham, Alabama, June 5th, 2011 by Roy Williams (Al.com / The Birmingham News)**

*In 2011 U.S. Census data: "Birmingham black businesses accounted for 1.2% of business receipts" (black population 73.4%)*

**Source: Birmingham's failure was not 'gentrification' March 23, 2016, by John Archibald (Al.com / The Birmingham News)**

*"Birmingham's biggest failure, since the Civil Rights era, has been its inability to cultivate black businesses." "Black owned businesses account for less than 2% of all sales in Birmingham" in a city 73%+ black. "Birmingham's failure was not 'gentrification'"*

**Source: Brookings Metropolitan Policy Program, June 14th, 2021 Birmingham's Tipping Point report**

*Among the 53 U.S. metro areas with populations over 1 million, Birmingham had the second lowest rate of job growth between 2008 and 2018, the second-highest increase in relative income poverty over the same period, and, as of 2018, the worst racial disparities in business ownership rates.*

**Source: The Color of Money: Black Banks and the Racial Wealth Gap by Mehrsa Baradaran** *(Biden / Harris U.S. Department of Treasury transition team)*

*"When the Emancipation Proclamation was signed in 1863, the black community owned a total of 0.5% of the total wealth in the U.S."*

## CHAPTER 2: THE AFFIRMATIVE ACTION, BLACK CONSTRUCTION FIGHT, AND RACIAL DISPARITY STUDIES

In 2020, a Pennsylvania newspaper reported the following about black contractors which is eerily similar to Birmingham, AL:

*Why are there so few black owners and workers in central Pa.'s construction industry? Published: Jul. 20, 2020, by Charles Thomspon, Penn Live Patriot News; Advance Local Media LLC*

*Over the past year, black leaders have regularly held protest marches outside the fences that surround the site on which the new federal courthouse building in Harrisburg is being built. They march for a bigger piece of a construction jobs pie that, in their view, has been largely unserved to residents of the majority-black city in which the courthouse is rising.*

*It's not a new complaint.*

*Labor historians, state studies and workers all agree that — for a variety of reasons — construction is a sector of the American economy that has historically been more resistant than most to calls for integration. That's a problem because the industry is a stepping stone to a solid middle-class life.*

Black contractors must understand the 50-year nationwide affirmative action fight involving their piece of the pie. I truly believe African American tradesmen, general contractors, and the families they support have faced one of their biggest economic barriers in construction across the country, where there are likely multiple intentional economic injuries and not just mere negligence in contracts with local industries and government. Either way, we must investigate this area legally because many families and communities are affected. The fight in Birmingham was an economic civil war between white contractors and a majority black city transitioning to its first-ever black mayor in 1979. The fight was nothing like Maynard Jackson's one in Atlanta, just 2.5 hours' drive away, that opened the doors to economic opportunity for black contractors. Before Maynard Jackson won his election for mayor of Atlanta in 1973, black contractors received less than 1% in contracts. In office, blacks had surpassed 35% in non-voluntary Affirmative Action set-aside contracts. Nowhere in the country in 50-plus years has there been a repeat of the Maynard Jackson economic impact, which is not a coincidence. Sleep if you want to when your families and communities are being locked out economically for generations because some committed entities and persons want to ensure you and your communities remain economically left out, imbalanced and deprived under equal protection of the law. Today, I'm concerned about the black leaders who have joined the ranks of those people, making sure black contractors don't win either.

Back in Birmingham, there was an all-out 15-year battle to keep black contractors at the bottom. The newly black-led government was beaten with time, resources, constitutional, federal, and state strategies led by the white leaders of construction in Alabama. Several involved in the original lawsuit are doing more today to help those at the bottom. Still, the reality is that black contractors never grew and have been crushed on the larger scale of things, affecting jobs that never were created and families that were never supported.

I had to read two newspaper articles in reverse that are 5 years apart to understand what happened in Birmingham.

***Source: The Birmingham Post Herald July 13th, 1982, article by Terry Horne***

*"Minority contractors put out of the ball game."*

*"Birmingham was pressured into enacting a minority participation program in 1977 by agencies such as the departments of Housing and Urban Development and Transportation." "The year before, minority contractors had received only $476 out of $20 million in city contracts, according to Roger White, an assistant to Mayor Richard Arrington."*

***Source: The Birmingham Post Herald December 2nd, 1977, article by Harold Jackson***

*'Suit Charges reverse discrimination'*

*"Mayor David Vann said Thursday a suit has been filed in Jefferson County circuit court charging the city with reverse discrimination through its policy of reserving 10 percent of any city construction contracts for minority businesses."*

*"The lawsuit was spearheaded by the Associated General Contractors of America" "Those filing suit include Brasfield and Gorrie Inc., Brice Building Co., Doster Construction Co., G.C. Colyer and Co., Hallmark and Bachus Inc., Moore Engineering & Construction Co., Richardson Construction Co., Rives Construction Co., Southeaster Porcelain & Construction Co., Sullivan, Long & Hagerty Inc., Guin Co. Inc., and Steve Russo Contracting Co."*

The 1982 article stated what happened in 1976 and 1977 when black contractors were shut out of minority contracts again in Birmingham. Roger White stated in 1977, "The year before, minority contractors had received only $476 out of $20 million in city contracts." When you merge the December 1977 article with the 1982 article, you see that white contractors sued immediately after black contractors received their first set aside. The city approved a 10% goal for set-asides under the Mayor David Vann's administration to help black contractors finally grow who had been locked out for the previous 100-plus years from their local government. Just think that black contractors only received $476 out of $20 million in contracts, and the giants of construction step in and sue to make sure they don't get a 10% chance to grow when they had a 100% chance for the previous 100 plus years since Birmingham was founded in 1871.

The City of Birmingham was in a court battle for the next 12-plus years until a court-approved consent decree was approved. Black contracts with the city appear to be the highest they have ever been after Arrington took office from 1979 to 1990. The numbers for black contracts dropped like the 40-foot bulletproof iron, H.L. Hunley, Confederate submarine which sank 3 times in the Civil War, killing those on board several times. The Civil War and the south rose again, but more covert than secession. Civil rights have always been ideal in the words of the U.S. Constitution, but when those rights meet economic rights and economic opportunity, the fight for justice has always been difficult. Black contracts dropped almost every year from a high of nearly 9 percent around 1990, to around 2% over the next 13 years and maintained the extremely low level for several additional years.

The white men of Alabama won again just as John T. Milner proclaimed what would be necessary to maintain supremacy in his 1893 book.

**In 'White Men of Alabama: Stand Together 1860 and 1890' written in 1893 by one of the founders of Birmingham, John T. Milner,** *wrote the following:*

*"In Alabama the struggle for supremacy will be long; and the issue will be doubtful, as the immense concentration of white people in our mineral region will render difficult the negroizing of Alabama."*

*"Two things are very evident, first: The Anglo-Saxon white man and the negro will forever occupy this island, so to speak, Alabama, whether as political and social equals time alone can tell. Second: judging the history and experience of emancipation on this continent, the white man must shape and absolutely control the political affairs of Alabama, or the civilization of the Anglo-Saxon white man will be destroyed, and such as can will move away, as they have ever done elsewhere, on this continent, and those remaining will deliberately consign their posterity to a civil and political hell."*

I do not believe the black community is aware of how critical the black construction fight was and still is in Birmingham and other similar majority-black cities across the country. Here is the response at the end of the 12-plus-year battle:

**The Birmingham News July 26th, 1988, article "Change is slow despite Arrington's election" written by Doug Demmons, Bob Blalock, Jeff Hansen and Rick Bragg.**

*"The first goal was political power."*

*"Once achieved, it could spawn more and better opportunities for blacks in Birmingham – especially for the city's wilting black business climate."*

*"We don't have any political leadership to assist minority economic development," said Willie Huff, chairman of the Minority Business Council*

*In 1988, "in the first 10 months only 2.5% of contracting dollars went to minority businesses. The city's goal was 15% through 1987, and that goal was raised to 35 percent in January.*

*"Over the past 4 years, only 6.4% of city's spending on construction has gone to minority companies."*

*"Arrington has told impatient critics that the history of 100 years of white domination cannot be undone in 9 years."*

*"But in Atlanta, 150 miles east, iron willed Maynard Jackson had a different idea when he became mayor in 1974. Jackson stunned the white business community in the mid 1970s by demanding that minorities share 25%."*

*"Atlanta has prospered and thrived." "It allowed minorities to get in the door." "In 1987, almost 37% of City of Atlanta business went to minorities."*

*"Court challenges by Associated General Contractors blocked Birmingham set-asides."*

*"I cannot run government with the sole purpose of improving black economic development." Mayor Richard Arrington*

*"It is a very big job to bring blacks into the economic picture." "It takes Corporate will."*

*When you read between the lines of what black Mayor #1 says in 1990 in the next article, you can sense the strain and defeat the black contractor fight had on the mayor. You will see his new focus as he prepares for his next 10 years in office.*

*Birmingham's black Mayor # 1 was quoted in an April 11th, 1990, Birmingham Post Herald article as saying: "Minority business can function best within an atmosphere of voluntary cooperation rather than one of constant court battles."*

*"Litigation has its place, but real progress will come when a community can marshal its efforts toward economic development."*

*That voluntary cooperation has benefitted the wealthy established contractors much more than Birmingham's historically disadvantaged businesses.*

**Fast forward to 2020, and let's see what has happened:**
Source: Birmingham Times: March 12th, 2020

*'Minority Firms Seek Part of Birmingham's $1B Construction Boom'*

*"A lot of disadvantaged [firms] are starving,"*

*"Construction Works won the bid to construct a new aircraft rescue firefighting station at the Birmingham-Shuttlesworth International Airport. The bid was the "lowest and best" offer — in the language of the public bidding world — among four companies vying for the $10.3 million project." "Washington's celebration was tempered, though, when he learned it was largest ever such prime contractor bid awarded to an African American-owned firm on a Birmingham construction project." "Really?" he asked. "That's sad. Now, let's fix it."*

*"No [minority-owned firm in Birmingham] can build a $50 million project," says Michael Bell, executive director of the Birmingham Construction Industry Authority, an oft-criticized entity that was created in 1980 in response to legal actions taken against the Birmingham Plan. "It's a sheer matter of cash flow. One could not even submit a responsive bid. They can build a building like*

*anyone; most just don't have the capacity to [bond more than] $5 to $7 million on a project."*

*"Some black contractors, simply and bluntly put, die from cash flow."*

Local companies never grew, while other companies had the luxury of Jim Crow to have 100% access to the market to grow their legacies. When black companies had a chance to compete, they didn't have a chance at all because of the barrier to entry. Guidelines in local and national policy made it a requirement that you had to have so much experience, and you had to have led projects over certain multi-million dollar amounts.

**Source: The Birmingham News December 18th, 1977 article 'Catch-22 for black contractors?' by Walter Bryant**

*"Black-owned Birmingham, area construction companies are battling what some of them feel is an industry version of Catch-22, they can't get big contracts without experience, but they can't get experience without big contracts." "The Alabama contractors suit against the city is similar to actions filed by such groups in West Palm Beach, FL., Pittsburgh, Pa., Washington D.C. and cities in Indiana, Michigan, Virginia, and Montana. All challenge the right of "quota systems to determine the awarding of a contract."*

Local industries and government contracts affect your home, your neighbors, your community, and surrounding communities, so when a major industry has barriers to entry intentionally added to make it tougher for African Americans to enter the market, then we likely have tortious interference with a business relationship and other potential violations. When you study the obvious racial disparities in construction, there are obvious signs of likely tortious business interference violations, antitrust violations, monopolizing trade violations, unfair methods of competition violations, color of law violations, civil rights violations, conspiracy against rights violations, equal protection of the law violations for local officials, due process violations for federal actors and more. If we feel like we don't have the capacity to go to lawyers or we don't feel like we have lawyers to go to, then deprivation of rights remains the norm.

We need economic deprivation of rights chasers just as we have ambulance chasers with car accidents. If you are a lawyer reviewing this, to expect the always deprived to seek you out after you learn of their story as a lawyer is hopeful but concerning because many who understand the laws of the land know that many entities have adopted deprivation of rights as a regular course of business just to eat the crumbs left on the table. The starvation that many small businesses face due to barriers to entry is a real situation destroying the heads of families that never get hired because they never grow. When the heads of families are deprived, their communities remain deprived.

Let's investigate the legal side of the situation from what the Supreme Court has done. The shift for affirmative action for set-aside programs came with Richmond's 1989 decision forcing a "strict scrutiny" standard for race-based programs. The first obstacle is overcoming "the need to demonstrate a compelling governmental interest," proving that a set-aside program is "necessary" to remedy or repair the effects of discrimination or deprivation of rights in the marketplace. In the Richmond case, percentage gaps based on race are insufficient to prove a government's compelling interest.

The City of Birmingham 2022 disparity study goes on to state:
*"The Court reasoned that a mere statistical disparity between the overall minority population in Richmond (50% African American) and awards of prime contracts to minority-owned firms (0.67% to African American firms) was an irrelevant statistical comparison and insufficient to raise an inference of discrimination." (The 2007 City of Birmingham disparity study also explains this court case in detail.)*

When less than 1% at 0.67% out of 50% of the total population is not compelling, we have a long fight ahead for the disadvantaged businesses. Whew! I get it, in any case.

Let's continue and see what else is written in the disparity study. The next arguments were related to maybe it's just "societal discrimination." Supreme Court Justice O'Connor gave a little bit of guidance on how to address the statistical disparity with the following statement: "[W]here there is a significant statistical disparity between the number of qualified minority contractors willing and able to perform a particular service and the number of such contractors engaged by the locality or the locality's prime contractors, an inference of discriminatory exclusion could arise. [Crosson, 488 U.S. at 509]." The case tells us we must look at the total available contractors based on race and not just population. Now, to the second part of strict scrutiny, the program must be narrowly tailored to redress the effects of discrimination. In Richmond, groups without evidence of discrimination could have been added through their loopholes, so the scope must be narrow. Richmond's 30% set aside goal was not enough, and now the city had to overcome whether the black contractor seeking participation was ever affected by past discrimination. The Supreme Court was critical to cities' effort to "consider race-neutral alternatives to remedy the under-representation of minorities in contract awards." Last, the Supreme Court was critical of "no sunset provisions for a periodic review process intended to assess the continued need for the program."

The next legal argument was for federal contracts. The Supreme Court reverted to the Richmond case for strict scrutiny but added a little to meet the government requirements. The Supreme Court stated, "the necessity for the relief and the efficacy of alternative remedies; the flexibility and duration of the relief, including the availability of waiver provisions; the relationship of the numerical goals to the relevant labor market; and the impact of the relief on the rights of third parties."

So, when you read between the lines, our black government has had the framework to help black businesses for 15-plus years now, and all administrations have looked the other way.

In 2007, when the City of Birmingham completed its first racial disparity study, the findings in the report were concealed from the public under black mayor #2 (Bernard Kincaid) administration, who ordered the report. The 2007 disparity study was released on the city website after the next mayor took office. Today, the current disparity study numbers are still bad. The document just happens to be concealed again through 2023. I do not believe it is a coincidence, and it's concerning when local black contractors and service providers are seriously deprived under black-led leadership.

I'm critical of the 2022 to 2023 concealment because too many people are hurting, and our black-led government is withholding needed critical information from the majority black city that is the most affected.

The Supreme Court's legal analysis for how to move forward is included in the 2007 and 2022 disparity reports. All associated administrations have dismissed the findings, and the second administration concealed the findings from the public.

The Supreme Court's Decision in City of Richmond v. Croson is discussed first, followed by the Supreme Court's Decision in Adarand v. Pena and Subsequent Circuit Court and the Eleventh Circuit's Decision in Engineering Contractors v. Metropolitan Dade.

The basis for Affirmative Action is here regarding local governments. I expect new legal fights after the 2023 Supreme Court decision in Students for Fair Admissions v. President and Fellows of Harvard College. The Court held that Harvard College's admissions system does not comply with the principles of the equal protection clause embodied in Title VI of the Civil Rights Act. The question that exists today is, what will change? Did Birmingham, with a black-led government, miss a 30-plus-year opportunity for Affirmative Action based on the previous rulings, or was the fight just too much to bear, leaving the historical disadvantage off the field?

This decision likely was a new obstacle added for Birmingham and other cities across the country, and soon after, Birmingham and the white-led contractors agreed to a consent decree creating the Birmingham Plan and the Birmingham Construction Industry Authority (BCIA). BCIA was designed with a staff of 7 full-time employees to help meet all the needs of the Birmingham market. The staff eventually was reduced to 2 full-time employees per the 2007 disparity study and, therefore, never could meet all the needs of the court-approved consent decree and the Birmingham Plan. BCIA 2 full-time employees were responsible for bid preparation, estimating, finance, contract, law advice, review, providing advice regarding job site performance, assisting in marketing of membership outreach, resolving preventing construction disputes, assisting in business planning, and providing bonding and insurance assistance. The organization was undercapitalized, and the disadvantaged contractors in the areas had an organization specifically created to help them that could not properly help them. Tension between the City of Birmingham, BCIA and black contractors increased.

The Birmingham fight for black contractors is what I believe is Birmingham's first black mayor's biggest loss. It doesn't appear to be a loss, as a consent decree was approved in 1989. In 1990, Birmingham Construction Industry Authority opened for service, allowing both sides to move forward, but the results 30+ years later speak differently. I do not blame black mayor number 1 (Richard Arrington, Jr.) or the last white mayor (David Vann) for this economic deprivation because they and their administrations were likely the first ever in Alabama to fight this construction economic fight, and they fought this fight for 12 years straight from 1977 to 1989. I am disappointed that no other mayors or local leaders continued this important fight for economic opportunity.

Per Westlaw: "Tortious interference with business relationship is a similar claim that typically arises when no valid contract exists and a defendant intentionally interferes with the business relationship between a third party and the plaintiff, resulting in damages to the plaintiff." Let's take the tortious interference definition and apply it to black contractors across the country where insurance requirements changed, apprenticeship requirements, multi-million dollar previous contract requirements changed or some specific statement in a local code, regulations or policy was added that is geared towards a certain wealthy demographic and the already suppressed contractor is locked out and have been locked out for years because of a single sentence in the policy. Their actions may be tortious interference as the entities or persons who caused the barrier to entry do not have a contract with you, and they have never met you. Still, they intentionally interfered with your future business relationship with the third party.

July 20th, 2020, Charles Thompson with Penn Live Patriot News published an article titled 'Why are there so few black owners and workers in central Pa.'s construction industry?'. This Pennsylvania article is very telling, and it is essentially a mirror image of the black construction concerns I have seen in Birmingham and many other cities and states. I have had the pleasure of visiting over 300 manufacturing plants across the country as I have worked as a construction field engineer as well as a regional technical business development manager for various manufacturing companies.

I can still remember the first time I walked into the first black-owned manufacturing company in Houston, TX, after visiting more than 200 other sites nationwide. I was taken aback with surprise and emotion and I didn't know what to say for what felt like forever, even though it was likely seconds. I was proud at that moment, and I was also disappointed at that moment because I had only met 1 black-owned manufacturing company out of several hundred. The same feeling was true for construction companies with access to the manufacturing companies I visited or worked for.

I am thankful for my experiences in engineering with a focus on mechanical systems in manufacturing, construction, and business development. I am equally thankful for my love for mentoring, volunteer work, and helping others in underserved communities. I now use both experiences to apply engineering principles in intentionally deprived communities with a vision and focus on correcting the parts of the community-constructed system that are damaging the outcomes in my community. I guess I became the community engineer without knowing it as I was being prepped for a long time to move back to my hometown and local community. I thought I knew, but I didn't know the deep roots of systemic economic injustice affecting my hometown and many other towns nationwide.

In the next section, I will dive deeper into black fronts for white businesses associated with the same disparity studies.

## CHAPTER 3: WHY ARE BLACKS ONLY RECEIVING 0.31% OF LOCAL CONTRACTS?

**We are in the era of black fronts for white business:**
As shown in the previous chapter, the 2022 Disparity Study is directly linked to the 1977 to 1990 victory for local white contractors. The 2022 Birmingham racial disparity study breaks this down even more. Still worse, the study admits to white companies using black companies as fronts so white companies can get more minority-related contracts. Remember, the city only has a voluntary program to reach 25% or more of contracts for black businesses, not a court-approved program. The major companies know the city will not challenge them when they put on paper that they plan to use minority contractors, and then when the project is over, they never use any at any decent rate.

The words of local black contractors are more silent cries for help. The following quote confirms what we thought we knew, but black leaders run the local government this time. So, what do black businesses do?

Pay attention to how black contractors sell their minority certifications to eat for a small amount as low as $300 in the following quotes from local businesses in their 2022 report:

*"There is a huge amount of pass-through opportunities where minorities are selling their ethnicity to obtain 2-to-3% of the business deal," he said. This leads to an overall reduction in growth for small and minority firms, he said."*

*"African American woman owned civil engineering and design firm AI-26 said she has been hired by primes to do either a small percentage of work or receive inconsequential assignments, only to learn that in many cases the prime has already self-performed. "Sometimes a prime will bring you on for 10% of the work, and when you get on the job all the work has already been done," she said."*

*"AI-24, an African American owned printing business, and Non-minority woman owned industrial cleaning firm AI-51 felt that*

*prime contractors often exploit small subcontractors, paying them a small amount, often to do jobs beyond their specialty, to countermand the sub's certification. "It's where a very large company will say, 'Hey, let me use your certification and I'll give you a percentage of the sales,'" he said. "I've been a victim of it. I've been out here struggling, so if I can get $300 a month for doing nothing but letting somebody use my certification, it happens." AI-51 also was engaged by a prime looking to circumvent participation goals. "Primes work hard to fill their percentages, and my company has been approached in the past by such firms to perform work that is outside the scope of our competency, specifically because of our MWBE status," she said when interviewed by the Study team."*

*"Study participants outlined ways that prime contractors worked to circumvent aspirational MWBE Construction participation goals established by the BCIA, including but not limited to, creating fronts and dropping subcontractors after winning bids. When asked in the GSPC Survey if sometimes prime contractors will include minority and woman owned subcontractors on a bid to meet participation goals, then drop the company as a subcontractor after winning the award, 45.9% of all respondents agreed or strongly agreed, which included 54.4% of minority owned firms."*

The conditions are awful here, and no one in leadership addresses the problems we see here while they conceal local evidence from the public.

## Did we miss our affirmative action opportunity when we had the evidence to meet strict scrutiny?

Let's switch to the 2023 Supreme Court Affirmative Action decision that will likely affect Birmingham's 40-year-plus missed opportunity to help black contractors.

This portion of the book has several key aspects regarding black contractors receiving contracts from their local government.

In the 2007 City of Birmingham Racial Disparity Study ordered under black mayor #2 (Bernard Kincaid), the report stated:

*"Income[s] for blacks are lower than incomes for whites in all areas and for all groups. However, self-employment earns higher incomes for both groups on average and in Birmingham blacks nearly close the income gap when they are self-employed. Economic theory suggests that, in Birmingham, the returns more than compensate for the additional risk of starting one's own company. The lack of increased business formation for both whites and blacks relative to the higher incomes earned indicates that there are other negative factors keeping the rate of business formation low. This is especially true for blacks where the income increase is even greater than for whites."*

The 2007 statement is profound, and the city leaders acted with conscious disregard or deliberate indifference to its impact and recommendation. When I interpret the statement, it means to me it's more than worth it to invest in black entrepreneurs and find a way to open the doors of economic opportunity as there is clear data in a 25%+ impoverished city that investing in self-employed entrepreneurs can help close the severe income gaps in this city. **To not invest in black entrepreneurs is to invest in continued deprivation, high unemployment, and underemployment.** When leaders choose not to take appropriate steps to help this historically disadvantaged group, the imbalance caused by the underfunded head of households trickles down to the whole family. Then, imbalanced conditions spread more and more through underserved communities. It is not trivial to dismiss economic and entrepreneurship development. It's almost as if our future increase in tax dollars is irrelevant, and the unaddressed crime on the nightly news has become the final stigmatized situation in our communities.

Black mayor number #3 vetoed the use of the disparity study implementation plan in 2009 (2007 – 2009). Black mayor #4 (2009-2017) spoke on the importance of using the disparity study to help more black businesses, but this never transpired. Black mayor #5 (2017 – 2023 and counting) ordered the 2022 disparity study, which covers the years of 2015 – 2019, completed in March 2022 and omits data from 2020 and 2021 concealed from the public through July 2023 and counting.

What is a Racial Disparity Study? (as defined in City of Birmingham 2022 study)

*Disparity Study ("Study"): A tool, identified by the Supreme Court as necessary for satisfying the strict scrutiny threshold for race conscious programs and demonstrating the compelling governmental interest by "factual predicate" that identifies discrimination and a narrowly tailored remedy to redress any finding of discrimination. Must adhere to the legal requirements of U.S Supreme Court decisions like City of Richmond v. J.A. Croson Company, 488 U.S. 469 (1989) and its progeny. Disparity studies are not designed to be an analysis of any current remedial programs but an analysis of race, ethnicity, and gender status and how it affects participation in the procurement process and in the marketplace.*

*"A&E: For the purpose of the Birmingham's Disparity Study means, architecture, engineering, Construction Management, and Surveying"*

*"Construction Services: For the purposes of the Birmingham Disparity Study means the construction, erection, repair, renovation, or demolition of a public structure, building, street, road, wharf, and other public improvements. Construction Services is one of the Birmingham's Study Industry Categories."*

*"Goods: For the purposes of the Birmingham's Disparity Study means commodities, materials, supplies, and equipment."*

*"City of Richmond v. J.A. Croson Company 488 U.S. 469 (1989) ("Croson"): – Laws that, on their face, favor one class of citizens over another, may run afoul of the Equal Protection Clause of the 14 Amendment of the U.S. Constitution even if those laws are meant to remedy discrimination. Such laws, including those that create race conscious programs, must withstand judicial "strict scrutiny" or they will be dismantled. In its Croson decision, the Supreme Court ruled that the City of Richmond's Minority*

*Business Enterprise (hereinafter "MBE") program failed to satisfy the requirements of "strict scrutiny" review under the 14th Amendment "Strict scrutiny" review involves two co-equal considerations to determine whether a race conscious program can withstand the Strict Scrutiny: First, the need to demonstrate a compelling governmental interest (which may be established through periodic disparity studies); Second, implementation of a program or method narrowly-tailored to achieve/remedy the compelling interest. In Croson, the Supreme Court concluded that the City of Richmond failed to show that its minority set-aside program was "necessary" to remedy the effects of discrimination in the marketplace."*

*Equal Protection and Levels of Judicial Scrutiny*

*The Fourteenth Amendment provides that "No state shall . . . deny to any person within its jurisdiction the equal protection of the laws". U.S. Const. amend. XIV, § 1. Courts determine the appropriate standard of equal protection review by "[f]irst. . . [determining] whether a state or local government has developed the program, or whether Congress has authorized the program's creation", then by examining the protected classes embodied in the statute. S. J. Groves & Sons Company v. Fulton County et al, 920 F.2d 752, 767 (11th Cir. 1991).*

*When a program or ordinance provides race-based policies or remedies, equal protection considerations are triggered, and the court will apply what is referred to as "strict scrutiny" in evaluating its constitutional legitimacy. When gender-based, the program (or policy) will be reviewed under the less-stringent "intermediate scrutiny" standard, as detailed below.*

There are 4 critical categories in the March 2022 Birmingham Racial Disparity Study that studies African American participation based on payments from the City of Birmingham from fiscal year 2015 through 2019. These areas include Construction, Architecture & Engineering, Professional Services, Other Services, and Goods. In Construction, African Americans received $10,165,142 out of $115,009,949 (8.84%). In the area of Architecture and Engineering.

Imagine being a super majority black city hovering from a low of 55.6% to a high of 73.5% black population from 1979 – 2023. Imagine being in a city with a black mayor for 44 years consecutively and a majority black city council from 1986 – 2023, and you learn in 2023 that the racial disparities are so bad in the last 2022 report, the city doesn't even share the disparity report with the public.

Griffin and Strong P.C., Attorneys and Public Policy Consultants, completed the City of Birmingham Disparity Study in March 2022. The racial disparity study has 5 critical categories (Construction, Architecture & Engineering, Professional Services, Other Services, and Goods) that show a high likelihood of black-led economic suppression from fiscal year 2015 through 2019.

There are several areas included:
- In the area of Construction contracts, African American received $10,165,142 out of $115,009,949 (8.84%). in a nearly 70% black city.
- In the area of Architecture & Engineering contracts, African Americans received $7,018,674 out of $19,291,220 (36.38%) in a nearly 70% black city.
- In Professional Services contracts, African Americans received $146,950 out of $16,974,896 (0.87%) in a nearly 70% black city.
- In Other Services contracts, African Americans received $1,403,652 out of $20,305,371 (6.91%) in a nearly 70% black city.
- In Goods (supplies) contracts, African Americans received $184,404 out of $60,133,191 (0.31%) in a nearly 70% black city.

Before we go deeper, let's evaluate what it means to receive less than one-third of a percent at 0.31% in the Goods category and less than one percent at 0.87% in Professional Services when black residents make up nearly 70% of the population in a black-led government for 40+ years.

Let's take the Professional Services contracts over 5 years, reaching $146,950 out of $16,974,896. This number tells me that over 99% of someone who is not black in a nearly 70% majority black city is contracted as a consultant and providing for their family and their employee's families. When blacks receive less than 1% of all professional service (consulting) contracts from the city, someone else receiving nearly 100% of all contracts is planning out the needs of 100% of the residents. Still, for some reason, black residents are left out of the growth of the city when black unemployment is high, crime is high, blight is everywhere, and distressed communities cover the majority of the city. **Imbalanced black communities stretch across the city in 3 directions, north, east, and west and almost no one is addressing the economic gaps of starved and deprived communities.**

Now, let's combine the almost no existence of professional service contracts with the even worse number of goods contracts within the city, and you have a total of nearly $331,354 out of $77,108,087 in contracts going to black businesses in a nearly 70% black city. Black businesses received less than one-half of a percent out of nearly $77 million from their majority black-led government in a nearly 70% black city.

**How can the deprived and underserved black community in Birmingham be anything but deprived and underserved when there is almost no real economic inclusion** in their black-led government in a nearly 70% black city? What happens to a **chronically deprived** community when people have no jobs and families are imbalanced in a decaying community? Americans know all too well what they see repeated on the nightly news. Americans know all too well which communities they would not dare drive through.

I believe it is critical to look at historical deprivation, too. September 28, 2007, The City of Birmingham completed its first racial disparity study that showed all contracts from 1990 to 2005. Pendleton, Friedberg, Wilson, & Hennessey, P.C. out of Denver, Colorado, performed the study. In 1990, blacks received just under 9% of all contracts, and then the chart looks like a crash is coming for the next 13 years when in 2003, blacks received approximately 3% for all city contracts. The number remained 3% through 2005 in a nearly 73% black city per the 2000 U.S. census.

In the area of construction alone, blacks received 9.61% of all contracts from 1990 – 2005. If blacks received 3% of all contracts in 2003 – 2005, then several areas must be well under 3%, which is no different than blacks receiving 0.31% out of $60 million plus in Goods and 0.87% in professional services out of nearly $17 million from 2015 – 2019. The 2007 disparity report calculated 0.6% of General Commodities from black businesses. Many will say that blacks and disadvantaged businesses don't own those businesses. Brian will say, if this is the largest area of disparity, what can be done to increase the ownership of disadvantaged businesses so we can spread the contracts out, which ultimately spreads the jobs out and supports more families and more communities? In the 2007 disparity study, the categories were slightly different, and they were: construction services, professional design (A&E in 2022 study), professional services, business services (other services in 2022 study), and commodities (Goods in 2022 study).

Remember, Birmingham has had a black mayor since 1979 and a majority black city council since 1985. The black community has turned a blind eye to their representatives. **We don't need any more social parties. We need economic opportunity.** If the community hurting the most is left out, put an action plan together to balance the scales of economic opportunity where you can legally do it.

In the Birmingham News, an American Demographics Survey published in 1987, Birmingham ranked last for black businesses in the country for 48 similar-sized cities in 1982. In 2018, the Brookings Institute released Birmingham's Tipping Point Report, and Birmingham was ranked last for business ownership rates for 53 similar-sized cities. So, let's get this right: in 36 years under black mayors and a majority black city council, Birmingham made no progress economically for black businesses but instead lost ground. It is not easy seeing this data, and I'm writing this book because others need to know so they can examine and determine a way to improve the economic conditions of truly deprived communities.

In June 2023, I was the keynote speaker on the topic of equitable communities, and after my presentation an older white lady asked me, **"Why is it that black leaders don't help black people** more? I just don't understand." I responded, "I often think about that exact question, and then I gave my quick thoughts and just chose one or two angles. First, I believe most black leaders are first or second in their families to have the position they have in government or some major corporation. Blacks, **knowingly or unknowingly, have created a caste system inside black America. The first people they separate from are those on the bottom. Those on the bottom are the chronically poor, unemployed, and underemployed. Blacks also have created a caste system between white-collar and blue-collar blacks, and it's extremely obvious when mingling in the different circles. Now, the last layer of the caste is the "clique" inside the white-collar class. This group gets preferential treatment, and they usually make up the 0.31% or 0.87%. They are local legends in their minds. They speak up for the clique but never those left out. Black leaders are often so highly strung on status, position, title, and prestige that they are blinded by self-gratification, not the work that must be done to make a true difference.**

As early as 1972, then City Councilman Richard Arrington stated the following in the Birmingham World: "Are NAACP leaders in such debt with the Birmingham downtown power structure that they can no longer speak against the wrongs committed against blacks?"

In 1980, Richard Arrington Jr., Birmingham's first black mayor, was quoted as saying the following in 'Back to Birmingham' by Jimmie Lewis Franklin about the black middle class. "Many focus on their own success, without remembering the 'hell holes, cotton fields and ghettos.'"

Franklin quoted Arrington again in his book with the following statement: "The failure of so called black leaders in this community to speak out about police abuse simply reconfirms my belief that there is really no such thing as black leaders in this community – they are people who are used by the white power structure in this community who take an ego trip because they are called upon by some powerful white citizens to fit their agenda."

So now, let me fast forward to 2023 after local black businesses have ranked last in business ownership rates for 40+ years now.

Many black leaders have placed themselves on pedestals, and unfortunately, the community has placed them on pedestals with no accountability. I also believe blacks are still learning government and repeating the actions of those who came before them, whether lawful or unlawful, instead of improving upon the past or even challenging the past. Many of these black leaders are treated like celebrities of Birmingham, and it's addicting and distracting despite the unfortunate numbers of those left behind.

Time is also very short, and the addiction to self-gratification and all the events invites that there is little to no time to focus on the hard fights and heavy lifting that must be done. People get elected, and some are there for just a few years and some much longer, but time flies for all of us, so we must do our absolute best when we can open the doors to the masses. For any politician to seek leadership coming from an underserved community and secure the role, it takes a very aware person, full of purpose, full of a public servant mind, and full of integrity not to get sidetracked by the million-dollar deals that come from the same people who have received the contracts decade after decade to look back and figure out a way to help those left out of economic opportunities legally. I then said the black community must hold black leaders accountable.

There is a racial disparity here, but majority black leaders lead this racial disparity against a super majority black city. I have often heard black folk say it's 'the system' or 'they,' but rarely have I seen black Americans call out black leaders for the huge disparities in places where black is the super majority. It's similar to an outrageous amount of crime but turning a blind eye when black does it to blacks and raising flags when someone of another race commits the crime.

I have decided to look deeper than the surface, searching for what can be done. We must use the legal system to sue where we can prove intentional economic injuries in federal court or negligent, carelessness, or unskillfulness-related economic injuries in state courts.

Over the last few years, I have been more exiled as I have spoken out against black-led economic suppression from the local black leadership class who push the narrative and the appearance of progress but constantly deprive those in majority black communities of economic opportunity. My mother taught me to stand on my truth. I have no desire to seek acceptance from those who operate with deceit, while the majority of their community suffers. I will continue to stand for what I believe in. It's disheartening to see our underserved communities being intentionally deprived of basic necessities.

During this period of being locally exiled, it has been surprising and sad at the same time when I receive phone calls from others who have been excluded. I have received calls from black construction general contractors, consultants, suppliers, restaurants, investors, property owners, residential investors, and multiple current and former NFL players all expressing the same complaints of not being able to get help from the City of Birmingham. One lady called and said, who can I call that has been exiled from the establishment and she thought of me. Another lady called after she thought of me as someone who has been intentionally suppressed, and you could hear the pain and tears of years of deprivation.

Another contact, a consultant with 30+ years of experience, has called multiple times, expressing concerns about no-bid contracts and the locking out of local consultants. Two of these contacts asked me for a few dollars because getting local contracts has been hard in my hometown. I gave it because others gave it to me when I was hitting roadblock after roadblock. **I don't have much, but I will stand for our rights, and I will stand for more opportunities for our community.**

I truly believe the Alabama A&M University and Alabama State University annual football game is another prime example of an imbalance when it comes to who controls the money for the largest HBCU football game in the country. I am a graduate of AAMU and it is disappointing to see articles expressing how no one will show the full details of where the money is going. This is one example that probably needs a full chapter by itself.

I remember watching one city council meeting on January 18th, 2023, where the current economic development director expressed how they were using a consultant for the Crossplex to preplan. A few minutes later, Carol Clarke confirmed the contractor's name (RPG, Riddle Project Group) and then Councilor Hunter Williams said has a contract been presented to the city council. Then, moments later, the economic director backtracked and stated, "No, we don't have a contract. RPG is not doing any work."

As I had anticipated, the contracts were approved prior to the upcoming meeting. However, I thought about the local black contractors being overlooked by Atlanta companies where the mayor and economic development director went to Morehouse. The actions are very concerning because our local businesses never grow.

A few months later, the economic development director helped the same consultant secure a building in Downtown Birmingham. The article was posted in Birmingham Times, titled 'AG Gaston Center for Entrepreneurship Planned for Birmingham' on May 31st, 2023, with the city backing it if necessary for the million dollars plus purchase as stated in interviews and during a city council meeting on May 22nd. After this, I wanted to stop looking at city council meetings because our local public servants are going out of their way to help non-Birmingham businesses while Birmingham businesses are starved.

I have informed multiple individuals who reached out to me regarding their difficulties with the City of Birmingham that you possess the evidence concealed from the public. In order to hold them responsible, you must either file a formal complaint or initiate legal proceedings. I've said that if what has happened to you is not uncovered, it will affect the next person and then the next person until we are all locked out. I've wished some who had more resources would file the lawsuit so it's easier for others with fewer resources to use their case as case law to hold the local government accountable if the actions continue. People are trying to eat and support their families and not risk too much, so the lawsuits or formal complaints never go forward, and many more are locked out because there are not enough of those with the right heart and focus on leadership.

I have been studying black-on-black discrimination vs. traditional racism. I truly believe we must stop looking at the leaders as black leaders but officials and employees of the local government. The local government is causing the deprivation of rights in their official capacity, and where you can't sue for blatant racism, you have to find the law that was broken in the process. Was it a bid law they broke when they did a no-bid contract with the person chosen over you? Was it fraud? Was it unequal protection of law? Was it tortious business interference? Was it unjust enrichment? Was it price discrimination by suppliers? Was it double standards in performance? Were you paid slower than the majority of subcontractors? Did you have trouble joining trade unions? Was it conversion? Was it a federal, state, or local violation? We must dive deeper into the laws that affect our business.

## CHAPTER 4: FED RESERVE, RACISM AND THE ECONOMY

I kept looking around after moving back to Birmingham in 2013, and I saw deprivation in the vast majority of 99 neighborhoods beyond the city's center. I kept wondering what had happened and what was happening?

During the Federal Reserve series on racism and the economy in 2021 there was a focus on the wealth divide, Neel Kashkari, President of the Federal Reserve Bank of Minneapolis, made the following statement:

> *"Its [Racism and the Economy is] only invisible because we haven't being looking. Once my eyes were open, now everywhere I look I see. And it's impossible not to see it… Once my eyes were open, I see so many examples where wealth has been given to whites by the government."*

### Federal Blight Money:

In Birmingham, I watched the 3/7/2023 city council meeting after I saw a $2,000,000 request go forward for money to "undertake a project to redevelop and rehabilitate" with the first $400,000 going towards blight from the American Rescue Plan Act (ARPA) funds. The black economic development director for the City of Birmingham present and state, the money will go towards "a blighted, neglected building in our Central Business District." Moments later, before closing his statement, the black economic development director contradicted his earlier statements regarding the conditions of the buildings being "blighted and neglected" and immediately stated, "This [building] is getting ready to be open. [The white owner] has done an amazing job with the renovation of this site." "This is a great project. We emphatically endorse and support it."

I had recently driven by the building and saw the beautiful transformations with lights lighting up the building's interior at nighttime, where any driver could see the non-blighted building conditions. When I saw the item go on the agenda, I went and took the attached pictures that night on 3/1/2023, and then I took them again the day of the final vote. Our black city councilor, who works in the construction family business, asked the black head of economic development the first question. It was a very soft statement. black Councilor Woods stated, "Yea, I was kind of thinking, it looks like it was pretty close to being done just in passing by, so they're about at completion, so that's good."

The former Sticks and Stuff building in the picture above on 3/1/23 was listed as blighted and approved for ARPA blight funds. I just kept thinking of the conditions in Ensley where blight is everywhere, and the property owners have been locked out of resources. Our blight is not pristine.

The former Sticks and Stuff building in its current condition was listed as blighted and approved for ARPA blight funds.

The former Sticks and Stuff building in its current condition was listed as blighted and approved for ARPA blight funds.

Then, the second white City Councilor, O'Quinn, states: "I think the product we have today is a thousand times better than the direction was headed." "It deserves this type of investment." Black City Councilor Clarke says, "It's been a long time coming. It's beautiful." "I want to applaud [white owner]." Chief of Operations Mitchell states, "The first payment will be [American Rescue Plan Act] ARPA." "Going forward, we will pull from City funds." All city councilors in attendance voted for the approval, even Woods, who had the initial concern for blighted money going to something essentially done.

Sitting in Downtown Ensley where I've learned of only one black building owner in 40+ years to get a loan to properly develop any of his commercial properties from a local bank, I was thrown for a loop. Then looking down the street lined with truly blighted and underdeveloped buildings written off by local leaders as local owners operate in a fend-for-yourself mentality where they know they don't have equal protection of the law regarding financing or government support. I became more bothered at our self-infliction. I marveled at how easy it is for local public leaders to support the wealthy and deny those who need a little push who look like them to get over true economic suppression to create spaces in underserved communities. I thought with consternation, "to only be white with enough money to renovate buildings without needing help," under a now majority black set of city leaders who will go before the city council to request money at the end of a Black person's process to ask them to return their money.

**Neel Kashkari, President of the Federal Reserve Bank of Minneapolis was right about the U.S., and he was right about Birmingham when he said during his speech on racism and the economy, "It's only invisible because we haven't been looking. Once my eyes were open, now everywhere I look I see. And it's impossible not to see it… Once my eyes were open, I see so many examples where wealth has been given to whites by the government."**

## Federal Blight Money with a Twist:

A few months earlier in late 2022, I witnessed an almost identical example of transferring money from the local government to white owners in the name of blight and potentially misrepresentation. I'm being nice about the potential misrepresentation and unjust enrichment because I want to let you, as the reader, determine for yourself and see if the Federal Reserve President of Minneapolis was right again.

On 11/28/2022 and 12/6/2022, 2 meetings took place on the same subject. Black mayor #5 (Woodfin) led the conversation with executive staff member Mueller, requesting $3.7 million in funds to redevelop an old, abandoned hospital site. I saw nothing wrong with the request to move the project forward with City funds, but the all-out effort of what looked like misrepresentation bothered me as one of the "people of the government." I'm being nice about the potential misrepresentation and unjust enrichment because you, as the reader, must determine if it is lawful in your eyes.

The black City Councilor (Woods) then speaks, who has a background in construction and starts the critical questioning about $3.7 million in taxpayer funds going towards this project for a deficit. What was the original budget?

The white developer project manager stepped to the podium for the Carraway Hospital redevelopment site and stated they had an original budget of $25 million (December 2020) to complete demolition in response to Councilman Clinton Woods's question. There are no concerns yet, but it is coming. Black Councilor Woods stated that if the project's original budget was nearly $25 million and the current cost to complete is nearly $17 million, then the project should have a surplus of $8 million and not a deficit of $3.7 million. The developer kept repeating that they had a deficit of $3.7 million, and black Councilor Woods asked how they could have a deficit if they saved around $8 million. White City Councilor Abbott inquired about the $3.7 million deficit versus a surplus near $8 million, confirming there were "inconsistent statements" and thereby confirmed that you can't have a deficit of $3.7 million when you saved $8 million. Black Mayor #5 speaks, and then another executive staff member speaks about the importance of this transformational project. Black City Councilor Woods stated, "Oh, I understand" and never asked another question. white Councilor Abbott was the only no vote from the City Council when the Federal public funds from the American Rescue Plan Act were approved for blight to make up for the surplus, oh, I mean the deficit.

**As the people of the government, we have the right to look away, and we have a right to stand for our rights.** When I saw the effort to make sure the affluent secure resources regardless of what anyone said, all I could think about was the conditions of some of the buildings in the Ensley business district, where owners have been intentionally deprived for decades by the same city government.

Regarding this same project in an article released on January 19th, 2021, written by Hanno van der Bijl, Real Estate Reporter, Birmingham Business Journal, who interviewed the owner of the Carraway Hospital redevelopment. The owner stated, "I've never seen a deal fall apart because the investment from the municipality was not there." This statement is critical because the owner was approved for nearly $13 million in city tax dollars when this project started. He immediately turns around and says, "I've never seen a deal fall apart because the investment from the municipality was not there." I'm not mad at the owner for seeking money from the city, which the city will give him regardless, while ignoring real obstacles from their communities. I say take advantage of it if it is within the law. I just don't understand why the same city leaders refuse to help those in communities they grew up in and heavily campaigned in who face undeniable economic injustice obstacles and just need a chance to get past unequal protection of the law.

I have been one of those people who have stood up for rights, and it has been a journey against friends, peers, and former associates. It is an unfortunate circumstance, but my soul can't take the deprivation and look the other way when my community has been intentionally injured for so long while we see our leaders go out of their way to sustain the wealth of the wealthy.

I was amazed one day when one of my neighbors told me to look at the new mural he had painted on the side of his vacant building. The left side of the image was dedicated to me and my stance. The muralist painted the words "Strength" with a side image of my buildings on the right at the closest intersection of where my buildings are, which is 19th St Ensley and Ave F. Under the word **"Strength," the quote states: "When you are truly strong, there is no need for words. Your strength will speak for itself."**

I remember when I took the following picture of my buildings, and I used the imagery of a penny, a brick, a crushed can, a glass beer bottle, and a plastic water bottle to show actual items that have a higher value than the fraud causing my buildings to be appraised at $0.00. Everyone I know in the City of Birmingham connected to real estate, banking, and local government has turned a blind eye and, worse, has blackballed me for standing up against undeniable economic injustice. My hometown has been awful to me, but my commitment to whatever community I am in is stronger than their injustice.

**"Strength" the quote stated: "When you are truly strong there is no need for words. Your strength will speak for itself."**

To sit in Downtown Ensley and watch the decay and abundance of blight from 4 decades of public disinvestment, all I could say was wow, to only be white with millions and maybe our deficit encumbered with economic obstacles after economic obstacle could be incentivized or subsidized for economic development. Was the President of the Bank of Minneapolis right again about opening his eyes and seeing racism operating in the economy to benefit white entities regardless of whether black or white was leading the government?

The last one for now, I was looking back at an old city council economic committee meeting from October 2018. The young 30-something-year-old white commercial developer Boone spoke on behalf of Orchestra Partners. His presentation was great, but then it turned when black City Councilor Scales asked the following question with black City Councilor Hilliard sitting to her right and white City Councilor O'Quinn sitting to her left: "If you are complete with construction for the lofts, why are you coming to us for taxpayer incentives? The developer responded, "Normally, this project will be brought to you much sooner."

City Councilor O'Quinn asks, "Normally, we would consider these types of abatements before the project is done, correct?

The white 15-plus year City of Birmingham economic development employee Lassiter responded and stated: "Right, yes sir, you right but um, but the change orders are what kind of put it out of the realm; made it tough on the [white] developers. Those change orders are what we are trying to help them fund. But they didn't happen until they got going."

The young white developer spoke immediately. "I can add some clarity because we are so new to this, we sort of shot from the hip from the beginning (while giggling), these old buildings have so many secrets in them."

I wondered why watching this on repeat for the developer as I know Boone, but my head turned sideways for people like me who are stopped from starting with gross redlining that has never stopped in this country. Boone stated, "We are trying to get some of our money back."

Councilor Scales closed out with questions, "I got a question." "So, this project is about $11 million?" "This $535,150 basically is in tax abatement over 10 years." "So that doesn't look right." "Did you mention what these probably will lease for?"

The developer then stated, "The condos are already sold." Councilor Scales then stated while laughing, "So they are not leasable, they are already sold, that's smart." "So, you would have loss money for you this time, this time it's going to be a profit because you have already made sure the property has been acquired, so basically, you are just maintaining the building."

Boone, "financing would have been easier if we would have leased them as apartments."

Scales, "You would have made more money." "I'll be honest with you; I could have more questions, but I'm going to support your item. I know in the back of my mind." "If you sell versus lease, then what exactly are we abating the taxes for? I mean, I heard in your honesty; you just didn't know you are before the government saying the fact that you trying to recoup your money (while laughing), okay." Scales then states: As long as you have [Wesley] with you, you will have my support." The vote went forward, and all were in favor, "I's have it". Funds move forward.

I am amazed at what white developers have requested and secured even when the projects are complete. I have absolutely nothing wrong with the developer asking for the funds, especially if they know they are in an environment where the government will approve them even when they know they don't need it. I want the developer to win just like I want my community to win. Congratulations to you for being white in Birmingham 50 plus years after the Civil Rights Movement with a majority black government. Now, come to Ensley, and maybe 1 of my neighbors will be treated as you and many others.

Was the Federal Reserve President of Minneapolis right again for the U.S.?

Now, to the citizens who have been met with roadblocks from your city leaders and the stacked deck of economic injustice systems, I ask you to be more involved in the accountability process. You have rights and options. These few examples show a government for white citizens and a government for black citizens. I watched every economic committee meeting that stretched back the last 3 years, and I only found one example where one black business owner went forward and, on that day, the person was turned down to speak. Eventually, a year or so later, that person, a fraternity member of black Mayor #5, got his approval to acquire the old bank. I saw white citizens go forth almost every other week or monthly, and I saw approval of what seemed to take place 100% of the time, if not 100% of the time, over the 3 years plus period I watched.

The black businesses community in the city is essentially not even at the table, but the question is why? Is it years of roadblocks and a loss of confidence from past mistreatment, or is it capacity, or is it awareness, or something else? If you can prove there is a separate government for white citizens, then you may have a civil rights case based on a protected class, but if you are black, you must sue black leaders, so now it gets tricky. Just remember, regardless of the race of the public servant, the institutional entity is not a color, and you may have a case based on a protected class in addition to other potential violations. There is so much to learn, but we must be interested in learning first.

To be the white citizen, Congress put in the federal statute 42 U.S. Code § 1982 – 'Property rights of citizens' is admirable where the full statute states: "All citizens of the United States shall have the same right, in every State and Territory, as is enjoyed by white citizens thereof to inherit, purchase, lease, sell, hold, and convey real and personal property."

It is important for those with limited resources to have a good understanding of the law, in order to stand up for their rights, with or without assistance. Stay encouraged and fight for your dreams and the improvement of your community, the health of your business, your body, and the stability of your family.

## CHAPTER 5: AMENDMENT 772 AND THE INTENTIONAL DEPRIVATION OF BLACK BUSINESSES.

Amendment 772 is powerful in the State of Alabama. I assume many other states have a similar amendment for cities and counties to use to support economic development at their pleasure. I have included the full text at the end of the chapter as it is easy to just glance over statutes. Still, this law kept popping up every time the City of Birmingham granted public funds property or significantly reduced the purchase price of properties. I learned of several properties that sold for $1 while using this amendment. Several buildings across the city were transferred for $1, but all seem to go to the affluent white business leaders. Properties were not always sold as low as $1, but the price was always minimal compared to the property's value. I started wondering what the city of black leaders did for black residents under Amendment 772, so I read through the end-of-the-year annual financial reports. I pulled the 2017 and 2019 report tax abatements first. 54 and 63 companies were shown respectively as receiving tax abatements, and some date back to 2009. There were ZERO black companies I could identify right away on the list. The same was true for almost every report I examined from 2004 to 2019. I eventually found 1 black company listed for tax abatements. Even if I am missing 1 or 2 or 3, the number is so low that it is essentially not measurable in a 70% plus majority black city and not making an impact.

Now, I started talking to my neighbors, who told me how the dollar store just 2 blocks away from my properties got their building for essentially nothing from the city. I then learned of the sweet deal the car dealership got down the street where the city granted them the land and then approved $315,000 a year to go to the dealership. There was deal after deal shown in these financial reports lifting up or at least making sure the successful white businesses have it much easier. It makes good business sense for the city, so I'm not knocking it, but I kept asking where black deals like these are in a 70% plus black city. When searching for deals others receive versus blacks, you often see less than 1%.

So, you are telling me when you look at the data, black leaders with a black mayor since 1979 and a majority black city council since 1985 have had this power while sitting at the table of opportunity. They don't use it to lift intentionally deprived businesses in communities they grew up in, and their families and friends grew up in. Yes, that is what is happening. A friend of mine said jokingly that they had perfected racism in Birmingham when discussing this subject one day. I said, wow, that is a powerful statement. The perfection of racism exists when black people take on the traits of traditional racism but towards their own. It's not all of them, but it is a significant amount of our supposed black leaders.

Now, back to the text of Amendment 772, I believe the most flexible and powerful ratified words in Amendment 772 are under section (a)(3), which state the (a) The governing body of any county, and the governing body of any municipality located therein, for which a local constitutional amendment has not been adopted authorizing any of the following, shall have full and continuing power to do any of the following: (3) Lend its credit to or grant public funds and things of value in aid of or to any individual, firm, corporation, or other business entity, public or private, for the purpose of promoting the economic and industrial development of the county or the municipality.

Let's have a moment here for a second. Let's say blacks have been obviously redlined in a majority-black commercial district, and blight and underdeveloped buildings are everywhere. Unemployment is high. Finished up-to-code spaces for small businesses are limited. Youth jobs are low. Mentoring programs are nowhere in sight. Healthy food and restaurant options are missing. Black doctors can't get local loans. black attorneys must sue to create a name for themselves to get loans. Workforce development programs are nonexistent. Crime is the talk of the town. The broken windows theory has taken full effect, and more crime is here. I wonder sarcastically why kids or young adults cannot see healthy businesses in their community, but they can see poverty, deprivation, blight, decaying buildings and death by homicide regularly.

So, what did black leaders do with Amendment 772? The policy clearly states that the local government "lend its credit to or grant public funds and things of value in aid of or to any individual, firm, corporation, or other business entity, public or private, for the purpose of promoting the economic and industrial development" in their jurisdiction. Let's consider other cities in the country where black leaders hold power and influence in their jurisdictions but, for some reason, deprived communities are not receiving economic opportunities through the use of public funds. It's important to assess why this is happening and find ways to address the issue.

Let's continue. I then saw the City award a $4 million grant to the out-of-state black developer a block away from my investments. At the same time, the city transferred the property for $1. This development is a special situation because my neighbor, 2 blocks away from me, sued the city for not using their financial capacity to maintain or develop properties in Downtown Ensley. Still, they always used their funds, especially Amendment 772, in other city areas. The lawsuit argued that the city was essentially intentionally causing the business district and community to lose value and fall into disrepair. The lawyer won. The lawsuit paperwork was worth the $1500 I paid Alacourt to download all the pages of the case file. I needed to know what was happening near me. The cost per page is 50 cents, which lets you know how many pages are in the case file. The other sad fact about the lawsuit is the fact that if the lawsuit did not exist, there would be essentially no reasonable city investment in this majority black business district. Consider that a black lawyer must sue the black-led government to invest in the largest majority-owned black commercial district in the City of Birmingham. Politicians always refer to Downtown Ensley during an election year as the next place to focus public funds, but roadblocks always come once the elections are over.

I believe the attorney learned a lot during his lawsuit. The other fact I pulled from his lawsuit was how the local government "were responsible for maintaining and preventing their property from threatening the air quality, health, safety, and welfare of citizens ."When I looked at the local zoning law under AL Code § 11-52-72 - Purposes of Zoning Regulations Generally, the policy states that city has responsibility for "Such regulations shall be made in accordance with a comprehensive plan and designed to lessen congestion in the streets, to secure safety from fire, panic and other dangers, to promote health and the general welfare, to provide adequate light and air, to prevent the overcrowding of land, to avoid undue concentration of population, and to facilitate the adequate provision of transportation, water, sewerage, schools, parks, and other public requirements."

Let's break down the relevant part of the statute and compare it to Amendment 772, where 772 can be used as needed to grant funds or lend its credit to improve economic conditions, but they don't use it for deprived communities. A firefighter walked up to me after they extinguished a vacant commercial building fire in Ensley and said, "Brian, there has been a series of fires here, and they are not just because." Now, this is interesting because people across the country, especially in areas like Ensley, have seen all too often where vacant properties became targets for fire. Sometimes, it's a homeless person sleeping in them and trying to stay warm, and they light a small fire, but the fire gets out of control. Sometimes, vandals and arsonists cause the fires in the vacant buildings. It is also known that certain crimes are more prevalent when underutilized and vacant buildings are abundant, so wouldn't that include panic and other dangers? We are in a food desert and missing so many needs related to general welfare and health. So, providing adequate light and air is important when the lights have not been turned on to dark buildings for years. Air is another concern because we know all too well who often seems to live adjacent to a high-polluting manufacturing plant. Now, I am wondering if Amendment 772 can be used to help us economically here.

Why won't black leaders help historically deprived businesses when they have the power at their fingertips? We are a government of the people by the people, but one group of people seems to be left out significantly more than others, regardless of what race the leadership is.

It is extremely easy to shake your head and ask why blacks keep killing themselves the way they do after the next death by homicide is displayed on the news. I say the same thing, and I'm not about to argue with the simple argument that whites kill whites because no one is killing at the rate we are killing in our communities. Now, I am not going to blame the killers. I am concerned with the intentionally created and deprived environment that fuels high death rates by homicide and blighted conditions to exist so easily.

When you see a malnourished person, you feed them. When you see a malnourished black community, you keep depriving them and then blame the community while unemployment grows, underemployment grows, imbalanced families grow, and unhealthy communities grow. The solution is not simply feeding now, as too many other factors have been allowed to grow. People say it takes 21 days to change a habit. A traumatized mind, a traumatized family, a traumatized community, a traumatized people who have been traumatized and deprived intentionally for every generation of relatives they know have a conditioned mind full of habits that probably can't be broken in 21 days. The conditioned mind can't be broken if those in a deprived community only see broken conditions. We must create spaces to help change the narrative. A better community has been the core of what I have fought for. I did not come to my hometown to fight but when leaders did everything possible to stop me from developing spaces in my buildings through fraud and denying me equal protection of the law, I was determined to find a way to create healthy places in my community. Seeing my dream of improving my community die on the vine of economic injustice, caused me to fight for my dream even more. I am a strong believer that our communities are worth fighting for. The humans who live there are worth fighting for. The families there are worth fighting for. Economic development is worth fighting for.

Now, Mayor Richard Arrington, Jr. made a very powerful statement about communities after he became the first black mayor in Birmingham in 1979 and was there until 1999.

In 1980, Richard Arrington Jr., Birmingham's first black mayor, was quoted as saying the following in 'Back to Birmingham' by Jimmie Lewis Franklin about the black middle class. "Many focus on their own success, without remembering the 'hell holes, cotton fields and ghettos.'"

Franklin quoted Arrington again in his book with the following statement: "The failure of so called black leaders in this community to speak out about police abuse simply reconfirms my belief that

there is really no such thing as black leaders in this community –
they are people who are used by the white power structure in this
community who take an ego trip because they are called upon by
some powerful white citizens to fit their agenda."

I truly believe Arrington did the best he could for his first 10 years in
office but based on my research and the racial disparity studies,
when he lost the affirmative action fight to help more black
contractors around 1989, the black community took a major hit
across all business areas the city supplied, and we have not
recovered from it. I believe Mayor Arrington and those around him
who witnessed the 13-plus year affirmative action fight took their
eyes off those "hell holes, cotton fields and ghettos" for a significant
period as they were beaten by continued economic suppression and
too many of those ghettos here remain the same and still
impoverished today.

I have wondered how black mayors #1 through #5 used Amendment
772 to improve the widespread unfortunate conditions across
Birmingham. If you are a leader, a business owner, or a property
owner who has suffered damages, how can you legally hold the city
accountable, like the attorney did in Ensley using amendments like
772? We need to find a solution, as several neighborhoods and
businesses are constantly losing while the government keeps
favoring the same winners over and over again.

## CHAPTER 6: STRUCTURAL ECONOMIC DEPRIVATION

**Imagine you are living in Ensley, and your first black mayor makes the following statement.**

### Garbage, Police and Fire:

In a May 31st, 1995 Birmingham article, our first black mayor, Mayor Richard Arrington, who was in his 16th consecutive year stated during a budget meeting:

> *"I know where the milk comes from, it's from the occupational tax, the sales tax and the business license tax," the mayor then said "The money that comes from someone who wants to locate on U.S. 280 (in north Shelby County) can be put into Pratt City or Ensley for garbage pickup, police or fire." (Pratt City is adjacent to Ensley and is suffering similarly to this day.)*

Imagine you are in Ensley, and your first black mayor made the statements above after his 16th year in office. The conditioned mind is experiencing more trauma knowingly or unknowingly by intentional "Municipal Disinvestment" You don't have to watch the news to know you must fend for yourself in an intentionally economically starved-out environment.

It has been 25+ years since that statement, and the mayor was right about 280 and wrong about keeping the sacred trust and turning his back on economic starvation in Ensley. Every mayor followed suit with garbage, police, and fire for Ensley. Crime has increased. Ensley has led the city in homicides or is perceived to have led the city in homicides for too many years. Like many other majority deprived black areas in Birmingham, the starved-out Ensley has had an abundance of house fires and homicides. Still, 2 days a week, the city continues to change out the garbage cans in Downtown Ensley, where many buildings are closed, severely blighted and underdeveloped.

City economic plans and actions have chosen "municipal disinvestment" for Ensley, a direct investment into less economic opportunity, more poverty, more blight, more abandoned structures, more homicides, more house fires than anywhere else in the city for several decades.

Arrington succeeded in several areas, so his entire career should not be judged on a few areas alone. US 280 Summit Development did become the main tax base for Birmingham. The taxes in Ensley didn't matter to many, and unfortunately, it has been passed down through city leadership.

In 1973, Arrington stated: "Organizations like the NAACP, ACMHR, Metropolitan Business Association no longer speak out on issues vital to blacks." Emory Jackson, July 1973, Birmingham World. It is 49 years later; those words ring true today, and our lack of economic opportunity has been entangled in structural economic injustice.

**What happens in a structurally disadvantaged Ensley for 40+ years when the standard of garbage, police and fire is the major form of municipal investment?**

In a 2005 Uncovering Ensley article, "Today, many know Ensley for its crime, but this Birmingham community has a past built on steel and jazz and residents believe it gets a bad rap."

Ensley has real concerns; there must be some real reflection and honesty about what can be done. Most importantly, we have to start doing something. If we have a government taking our taxes, we can't keep celebrating for 40+ years for stadiums and shopping centers in other communities. There has been mixed applause regarding Woodfin and his first major investment in office, which was to build the UAB Football Stadium, now called Protective Stadium. Yes, there have been serious wins with the stadium, but the reason for the mixed emotions was that Woodfin campaigned on investing in neighborhoods that had been left out first and immediately after being elected, he supported the largest employer in the state and largest funded university in the state with annual budget well north of $4 billion, roughly 10 times bigger than Birmingham. Birmingham had a budget hovering around $400 million, with roughly 80% going to personnel, so there wasn't much left. He chose to cover roughly 50% of the cost of a new stadium where the city has no ownership and the citizens are putting in $90 million. What was amazing was that 3 years later, after the stadium was complete, he returned to the city council and asked for $100,000 for UAB Football boosters and $100,000 for tickets for city employees, and the council approved it. I said wow when we realized our leaders with almost no entrepreneurship background approved $90 million but not ever thinking of a simple request in return for their investment and the money taken from communities. It is great to see shiny developments, but if the community is forever using a 40+ year manipulation strategy to get votes, there is nothing in the next deal for those left out. Public and private corporate leaders are manipulating our leaders at the expense of our underserved communities.

It is critical that you understand death by homicide. Under the black mayor #2 administration 1999- 2007, Ensley led the city in homicides. Under the black mayor #3 administration, who was in office for a very short period, it is hard to say as the moment he arrived in office, he was facing a major federal investigation that removed him from office. black mayor #3 is loved and hated in Birmingham.

Under the black mayor #4 and #5 administrations from 2017 through April 2020, Ensley led the entire city for homicides, and it's normalized. Now, it is critical to note that just because Ensley led, it doesn't mean the other areas weren't far behind. If you look at the maps, homicides engulf the underserved communities in Birmingham, and then relief stretches across the neighborhoods adjacent to Red Mountain and over the mountain as people say here. Ensley also has another major concern. Ensley once covered twice the area, now Ensley today, so streets in the old Ensley footprint still read Ensley, and Ensley is labeled with most of the murders from the 5 Points West Community in the media. Unfortunately, even when homicides happen miles away, Ensley is still blamed. Birmingham needs to change the street names for all neighborhoods that still read Ensley, and maybe the news will adjust. I never hear the news say 5 Points West Community, but always Ensley for crime.

City councilors and residents react in an article titled 'In 2021, Birmingham homicides neared all-time high'

(https://www.birminghamtimes.com/2022/01/in-2021-birmingham-homicides-neared-all-time-high-councilors-residents-react/ )

> *City Councilor Latonya Tate: "We have to reimagine what it looks like to fully fund community safety, what it means to address structural, systemic challenges that communities are facing," Tate said, "and we have to come to some type of common bond across the state of Alabama, where we realize healing is just essential for real, true justice, and stand together." In addition, Tate said "restorative justice" is one of a number of initiatives she would like to implement in Birmingham. Restorative justice is a process of bringing victims and perpetrators together, so that the "healing process can begin," she said.*

In 2021, Ramsey Archibald wrote a key article titled *"Birmingham has a homicide problem."*

> *"Everyone knows there is a problem, but so little has been attempted to alter the problem."*

In 2022, Birmingham homicides reached a record-breaking high, and 2023 is on track to come extremely close to the 2022 record. On 1/1/2023, the homicide article was titled *"A tragic year for the Magic City: Birmingham's historic 2022 homicide toll, by the numbers,"* the truth is repeated for all the underserved black neighborhoods. The article went on to say, 'Homicides have taken siege.'

Death by homicide has been normalized. Death by homicide has conditioned the minds of those who live in the community. To die by homicide, whether justified or not, is a way of life. To cry and to see no change and no attempt at change is a way of life. To use crime in election campaigns is a way of life to reach the longstanding trauma-filled, structurally devalued blacks who have never seen equal protection of the law. Leaders tap into the emotions of the deprived for their support, and they never help the deprived is an evil form of manipulation.

I learned the sounds of single vs. multiple guns in a gunfight in this community. I learned the sounds and looks of humans damaged by synthetic-laced drugs through those walking through the alleys who took the drugs. I learned the voice of mental illness walking the sidewalks of Downtown Ensley. I learned more about poverty and the desire most people have to work when there is no workaround. I learned the distrust of blacks against blacks in the community. I learned the distrust blacks in the community have with the local government and the many years of deceit led by black leaders in the last 44+ years.

I learned of a government where blacks receive less than 1% of professional services and less than one-third of a percent in other areas where we have small businesses in a nearly 70% super majority black city under black leadership. Black businesses are often starved out and manipulated by social media. You must know that a community cannot be healthy if it is starved out at almost every level of opportunity. The choice of adding more trauma in a trauma-filled community is easy when too many sitting at the table of opportunity devalues your life. A property owner looking for healthy small business owners cannot find a good supply of healthy small businesses if they desire to be in this community, and they have been locked out of the chance to develop their businesses for 40-plus years.

Death by homicide is just one of the symptoms of a trauma-filled, systemically deprived community. A family cannot be healthy if the parent or head of the household is economically starved and stressed out in a trauma-filled environment. A child growing up in a trauma-filled, starved household and community will select something to insert in their mind, and many people may not like the limited choice they have in their developing mind.

I was trying to renovate buildings to put an art studio and gallery, workforce development space, entrepreneurship development space, lofts and much more that would be one step in a positive direction for the **sea of injustice** that has taken place against communities like Ensley.

It takes a **<u>special kind of evil</u>** to mount every resource possible to stop a person from trying to create a few positive places in an extremely underserved community. I strongly believe that our communities and the lives of those extremely deprived are worth fighting for. I was met with an all-out attack of economic injustice to ensure I didn't develop in this extremely deprived, malnourished, blighted, underserved community. I had never bothered anyone in leadership, but when I went to Ensley, I learned that there are people who prefer death by homicide to be the narrative than to help or support or remain hands-off to give black people here a chance under equal protection of the law to improve their communities. The darkness in that energy is the evil of darkness that persists, hovering over too many intentionally underserved communities.

I'm not an admirer of any leader who choose to oppress others. There is much work to be done and a lot are watching. I must recite the words of Proverbs 22: 22-23: "Do not rob the poor because he is poor, nor oppress the afflicted at the gate; For the LORD will plead their cause, And plunder the soul of those who plunder them." I want others to win, but don't intentionally rob me and my poor neighbors when we all can win.

My Why: I have kept the article and picture close to me for years as a reminder.

The May 2010 'killing years' picture with the faces of 140 alleged murderers, pictured around 130 murderers that were black from an article titled 'The killing years, Part One: Accused killers in the Birmingham area, and victims, often under age 25' is one of my why's for moving back to Birmingham. I was determined to try to find a way to make a difference. The actions of those in leadership are causing the homicides to increase in this area.

I have lost friends who are participants in the economic obstruction in my hometown because I never forgot that this picture was my why for moving back home. Elite Birmingham blacks have exiled me for speaking up regarding the suppressed economic conditions in Ensley. I'm okay with that, as the cost of the people we have lost is worth more than their acceptance and denial of the truth.

I didn't think I would be writing an open letter to the FBI, local officials, state officials and the citizens when it came to the subject 10+ years later. My why became very heavy on me. I have kept this picture close to me for 13-plus years as a reminder, so when I was locked out of resources for trying to create a better alternative, I will be more determined.

When I learned that politics added to the problem, I sought to do my part to address a portion of the problem, even if I had to step out of communion with my friends of today and my former friends.

What is the economic cost of the intentional deprivation of entire communities? What is the cost of death by homicide to families and loved ones? Their lives are worth everything to many of them.

Birmingham, AL Death by Homicide: *record year – the numbers have been increasing 5 years in a row.

| | | | |
|---|---|---|---|
| 2022: 152* | 2021: 141 | 2020: 125 | 2019: 115 |
| 2018: 110 | 2017: 117 | 2016: 109 | 2015: 100 |
| 2014: 63 | 2013: 67 | 2012: 77 | 2011: 64 |
| 2010: 64 | 2009: 72 | 2008: 88 | 2007: 93 |
| 2006: 110 | 2005: 105 | 2004: 64 | 2003: 87 |
| 2002: 71 | 2001: 80 | 2000: 89 | 1999: 81 |
| 1998: 85 | 1997: 108 | 1996: 113 | 1995: 121 |
| 1994: 135 | 1993: 129 | 1992: 148 | 1991: 141 |
| 1990: 129 | 1989: 100 | 1988: 92 | 1987: 84 |
| 1986: 88 | 1985: 97 | 1984: 60 | 1983: 70; |
| 1982: 91; | 1981: 90–97; | 1980: 88; | 1979: 93; |
| 1978: 74; | 1977: 87; | 1976: 76; | 1975: 89; |
| 1974: 76; | 1973: 63; | 1972: 76; | 1971: 82; |
| 1970: 63; | 1969: 92; | 1968: 66; | 1967: 51; |
| 1966: 56; | 1965: 56; | 1964: 56; | |

As recorded by Birmingham Wiki

## CHAPTER 7: TO CRUSH YOUR OWN IN THE AGE OF BLACK LEADERSHIP

### *Freire, Paulo. Pedagogy of the Oppressed. Bloomsbury Publishing.*

*"Almost always, during the initial stage of the struggle, the oppressed, instead of striving for liberation, tend themselves to become oppressors, or 'sub-oppressors.'"*

*"In order for this struggle to have meaning, the oppressed must not, in seeking to regain their humanity (which is a way to create it), become in turn oppressors of the oppressors, but rather restorers of the humanity of both."*

To be oppressed and crushed by your own economically while you and your community are already being crushed is economic oppression inside 400 years of external oppression. To be double oppressed.

When I could finally see and realize that those closest to me were also involved, Judas was repeated in my mind. I'm convinced that betrayal from the inside is the worst form of betrayal.

The oldest enemy and likely the worst enemy against the African American (African Descendant of Slavery) is not racism or white racism; it is their division, self-gratification, self-destruction, self-hate, self-deceit, tribalism, internal classism, and choice to suppress and destroy their own alongside traditional systems of injustice. Self-destruction does not dismiss the damaging, longstanding, sustained trauma forced on the African Americans from slavery to marginalization built into the laws of this country, convict leasing, separate but not equal Jim Crow, lynching, mass incarceration, environmental injustice, economic injustice and all the other injustices led by other races. The longstanding human damage is part of the critical race theory this country wants to conceal and hide.

**Today, as I write, I'm concerned with self-destruction more than external destruction.** Now, as I close out this section of this book, I am certain that the greatest success of what the black community often refers to as "The Man," "They," or "The System" since the Civil Rights Movement is keeping the black community divided for a minimum of 60 additional years. Our division is our greatest weakness, and it's centered around deceit inside ourselves, self-hate, self-destruction, elitism, and learned helplessness all at the same time.

Today, the man, the system, and the racism of old have been perfected, especially in places like Birmingham, AL. 'The Perfection of Racism' is perfected when the conditioned mind of the historically oppressed African American chooses to oppress their own for the benefit of themselves and others who benefit from the oppression of their community. In Birmingham and across America, racism has been perfected in many cities through leaders who have African descendants of slavery DNA running through their veins.

I don't know who cares about the intentional economic deprivation of rights of black Americans and the unfortunate conditions that erupt as the last symptom through countless cases of 'Death by Homicide.'

There is no one area alone that must be addressed to improve the conditions of black communities, as many areas must be addressed simultaneously for a minimum of 2-3 generations straight in any targeted community to overcome the amount of intentional deprivation placed on a community for many generations.

Conflict resolution and mentoring are approaches that would not make a ripple by themselves. Education is a catch-all as so many types of education could become the focal point. Now, we know how controversial education is in this country when it approaches race. Education truly is a key area from birth to k-12 to college, trade to business through retirement to pass down knowledge. Education can make waves, but by itself, it isn't enough, but it is a root to all the other areas. Economics is not a catch-all, but a community that has been intentionally and specifically economically suppressed since entering this country can make waves if due process and equal protection of the law are honored per the U.S. Constitution. There are other areas, but I will hyper-focus on economic injustice in this book and legal rights.

When I started this journey, I had only read but never used the word deprivation in context before. I didn't understand systemic injustice or even the systems at play depriving many of us of our legal rights where we can legally sue. I didn't understand systemic vs. institutional injustice, racism vs. discrimination, good faith vs. bad faith, governmental immunity, lawful vs. unlawful, racketeering vs. conspiracy, color of law, and many other legal terms.

In 2018, when I decided to invest in my hometown, I could not shake the images of blight or boarded-up buildings I saw in the majority black commercial corridors from Birmingham, AL or in Baltimore, MD, beyond the Inner Harbor or Farish St. in Jackson, MS or San Francisco vs Oakland CA or Over the Rhine in Cincinnati OH or the north side of Milwaukee WI or Lockland OH vs. Wyoming OH or the eastside of Knoxville TN or the multiple corridors of deprivation I saw in Detroit MI and so many other cities.

Black public leaders of majority super majority black city, Birmingham, AL:

### Black Mayors for the City of Birmingham
- 1979 – 1999 Richard Arrington, Jr.
- 1999 – 2007 Bernard Kincaid
- 2007 – 2009 Larry Langford
- 2010 – 2017 William Bell
- 2017 – 2023? Randall Woodfin

### 3 Interim Black Mayors:
- 1999 William Bell (interim)
- 2009 – 2010 Roderick Royal
- 2009 Carole Smitherman (interim)

### Black Police Chief:
- 1991 – 1998 Jimmie Johnson Jr.
- 2003 – 2007 Annetta Nunn
- 2007 – 2018 A.C. Roper
- 2018 – 2022 Patrick Smith

### Black City Council:

- 1968 – 1977 Attorney Arthur Shores
- 1971 – 1979 Richard Arrington Jr.
- 1975 - 1981 Bessie Estell
- 1977 - 1979 Larry Langford
- 1979 – 1989 Jeff Germany
- 1979 – 2001 William Bell (D5)
- 1983 – 1997 Eddie Blankenship (D6)
- 1985: (1st year with black majority city council vote led by a black mayor, which has lasted from 1985 – 2023 and counting)
- 1985 – 1997 Roosevelt Bell (D8)
- 1985 - 1997 Linda Coleman (D9)
- 1987 – 1997 Antris Hinton (D7)
- 1989: First year of City Council districts after Yarbrough v. City of Birmingham Voting Rights Act lawsuit on local redistricting maps in a successful effort to preserve white voting in the city with 4 majority white districts created out of 9
- 1989 – 2001 Aldrich Gunn (D4)
- 1997 – 2001 Sandra Little (D7)
- 1997 - 2001 Pat Alexander (D6)
- 1997 – 1999 Bernard Kincaid (D8)
- 1997 – 2001 LeRoy Bandy (D9)
- 1999 Frank Adams Jr. (D8)
- 1999 – 2005 Lee Loder (D8)
- 2001 - 2005 Elias Hendricks (D5)
- 2001 – 2013 Carole Smitherman D6)
- 2001 – 2013 Roderick Royal (D9)
- 2001 – 2005 Gwen Sykes (D4)
- 2001 – 2005 Bert Miller (D7)
- 2005 – 2013 Maxine Parker (D4)
- 2005 – 2009 William Bell (D5)
- 2005 – 2009 Miriam Witherspoon (D7)
- 2005 – 2021 Steven Hoyt (D8)
- 2009 – 2017 Johnanthan Austin (D5)
- 2009 – 2018 Jay Roberson (D7)
- 2009 – 2018 LaShunda Scales (D1)
- 2013 – 2017 Marcus Lundy (D9)

- 2013 – 2018 Sheila Tyson (D6)
- 2013 – 2021 William Parker (D4)
- 2017 – 2021 John Hilliard (D9)
- 2018 – 2023? Crystal Smitherman (D6)
- 2018 - 2023?Wardine Alexander (D7)
- 2018 – 2023? Clinton Woods (D1)
- 2021 – 2023? J.T. Moore (D4)
- 2021 – 2023? Carol Clarke (D8)
- 2021 – 2023? LaTonya Tate (D9)

**Alabama State House districts:**
State House District 38
- 1974 – 1982 Ronald Jackson

State House District 39
- 1974 - 1977 John T. Porter
- 1978 – 1983 Fred Horn

State House District 41
- 1983 – 1981 Chris McNair

State House District 43
- 1974 Jerome Tucker

State House District 44:
- 1974 - Tony Harrison

State House District 45
- 1974 – 1980 Earl Hilliard, Sr
- 1982- 1983 Sundra Escott

State House District 52
- 1974 – 1982 Ronald Jackson
- 1982 – 2023+ John Rogers

State House District 53
- 1983 – 1986 Fred Horn
- 1986 – 2013 Demetrius Newton, Sr.

State House District 54 / 44:

- 1974 – 1982 Tony Harrison
- 1982 – 1986? Jarushia Thornton

State House District 55
- 1994 – 1998 Warren Minnifield
- 1998 – 2006 Eric Major
- 2006 – 2022 Roderick H. Scott
- 2022 – 2023 Fred Plump
- 2023 - ... Travis Hendrix

State House District 58
- 1994 – 1998 Earnest Johnson
- 1998 – 2016 Oliver Robinson
- 2017 – 2023+ Rolanda Hollis

State House District 59
- 1983 - 2002 Lewis Spratt, Sr.
- 1998 – 2002 William Parker
- 2002 – 2023+ Mary Moore

State House District 60
- 1983 – 1994 Sundra Escott
- 1994 – 2002 John Hilliard
- 2002 – 2006 Linda Coleman
- 2006 – 2010 Earl Hilliard Jr
- 2021 – 2023+ Juandalynn Givann

At Large State Legislature delegates at large:
- 1974 – 19?? Theodora Shores
- 1974 - 19?? Gladys Thomas

Alabama State Senate:
State Senate District 13
- 1974 – 1983 J Richmond Pierson

State Senate District 15
- 1974 – 1980 U.W. Clemon
- 1980 – 1984 Earl Hilliard Sr.

State Senate District 18

- 1983 – 1990 J. Richmond Pearson
- 1990 – 1994 Fred Horn, Sr.
- 1994 – 2023+ Rodger Smitherman

State Senate District 20:
- 1984 – 1990 Earl Hilliard, Sr (reassigned from District 15)
- 1994 – 2006 Sundra Escott Russell
- 2006 – 2023+ Linda Coleman

**7th District U.S. Congressman**
- 1993 – 2003 Earl Hilliard, Sr
- 2003 – 2011 Artur Davis
- 2011 – 2023+ Terri Sewell

**Jefferson County Commission**
District 1
- 1986 – 1990 Reuben Davis
- 1990 - 2002 Jeff Germany
- 2002 – 2007 Larry Langford
- 2007 – 2008 George Bowman
- 2008 – 2010 William Bell
- 2010 – 2018 George Bowman
- 2018 – 2023+ LaShunda Scales

District 2
- 1986 – 2001 Chris McNair
- 2002 – 2010 Sheila Smoot
- 2010 -2018 Sandra Little Brown
- 2018 – 2023+ Sheila Tyson

**District Attorney**
- 2018 – 2023? Danny Carr (campaign headquarters in Downtown Ensley)

We have the leaders, and there are many more when we start naming critical positions within the local and state governments and the corporate community.

# Part 2: Real Estate Injustice

## CHAPTER 8: ENSLEY HOUSING ECONOMIC INJUSTICE 1899 – 2000

We must know the history of redlining. I didn't know the 101-year housing history from 1899 to 2000 of one of the black areas just a few blocks from where I purchased my commercial property. I kept asking why are there no homes in this portion of the community.

When I received my $0.00 appraisal on my commercial buildings in what is likely the largest concentration of black owners of any commercial buildings in the State of Alabama, I sat still many nights wondering what else was going on in this majority black and shunned neighborhood beyond the surface statements of politicians. Sitting still allowed me to realize that there was a web of inequality full of injustice all around me. I kept thinking of this area just a few blocks from my investment, where several hundred homes have been removed since I went to college around 2000. This area is called Tuxedo Park, and its story is a true example of environmental and economic injustice for black Americans.

When I searched for history, I found real estate advertisements as early as August 1899, but I was not concerned about 1899 but needed to learn about it. I was concerned about what happened around 1999, 100 years later.

April 19th, 1900, is the first reported flood I could find on record for Tuxedo Park, less than 1 year after lots started selling there, but many floods happened before. What happened here was an American financial disaster for the black residents. The lots were not advertised to blacks initially, but the constant flooding changed that.

The Birmingham Post Herald April 19th, 1900, "Village Creek A Veritable River" article stated:

> "April 18th, The heavy rains of Monday turned Village Creek into a raging, roaring torrent. In the memory of the oldest settlers it had never been so high, commencing above the Thomas furnace to below Ensley, all the low places were inundated and the sheet of water in many places was a half mile wide and several feet deep."
> "The road at this place should be raised at least three feet, as this

*is the second time this month the rains have flooded it. Many*
*houses in Ensley and Tuxedo Park are entirely surrounded several*
*feet deep, and in some instances, families have attempted to move*
*out."*

By 1904, I only found articles about black residents living in flood
waters. I found articles almost every year for 100-plus years talking
about rain and heavy damage from flood waters from the adjacent
Village Creek. I repeatedly saw economic and environmental
injustice articles for 10 decades through the 2000s.

The Dursban chemical spill and the lost blood samples that took
place here in 1997 are also at the top of the list. When I rewind time
just a few years ago, repeated articles talk about smog, blight, air
pollution, slum conditions, and poverty for black residents in this
area.

These are surface items and require us to dig deeper to see how this
affects the black community economically and physically through
the 2020s.

In 1925, the Olmstead Brothers, the famous designers of American
parks, proposed to the city that the heavy flooding area in Ensley,
called Tuxedo Park, should be a park. The city did not choose a
park; they chose black homes to be flooded continuously for another
75 years.

The Birmingham Post Herald May 20th, 1983, article by Sidney
Bedingfield, you see a picture of an elderly black man named
Goldman walking through knee-high waters looking for higher
ground. Then, behind him in the picture, you see a white cat hanging
out on the roof. The cat found higher ground on top of the flooded
house, but Goldman didn't because his home was built in a known
100+ year flood zone. The article goes on to state:

*"Ensley residents, who experienced similar flooding this winter,*
*said it takes about two to three hours of hard rain to flood the*
*creek." One resident said, "The water had gotten in his house and*
*ruined some furniture, but, he said, "I've gotten use to this."*

The March 3rd, 1991 article titled "Dusky memories prompt modern hope for BEAT" by Nancy Bereckis. This article comes out of one of the poorest areas in the City of Birmingham, which is in one of Birmingham's most shunned majority black communities in a small area called Sandy Bottom just blocks from the Historic Downtown Ensley Business District. The article stated:

> *"U.S. Steel's Ensley Works plant is also lifeless. But Mrs. Askew can still smell the thick heavy smoke that sometimes was so heavy in the Sandy Bottom neighborhood that she and the other children would have to stay indoors and play. That smoke, however, was the oxygen needed to keep the neighborhood alive."*

When industrial steel environmental pollution is oxygen needed to keep the neighborhood alive, and it becomes normalized, you must ask yourself what else is growing out of this community. What other trauma from structural disadvantages are taking place? I was told that the Ensley neighborhood is called Sandy Bottom because that is where the soot fell that placed sandy dust over the unpaved roads from the adjacent US Steel plant (formerly Ensley Works, T.C.I.), adjacent to the train tracks. Bottom also became synonymous with the poorest of the poor, but in the essence of history, it was because it was a low point next to the train tracks.

The more I read and researched, the more I learned about 100-plus years of trauma placed on African Americans after slavery. The trauma endured throughout these neighborhoods eventually spills into other neighborhoods. When people are forced to be poor, forced to live and die from environmental pollutants, something must happen to the human mind of these African Americans. There is nothing healthy about this environment. You can call it critical race theory, but it is constant American injustice. I stopped looking at the final symptoms that show up in the nightly news as death by homicide. Then I started looking at the created underserved, blighted, polluted, nerve gas-damaging environment and what it does to humans stacked under Jim Crow and a never-ending caste system.

I often have dinner with a retired Vietnam veteran in Birmingham who is close in age to my father, who was also a Vietnam veteran.

One day, he said economics alone can't solve the problems. Then he said, "Brian, you are lucky you are not an imbecile as most blacks for generations have been placed next to railroads, plants, landfills, and airports where the environmental pollution is damaging your nerves." He then said, "A person with a busted nervous system can't deal well with conflict, and they act irrationally. Next to airports, they dump jet fuel to balance planes right before they land and guess who lives next to airports. Our nervous systems are damaged," and then he said, "Pollution is also spread on train tracks and guess who lives next to train tracks. Then he said, "Us".

I sat there thinking about the black neighborhood I grew up in on the north side of Birmingham, and then I realized there was a landfill at the entrance, and then I realized there were 2 other surrounding landfills. He said, "You are lucky you are not an imbecile." North Smithfield Manor was built on or immediately adjacent to a landfill where they covered it up. Lookup New Georgia Landfill. I searched for evidence but couldn't find evidence that the community was built on a landfill, but 3 landfills surround the community.

I researched one of my friends' properties in Charlottesville, VA, and the same was true for the Virginia black neighborhood. I then thought about all the EPA Superfund sites I've learned of, with the North Birmingham, Collegeville, Harriman Park, and Fairmont areas as the worst in the City of Birmingham. I then thought that I grew up close to that area, but this area was the worst of the worst as African American homes were built directly in the middle of 4 to 5 crossing train tracks. There is no way in without crossing a train track. This type of area is truly industrial, but blacks live there and have died from horrible diseases and all types of lung damage. There has been no significant lawsuit of note where I have seen the residents be compensated properly for the death of so many family members and the injuries sustained by those still living under the ideals of America. Life, Liberty, or Property don't have the same equal protection here, and it is more critical to learn how to stand up for their rights and be compensated properly for their injuries. This area is truly an environmental sacrifice zone.

I recently learned that some accepted settlements near $300 once before post-2000. I thought to myself, when people are deprived historically for generations, and their lives are confirmed to be essentially valueless by the polluters, health department, the city, county, the state, and even the federal agencies, then $300 appears to be a godsend. That is not of God. That is inhumane and a stall tactic until the next group dies off in one of the wealthiest countries in the world. What happens to a mind when people accept that their lives have no value?

Is it a coincidence that life and death and prison time become synonymous with areas forced into the worst conditions in this country? Valuelessness is hard to overcome when it surrounds you at every angle. To those who made it out and are now competing for some of the top jobs in this country or entrepreneurship, their story is worthy of recognition as there were no high private schools and a regular set of youth development programs for them.

Now, back to one of the other black areas in Birmingham, just blocks away from my investments. On October 8th, 1997, a Birmingham Post Herald article titled *"Poison on the Move"* by Steve Joynt covered the fish and other water animals and how their bodies started to float to the shore. Within days, other articles pop up. A lawsuit pops up from the white residents downstream of Village Creek. The alarm goes off in people's minds that black residents live next to Village Creek, where the Dursban insecticide, a known nerve gas, has contaminated the waters. The same nerve gas is used in chemical warfare. Around 150 blood samples were taken from mostly black residents in the adjacent Tuxedo Park neighborhood. Less than 6 weeks later, many of the blood samples are lost.

In a separate article Birmingham Post Herald article on October 15th, 1997, by Jim Day, Ensley resident Ethel stated:

*"I was real worried last night when it rained hard." "It doesn't take much for the water to overflow, and once it overflows it goes everywhere." "Ethel stated she felt so ill last week from the stench wafting from the contaminated stream across the road that she had to go to bed with headache."*

In another Birmingham Post Herald article on October 18th, 1997, by Dave Parks, John Archibald, and Jeff Hansen, residents were angry as the article stated:

*"Residents said they were sickened by the pesticide, and said they believe the spill would have been taken more seriously if the creek ran through a richer neighborhood that was not mostly black."*

In another Birmingham Post Herald article on November 12th, 1997, by Jim Day, the article states that over 15% of the blood samples were lost, and it didn't matter if residents retook the test as the insecticide is only detectable for 4 to 6 weeks per the Birmingham Post Herald articles. I was furious when I learned this, and it was nearly 25 years after the fact, around 2022. I thought to myself, who was there for the residents? Who legally took on the cases properly for the residents? What did the 18-year-plus black mayor do? What did the majority black city council since 1985 do to help the residents properly? The articles went away quietly, and I could not find any success stories from the follow-up from the injured black residents regarding the chemical spill.

Birmingham Post Herald, March 3rd, 1998, article titled "Haven from high water" by Lewis Kamb stated the following words of Mrs. Turner:

*"Down there, I didn't sleep." "I was afraid if I did the water would come up in the night and trap us." Turner was being interviewed in her new home and new neighborhood when she stated with a smile, "Now when it rains, I go to sleep at night." "Many Americans have no idea what it is like to be fearful of every rainy night."*

Birmingham Post Herald, May 4th, 1999, by William C. Singleton III, article confirms there was a FEMA and City of Birmingham $5 million buyout for 165 homes and a $2.6 million buyout for the second phase of homes. Now, let us think about this legally. I get that the federal government has laws for how they do buyouts, but let's think about negligent injuries in state court or intentional injuries in federal court, and this is where I'm bothered. America's white middle class and upper class have benefitted from this

American dream more than anyone. Just a short 2 to 5 min drive away from the Tuxedo high prone flooding area racially zone for Black families, white families live in a non-flood zone area where their houses were built and sold to other white families under federal government-backed loans from circa 1934 through the 1960s through the Home Owners Loan Corporation (HOLC), Federal Housing Administration (FHA), GI Bill at the same time blacks were redlined and forced to live in flood-prone areas all backed by the local and federal government.

White families saw their equity increase, and they used this equity to send their kids to college or invest in however they chose, but blacks were hit with economic suppression and environmental injustice for 100-plus years in the areas they were forced to live in. Let's say your grandfather or great-grandfather bought a house in the black area from 1899 to 1968 in the raced-based redlined neighborhood. 10 years go by, and the value doesn't increase. 100 years go by, the value of your family home reaches, on average, $30,000, but the average home for the neighborhood you want to move to home post-2000 is $100,000 to $150,000 plus, but you have no property value appreciation. Newcomers who move to the area are not choosing your property because they know it is in a flood zone.

Others looking for an upgrade are not moving to your property because they know the land and air is polluted, so your property is repeatedly damaged. You are living the American dream, and you see commercials on TV about using your home equity line of credit to invest back in your home or your family or your business or whatever, so you go to a bank. You see the commercials talking about your home as your greatest investment. The bank then tells you that the minimum value to receive a home equity line of credit is $50,000, but your home and none of your neighbor's homes ever appraised at that amount, so now there are no upgrades in your community. You and your neighbors just ride life out together because, you know, it truly is messed up. You learn to smile in your situation and enjoy life as best as possible. Now you pass your house to your kids, and now your kids are stuck with a house they can't get a rehab loan on, so the property decays and decays until the home and neighborhood are not desirable in their eyes. Now, I must ask the question: who fought for economic damage to an intentionally injured community? Who fought for the loss of equity you could not use to send your kids to school? Redlining and racial zoning maps forced your family to live there with known pollutants, flood waters, and depressed property values, which means the government and the banks intentionally injured you. They all know pollution and flooding hurt property values. They all know that when the buyouts finally come, the value is based on what a person would pay for it in that condition. They all know there was no real appreciation of property value for 40, 60, 80, or even 100 years, but who put the lawsuit together to fight injury to Life, Liberty, or Property? African Americans need a strong legal defense fund that's a visit away or a phone call away to help you and your family navigate the historical injuries against you, your family, and your community. Americans from all backgrounds need to use the law as it is written to stand for the most recent injuries in their life.

On March 18th, 2008, I watched a City of Birmingham City Council recording when former Mayor Larry Langford stated:

*"We have devalued people's property in Airport Hills." "All we did was bring the property values down"* one by one. Langford continued, *"We have caused people property values to be so low they can't even buy another house with our purchase amount. Every time we buy a property in phases all the remaining property values are reduced and we hurting the people of the city."*

If I were a lawyer, I believe this would have been a great time to sue the city for admitted property damage on behalf of those remaining and those who recently sold their properties. Who is fighting for economic injuries?

Please think of the emotional distress of being unable to sleep every time it rains. That is an injury to your life and your property. Think of cancer-causing pollution; this is an obvious injury to your life and property. Think of your dying relative coughing up blood or gasping for air or using a portable oxygen canister to breathe because they have been injured their entire lives by local pollution. These are injuries, and I'm convinced that until you find a lawyer who truly cares about you and your family, you may have to become the lawyer to represent you, your family, and your community. No group of people should settle for $300 payments when lives have been lost and property has been damaged.

What did Richard Rothstein say in his book Color of Law?
*"We have created a caste system in this country, with African Americans kept exploited and geographically separate by racially explicit government policies. Although most of these policies are off the books, they have never been remedied and their effects endure."*

*"We lost sight of the fact that housing discrimination did not become unlawful in 1968; it had been so since 1866. Indeed, throughout those 102 years, housing discrimination was not only unlawful but was the imposition of a badge of slavery that the Constitution mandates us to remove."*

I strongly believe 'Color of Law' by Richard Rothstein is an extremely important book to American history on race and housing, race and freeways, race and deprivation of rights under the color of law. I had never heard the term "Color of Law" used in context with aspects of any concerns I was seeing in our communities. The color of law is the most important term that must be used. After reading Rothstein's book, I looked up the color of law, and my answer to my federal litigation fight was right there. I strongly recommend the reading of 'Color of Law' so you will understand what redlining is, the wealth it created for white families, and the deprivation of rights it created for black families.

Now, for those lawyers and those with resources or in key positions who look the other way today, when you see housing discrimination separated by a known line in your city take place, please think of the time when African Americans had no one to go to for help. At the same time, you watch the injustice from your vantage point and legally prepared position.

Please don't say they didn't contact you. Maybe their agony is so bad that they can't even process who to contact because they are traumatized by the known overwhelming oppression and associated state and federal violations that they have not been trained to fight. **Black Americans have been intentionally injured for a long time,** and they don't know whom to go to for help because they don't see anyone around them getting help.

## CHAPTER 9: WE ARE REPEATING 1930S ERA REDLINING POST-2020.

### We are repeating 1930s Era Redlining post-2020.
### Circa 1933 – 2023 The Nationwide Redlining

In this section, I have shared critical historical articles starting around 1933 that most living today have never seen that are identical to economic injustice today post-2020.

I have written and sent over 2000 pages of complaints to state and federal agencies for modern-day redlining. America's redlining robbed many grandparents, great-grandparents, and great-great-grandparents that trickled down through history and robbed black descendants today post-2020.
Redlining and the head of the United States Department of Justice 2021

### Oct 22nd, 2021, Attorney General Merrick B. Garland Delivers Remarks Announcing a New Initiative to Combat Redlining:

*"Welcome to the Justice Department's Great Hall. This space and the building that we are in were constructed at the height of the Great Depression in the early 1930s. At the same time that the federal government was constructing this monument to justice, it was instituting a profoundly unjust nationwide real estate practice known as redlining."*

*"Redlining is a process by which lenders deny services to individuals in a neighborhood because of the race or national origin of the people who live in those communities. Redlining has its roots programs that were designed to make homeownership widely available for the American people, but that purposefully excluded minority neighborhoods from accessing those benefits."*

*"Much has changed since the federal government engaged in Depression-era redlining, but discriminatory lending practices by financial institutions still exist. Unfortunately, redlining remains a persistent form of discrimination that harms minority communities."*

*"Lending discrimination runs counter to fundamental promises of our economic system. When a person is denied credit simply because of their race or national origin, their ability to share in our nation's prosperity is all but eliminated."*

*We are here today to announce that the Justice Department has launched an Initiative to combat modern-day redlining. Redlining contributed to the large racial wealth gap that exists in this country. The practice made it extremely difficult for people of color to accumulate wealth through the purchase, refinancing, or repair of their homes.*

*When lending institutions deny or avoid providing loans to minority communities because of the racial or ethnic demographics of the relevant neighborhoods, they contribute to these inequities. Such lending practices also violate federal law.*

As the current U.S. Attorney General speaks about redlining, he is speaking about the forced economic suppression of the lives of most African Americans' parents, grandparents, and great-grandparents when there was no significant legal representation to fight the known U.S. Constitutional violations to Life, Liberty, or Property.

On September 20, 2020, the U.S. Senate Committee on Banking, Housing, and Urban Affairs presented the Minority Staff Report titled 'TURNING BACK THE CLOCK - How the Trump Administration Has Undermined 50 Years of Fair Housing Progress.'

The 'Turning Back the Clock' federal document stated:

*"FROM 1934 TO 1968, 98 PERCENT OF FHA-BACKED LOANS WERE MADE TO WHITE APPLICANTS".*

*"In 1929, the Great Depression triggered a crisis that began the federal government's involvement in the housing market. Until that time, housing policy largely was controlled by state, local, and private actors, making discrimination localized and ad hoc.8 But as the depression deepened, the number of real estate foreclosures*

*ballooned from 68,100 in 1926 to more than 252,000 in 1933. Half of all mortgages in urban areas were in default by 1934, and families, banks, and the housing industry suffered. With the housing market in free fall and the banking system collapsing, states, localities, and private actors were unable to address these problems."*

*"To reinvigorate the housing market, President Franklin Roosevelt created the government-sponsored Home Owners' Loan Corporation (HOLC) to purchase mortgages nearing foreclosure and refinance them into longer-term, more affordable loans, or to fix up and rent or sell homes when foreclosure did occur. This strategy was a first step to stabilize neighborhoods across the country. To assess and value properties – including the properties it had purchased – HOLC partnered with local real estate agents and appraisers to make "Residential Security Maps." These maps used color-coding to differentiate between high and low risk neighborhoods, with green signifying the "Best" neighborhoods and red indicating a "Hazardous" area.12 Neighborhoods that were home to people of color, even a small percentage, were marked "Declining" or "Hazardous."*

*"The Federal Housing Administration (FHA) similarly was created to rejuvenate the housing market by providing access to more affordable homeownership by insuring mortgages. Like HOLC, FHA relied on maps, similar to the HOLC maps, as well as appraisers and its own underwriting manual to determine the viability of a loan."*

The first known mention I could find in my hometown of Birmingham for the federally backed program called Home Owners Loan Corporation in local newspapers was November 6th, 1933, which was not designed for black citizens.

*"HOLC - Home Owners Loan Corporation, the purpose of which is to prevent the city or small town homeowner from losing his property through mortgage foreclosure" at the end of the Great Depression.*

The Birmingham News: Birmingham, Alabama · Monday, January 08, 1934. Article title: *'750 HOLC Loan Pleas Approved':*

*"Approximately 750 loan applications aggregating $2,100,000 have been approved by the Home Owners Loan Corporation to date in Alabama, E.H. Wrenn, Jr., manager of the state office at Birmingham." "About $1,500,000 in applications has been approved and acted upon within the last 30 days." "The State office has received 12,000 applications representing loans which would total $25,000,000."*

The Birmingham News: Birmingham, Alabama · Friday, March 16, 1934. Article title: $7,012,000 HOLC Loans Granted.

*"Additional appraisers and others needed to speed up the loans have been added to the staff." "The necessity of person seeking refinancing of mortgages to continue their mortgage payments after they have made application for HOLC."*

The Birmingham News: Birmingham, Alabama · Sunday, June 24, 1934. Article title: '20,942 Ask HOLC Loans in State'

*Montgomery, AL - Applications for loans made to the Hom[e] Owners Loan Corporation during the week ending June 15 totaled 20,942. In the same period, 16,442 were completed with an aggregate of $52,308,676. Total applications for loans throughout the country up to June 15 were 1,465,941, amounting to $4,702,441,796). The homeowners act authorized $2,200,000,000 in bonds and cash for the relief of distressed homeowners, and the corporation began business in September 1933.*

Think about those black citizens who could read and afford a newspaper with a little bit of consciousness when they saw $4.7 billion-plus in loans that had been approved in 1934 backed by the federal government take place just months after the program started. $4.7 billion in 1934 would be over $107 billion in today's money. Black citizens are watching with no practicing courtroom attorneys from their community in Alabama while the 3rd greatest transfer of wealth this country has created occurs. The first greatest transfer of wealth was created on the backs of slaves, and the other is all the homesteading that took place, granting millions and millions of acres of land to the super majority white recipients of this country. Yes, the 5th and 14th Amendments of the U.S. Constitution granted black citizens due process of the law and equal protection of the law during the Jim Crow era, but who was there to fight for their rights?

Acting U.S. Attorney General Merrick Garland's statements after creating a Department of Justice Modern Day Redlining Initiative in 2021 addressed these unfortunate economic truths for black citizens from the 1930s to the 1960s. Who was there to protect the rights of black citizens?

In the white Birmingham newspaper and when referring to the white populations, The Birmingham News on January 27, 1936, quote:

*"State FHA loans show sharp gain ."*

*"Homes here get modernization treatment."*

***"Loans under FHA easily obtained."***

The article states what modernizing loans can also be used for.

*"To repair, alter, or improve a manufacturing plant, hotel, or any home, farm, store, church, school, other type of property, or to purchase and install approved equipment or machinery in any type of property."*

In Birmingham, I have listed the first known legal redlining fight I could find. It was in 1947, and the only black practicing attorney in the State of Alabama took the case. This case also was the first bombing of a black residence in the Enon Ridge / Smithfield area of Birmingham, which we now call "Dynamite Hill."

The largest mass meeting in history in Birmingham for blacks, didn't take place for 2 more years per The Weekly Review, Birmingham, AL 8/26/1949. The mass meeting took place during the second legally represented court case related racial zoning bombings in the Smithfield area.

Article titled: "Negroes Sue Again Against Zone Law" (Saturday, July 26th, 1947, Birmingham Post Herald)

*"The new suit challenges the constitutionality of the city laws dealing with property." "This is the second suit filed by Arthur D. Shores, Negro attorney, on behalf of Samuel Matthews… and his wife, Essie Mae Matthews." The Matthews were denied a building permit. "An injunction and a declaratory judgment to determine the constitutionality of the zoning laws is being asked."*

Less than 1 month later, the home was bombed, and the article is titled, "House in Zoning Dispute Blown Up," Dynamite believed used to crumple Negro home built in 'white' area.' Birmingham, Alabama · Tuesday, August 19, 1947; The Birmingham News

Now, I jump to homes being sold "For Colored Homes" by W.R. Rush, one of the early owners of the Birmingham black Barons of the Southern Negro Baseball League.

1937 Advertisement state: (The Birmingham New: Birmingham, Alabama Sun, Jul 18, 1937)

*"Colored Homes," Ensley, Pratty City, Sherman Heights, Lomb Blvd. "Homes can be bought on rent terms," W.R. Rush.*

*There was no mention of any federally backed financing offered to other Americans.*

Why is it important that the Colored newspaper said rent terms? It is because blacks were locked out of the federally backed banking system, and almost all the billions the government put into the New Deal went to white families, creating wealth for the next 100-plus years that sent their kids to college and created business loans out of their equity while also passing wealth down.

What was happening to black citizens in other American cities?

### Chicago, Illinois
In Chicago, IL, what was happening to black families there?

"In the Plunder of Black Wealth in Chicago" by Bob Chiarito, posted on NPR on June 5th, 2019.

*"In just two short decades — while the post World War II housing boom created the wealth of the white middle class — blacks in Chicago were ripped off to the tune of $4 billion on land sale contracts, a common practice at the time that has been since outlawed but whose damage is still felt."*

*"A recent study from Duke University's Samuel DuBois Cook Center on Social Equity estimates that "the total amount expropriated from Chicago's black community due to land sales contracts is between $3.2 and $4 billion in today's dollars.*

*The study "The Plunder of black Wealth in Chicago: New Findings on the Lasting Toll of Predatory Housing Contracts," is the first report to put a dollar amount on the practice." "During a time when blacks could not get mortgages because of redlining, buying homes on contract gave the illusion of a mortgage payment without any protection. Simply put, it was often the only way for black families to buy a home in Chicago during the post-World War II boom."*

143 redlining maps were located and compiled by Esri and the University of Richmond's Digital Scholarship Lab, which feature 7,148 neighborhoods in the U.S. and cover more than 200 cities HOLC redlined in the 1930s. Just think of an all-out White House-led economic wealth creation plan for white families and all-out economic suppression of black communities and families that lasted 30 to 40 years openly from 1933 to 1968.

Every decent-sized city in this country had a map banks and realtors were using backed by federal money while black families were systemically locked out of resources to provide for their housing.

*Chicago, Seattle, Tacoma, Portland, Spokane, Omaha, Denver, Pueblo, Salt Lake City, Birmingham, Jackson, Knoxville, Chattanooga, New Orleans, D.C., Houston, Dallas, Galveston, St. Antonio, Waco, Beaumont, Port Arthur, Ogden, Minneapolis, Duluth, Saginaw, St. Paul, St. Louis, East St Louis, Mobile, Tulsa,*

San Diego, Los Angeles, San Francisco, Oakland, Phoenix, El Paso,
Ft. Worth, Amarillo, St Petersburg, Miami, Tampa, Jacksonville,
Savannah, Norfolk, Durham, Baltimore, Little Rock, Austin, Atlanta,
Charlotte, Greensboro, Asheville, Columbia, Augusta, Montgomery,
Pittsburgh, Nashville, Knoxville, Memphis, Macon, Shreveport,
Huntington, Louisville, Peoria, Des Moines, Waterloo, Lansing,
Battle Creek, Kalamazoo, Muskegon, Pontiac, Ft Wayne, Racine,
Kenosha, Detroit, Rochester, Milwaukee, South Bend, Toledo,
Columbus, Dayton, Davenport, Dubque, Madison, Oshkosh,
Covington, Indianapolis, Terre Haute, Springfield, Decatur, Aurora,
Joilet, Rockford, Fort Wayne, Muncie, Lima, Akron, Canton,
Wheeling, Charleston, Portsmouth, Wilkes-Barre, Elmira, Buffalo,
Niagara Falls, Altoona, New Castle, Youngstown, Erie, Lorain,
Lynchburg, Roanoke, Kansas City, Haverhill, Manchester, Boroughs
of NY, Greater Boston, Brockton, Philadelphia, Providence
Camden, New Haven Hartford, Schenectady, Utica, York, Chester,
Newport News, Atlantic City, Syracuse, Waterbury, Poughkeepsie,
Trenton, New Britain, Bethlehem, Brooklyn, Queens, Staten Island,
and many I didn't list.

The below map injuring Birmingham black communities
intentionally during the New Deal era is just 1 map that caused the
greatest wealth creation for white families simultaneously
nationwide for 35+ years.

1940 Birmingham Alabama redlining map. (University of
Richmond, Mapping Inequality, Redlining in New Deal America)
https://dsl.richmond.edu/panorama/redlining/#loc=12/33.516/-
86.884&city=birmingham-al

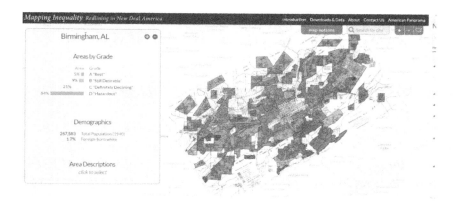

Fast forward to 2018 to 2028, I have been on the front lines in Birmingham, AL, screaming about the actions of the local government to cause the federal opportunity zone map to be created out of fraud injuring Ensley and surrounding black communities on the western side of Birmingham. The actions are identical to writing red on a map in 1933 and allowing it to remain through 1968 and excluding black areas because "They" want to steer federal funds based on unequal protection of the laws to those they choose.

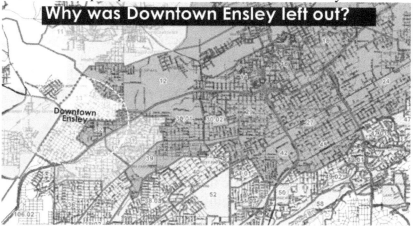

Now, let's jump back to the Deep South and what black real estate agents said during this historical period. (Note: Pay attention to the thought process of this December 1948 article and compare it to the February 1949 statements just 2 months later after the black realtor recognized the economic injustice in "The System" against his community. My question: How to Sue a System?)

T.L. Forrest, Real Estate Editor for The Weekly Review
Birmingham, Alabama · Friday, December 3rd, 1948 (Colored
newspaper):

*What is the best procedure for buying a lot for a home site?*

*The selection of the site is extremely important, especially if you
contemplate building a home at a contract, be sure later date.
Before signing any [contract make sure] that the lot will meet FHA
requirements as to size and location. "Check the property for the
following things: Is the neighborhood desirable? Is gas available?
Is transportation adequate? Are schools and churches near by?*

*"If the FHA does approve, the lot and neighborhood, it will be
much easier to build a home without paying cash for the
construction. The new housing law makes it possible for the
extension of mortgage payments up to 30 years at a low rate of
interest. After the lot has been purchased and is free of debt, you
may then apply for a FHA loan, however rigid, in that your credit
rating must be very high and your income substantial."*

Let us put this in context with today's concern related to lawyers
who see the violations but turn a blind eye to the violations. I have
had dozens of people who have approached me in my small circle
stating they can't find legal help to fight the economic injustice
against them.

The black real estate broker in 1949 is sharing with his readers the
problem with "The System." During this period, only one black
attorney was practicing in the State of Alabama courts, so there was
a gap for help. For about a decade, the NAACP started to take on
more cases, but their legal capacity was limited, and the attorneys
were few, while the cases were many. Attorney Arthur Shores of
Birmingham had already fought and won Birmingham's first racial
zoning case. Each deprivation of rights had to be fought individually
across the country when local governments, banks and realtors were
banking on blacks not being able to fight and take them to court and
win.

No one in the country had mounted a successful fight against the federal government and the ongoing redlining tactics to remove the ongoing property rights violations altogether against black citizens until the passing of Martin Luther King, Jr. almost 20 years later. Today, many are turning a blind eye to these rights still.

On September 20, 2020, the U.S. Senate Committee on Banking, Housing, and Urban Affairs presented the Minority Staff Report titled 'TURNING BACK THE CLOCK - How the Trump Administration Has Undermined 50 Years of Fair Housing Progress'. The report stated:

*"Facing the pressure of continued social unrest, the Kerner Commission's report, and the assassination of civil rights leader Reverend Dr. Martin Luther King Jr., Congress and the Johnson Administration passed the Civil Rights Act of 1968. This law included the Fair Housing Act, which for the first time prohibited anyone from refusing to sell or rent a property to someone based upon the protected classes of race, color, religion, or national origin."*

Now, it is critical to understand the evilness of unequal protection of the law regarding property for black citizens across the country.

Attorney General Janet Reno (1993 – 2001):

*"To shun an entire community because of its racial makeup, is just as wrong as to reject an applicant because they are African American." "Some neighborhood banks may turn away blacks because of their race, but other neighborhoods may not even have banks to which blacks can turn."*

Assistant Attorney General for Civil Rights Deval L. Patrick (1994):

*"You can't be refused service, if there is no service being offered."*

If you don't know the history of systemic injustice, then you repeat it, and it is widespread today.

T.L. Forrest, Real Estate Editor for The Weekly Review
Birmingham, Alabama · Friday, February 11, 1949 (Colored
newspaper):

*"Are there any sub-divisions being built by Negroes in the city of
Birmingham?*

*Answer: So far, land sites have been purchased and developed by
one Negro real estate broker, but to date there has been no
building program enacted.*

*The principal reason for this is lack of financing. In order for one
individual to buy sizeable tracts of land and pay the cost of
completely building homes, that individual must possess an almost
unlimited amount of cash which few of us ever accumulate.*

*During the two years there has been several requests made from
various sources to obtain FHA financing which makes it easier for
a developer to market his property in the form of ready built homes
with a down payment within the reach of the prospective
purchasers.*

*In short, as before stated, our dual system of living is the primary
reason for the uneven treatment of the dire problem."*

Comparing black realtor comments separated by December 1948
and February 1949, the separate and unequal economic systems in
America are glaring to him, but was he thinking about the loss of
billions in wealth for African Americans from 1949 to 1999? He
probably had no idea the number would reach the billions, but he
did know it affected black households.

December 1948: There are 3 obvious concerns for the black realtor
statements that became an unfortunate economic injustice reality
just 2 months later. The black realtor stated: (1) "The selection of
the site is extremely important." "Before signing any [contract
make sure] that the lot will meet FHA requirements as to size and
location." "Check the property for the following things: Is the
neighborhood desirable?"

Now, how can a black purchaser make sure the property is desirable if you are black when banks, real estate agencies, and federal agencies across the county approve hundreds of redlining maps for FHA use in every state and descent size city in this country that outline black zoned areas as red or shaded gray for Negro concentration for areas where they will not approve loans? Red is defined as Hazardous. Everyone knows that black homes dominated the population adjacent to hazardous smoke and air pollution of neighboring manufacturing plants and landfills and more.

In the February 1949 article, the same black realtor explained the dire economic problem as no blacks could get financing even after a black real estate broker purchased the land. The black realtor wrote, "So far, land sites have been purchased and developed by one Negro real estate broker, but to date there has been no building program enacted." "The principal reason for this is lack of financing. For one individual to buy sizeable tracts of land and pay the cost of completely building homes, that individual must possess an almost unlimited amount of cash which few of us ever accumulate." The realtor closes with a truthful example of being black and locked out of federal programs investing in white families' assets. The black realtor wrote: "Our dual system of living is the primary reason for the uneven treatment of the dire problem."

There was a hope for federally backed financing for blacks, and then there was a reality of that hope being removed. At the same time, he and many black citizens across the country watched the greatest source of wealth creation for white families from 1865 to 2023 plus.

The black realtor's final statement in December 1948 is also critical to both real estate injustice and unjust labor conditions in Birmingham. "If the FHA does approve, the lot and neighborhood, it will be much easier to build a home without paying cash for the construction. The new housing law makes it possible for the extension of mortgage payments up to 30 years at a low rate of interest. After the lot has been purchased and is free of debt, you may then apply for a FHA loan, however rigid, in that your credit rating must be very high and your income substantial."

The black realtor states your income must be substantial, but how can black income be substantial for the majority when under de facto segregation, every major industry makes sure you have the most dangerous lowest paying jobs possible while your white counterparts are always paid more and are the designed leadership."

In the March 10, 1993 'Part I of a Study of Alternatives,' Prepared for the National Park Service, Department of the Interior Cooperative Agreement CA-5000-1-9011; Birmingham Historical Society; Birmingham, Alabama; (The following conditions made about 1887, followed blacks through the civil rights movement through 1968.)

*"Informal distinctions were soon made between what was "white work" and what was "black work," with the latter covering the low paid, menial and hot jobs. In an 1887 publication, Birmingham businessmen sought to allay the fears of a multiracial industrial work force. Many company officials listed in this guide to Jefferson County and Birmingham stated:*

*"As to labor, about three fourths employed are southern whites. Negroes, as a class, will not become skilled laborers. All labor is southern born. Negroes are not to be relied on except for lower grades of employment."*

When I kept reading the repeated examples where property rights were removed from black citizens, I became more determined. However, I became more disappointed regarding the former friends and associates in my 2018- 2023-plus fight. Today, the layer of black gatekeepers pushing the white racist agenda of others and keeping their communities down is extremely tragic. I remind myself that our communities and livelihoods are worth fighting. We have lost too much and need the door of opportunity opened to our communities.

The Weekly Review: Birmingham, Alabama · Friday, March 04, 1949:

*"W. H. (Chief) Atkins of Atlanta, GA, President of the National Builders Association, in the keynote address at the regional*

*conference on building experts convened at Smithfield Court [in Birmingham, AL] and he said his organization would call on President Truman in a few days to solicit his aid in breaking down the discriminatory practices of agencies who refuse to lend money to Negroes to build homes solely on the basis of race. It seems that lending agencies in many instances are conspiring to keep Negroes in slum and blighted rental house areas by denying them loans after FHA approval has been obtained."*

Some blacks and whites were standing up, but nothing changed for black citizens across the United States until the passing, of the Fair Housing Act of 1968, roughly 20 years later. I have realized that the economic injustice got harder for black citizens.

The Alpha Phi Chapter of Omega Psi Phi fraternity members in Birmingham wrote a resolution in 1949. They published the resolution in the local newspaper after multiple racial zoning bombings because blacks were just looking for quality housing. (The Weekly Review: Birmingham, Alabama · Friday, April 08, 1949)

*"Whereas, three homes purchased by Negroes were bombed about midnight' Thursday, March 24, 1949, and,*

*Whereas, this bombing did cause serious damage to the property involved, and has also caused irreparable financial injury to the owners of these dwellings, and,*

*Whereas, this is not the first of such bombings to occur in this vicinity, and has therefore, aroused the dignity and sensibilities of all peace-loving citizens in this community, and,*

*Whereas, person living in this vicinity have been put in fear of their lives and their property because of this outrage.*

*Now, therefore, therefore, the undersigned members of the Alpha Phi Alpha Chapter of Omega Psi Phi fraternity have adopted the following resolutions:*

*1: That it be declared to all the world that racial zoning laws are contrary to the letter and the spirit of our Federal Constitution,*

114

*and are in abomination to all farsighted and reasonable human beings.*

*2: That all people regardless of their race, color, or creed have a right to live in peace and security where they are able to buy.*

*3: That we will use all in our power to search out the guilty party or parties. We further request the cooperation of all law enforcement agencies, or groups to join with us in our crusade to bring the dynamiters of justices.*

*Signed: E.J. Oliver, C.W. Lee, James G. Heath, James C. Johnson, Henry J. Williams, William E. Heard, Paul L. Ware, William H. Jackson, R. Reed, R.C. Johnson, Leon White, Abraham Jones, Thomas O. Jenkins, M.H. Caswell, N.J. Terrell, Arthur Reed, J.L. Lowe, E.J. McDaniels Jr., Wm Merriweather, Wilfred W. Howell, Oscar W. Adams Jr, Emory O. Jackson*

The 1949 open letter by the men of Omega Psi Phi Fraternity, Inc. is another supercritical historical example that links to economic justice today post-2020.

Button Gwinnet of the Shades Valley Sun wrote on June 9, 1949, and published in The Weekly Review: Birmingham, Alabama · Friday, June 10, 1949, the following article titled.

*'Crisis in Smithfield'.*

*"The Smithfield zoning crisis is a challenge to the Birmingham community. It involves us all in the necessity for a local solution to what is the most difficult domestic problem of our country and time."*

*"It is a problem which does not permit of a legal or legislative solution. Under the 14th Amendment to the Federal Constitution any provision of an ordinance attempting any zoning classification based on race or color is absolutely void. Our own Federal District Judge Mullins has so ruled with respect to the very Birmingham ordinance which until his ruling was the basis of our local segregation. That ordinance is invalid and any further*

*attempt to force any person charged with its violation to take his case to the Federal Courts would be a grave injustice to him and nothing short of an attempt to nullify the Constitution."*

*But to say that no legal steps are open to solve the problem does not necessarily mean the problem is insoluble. The customs and traditions of the southern people on the race issue have yielded only slowly to the 14th and 15th amendments since they were adopted 80 years ago. Feelings are very deep, and if we ignore them, serious trouble is likely to occur again in probably aggravated form. We have got to try to find a solution based on something other than the law.*

*Under such circumstances, what better reliance can be found than the common sense of our people? In the gradual evolution of the Negro over many decades toward more equal and responsible participation in our common life, the Negro and white elements of the community have gotten along well simply on the basis of agreement as to what is and what is not practically possible. Why should not the Birmingham City Commission in the present situation call in the Birmingham Urban League, the Alabama chapter of the Southern Regional Council, and leaders among the clergy, the teachers, the business men and other Negro groups and reach agreement with them as to fair and reasonable areas which may be allocated to Negro residential purposes? Some concessions to the Negroes to give them more adequate room for living should undoubtedly be made, but when the agreement has been reached there can be little doubt that the rank and file of the Negro population would follow their leadership in accepting it. Then it will be up to the Commission and all the white citizenship to enforce the agreement among white die-hards who may see to resort to violence."*

*Signed Button Gwinnett, Shades Valley Sun, June 9, 1949*

I was extremely concerned about this 70-year-old article when I first read it because it reminded me of my battles in the majority black business district and community in the Ensley area of Birmingham that started in 2018 and continues through 2023. I have been economically suppressed in Ensley for 5 years and counting, and the black community there has been economically suppressed since 1883, when Enoch Ensley first came to the region before Ensley became a part of Birmingham. I had no idea of the economic injustice I would face for several years as it often takes time for violators to violate your rights, and then for you realize your rights were violated. I filed state and federal complaints, and all agencies up to this point have acted with deliberate indifference or failed to investigate meaningfully or failed to discipline or failed to correct known violations.

Redlining is a very well-known illegal practice in this country that dates back to this period in the 1930s to 1960s. This practice mostly stole generations of wealth and opportunity from black citizens while white citizens were sending their kids to school, investing in businesses and passing generational wealth down, a practice denied to blacks. The local government, state government and federal government have allowed the practice to continue where there are some held accountable but very few in comparison to the economic suppression that has caused irreparable damages to black communities and those millions who have passed away never enjoying equal protection of the law for their property related economic rights.

Many of our fights continue because those "dynamiters of justice," as the writer wrote in 1949, are watching our rights being suppressed in 2023 and beyond under the watch.

I have learned that petitioning the government is a good first step, but if the government doesn't act or act with deliberate indifference, you have no choice but to prepare to stand in the courtrooms of justice with or without a lawyer. You may just have to represent yourself, and if that is the case, with enough preparation, you are more than capable of learning the law, the procedures, and the customs to stand up for your rights.

The 1949 writer means well when he suggests "concessions" and "We have got to try to find a solution based on something other than law." The mere acceptance creates many concerns for the future of the black community here. Mind me, this is 14 years before the 16th Street Church bombing that killed 4 little girls, so that is at least one form of "serious trouble" that was likely to occur, as he stated that bombing buildings and homes was a way of life for the die-hards in Birmingham and other cities across the country but worst in Birmingham. Now, for black citizens to agree to concessions is to agree to a dismissal of their Federal Constitution rights that are guaranteed rights. Blacks had to concede their rights to live in a Jim Crow America, which was a common de facto practice, and this practice prolonged Jim Crow and made Separate but Unequal under the Plessy vs. Ferguson decision last longer. The timing wasn't right, so blacks who could not mount federal court litigation had to deal with it until 1968 and beyond in many cases.

When I moved back to Birmingham, I often drove through the most deprived neighborhoods in Birmingham, and I kept seeing a few patterns repeat. We have an area called Woodlawn, and it's a great model for restoration. There has been much effort put in by various non-profits, foundations, community development corporations, churches and the local government, but one pattern stuck out post-2013.

On the south side of 1st Ave North in the Woodlawn area, I noticed that houses were being renovated left and right, and values were soaring well north of several hundred thousand. The as-is properties were getting as-is appraisals above $50,000, and many of the same as-is houses on the north side of 1st Ave North values never would reach $50,000. I spoke with a banker one day, and he made a statement about pulling equity from your home, but it has to appraise over $50,000. The light bulb started to go off, and all I could think about was those locked out, separated by a single road. One of my friends complained about his values, but several years passed. A white church bought a former school on the north side of 1st Ave N, and the values he complained about began changing. Many know all too well what is going on to deprive black communities, and they ignore it and blame the people within for being unable to improve their conditions.

I received a call from a friend who bought several houses in the Norwood neighborhood, and she expressed the same concern, but no line was drawn on the ground; there was a color on the application. The friend never mounted a lawsuit, which is understandable because it frustrates life, and people must weigh their options. Many know fighting these fights is hard, so many never mount the stand for equal protection of the law. Many in leadership know these conditions exist in decaying neighborhoods, and many in leadership just turn a blind eye. The issue with Norwood is that the neighborhood is actively going through gentrification, and house values have gone from under $75,000 to well over $250,000 to $400,000 in many cases once renovated. I'm not even focused on residential issues, but I saw the obvious injustice, and others know the injustice is there, too.

**Let's close this Chapter with G.I. Loans**.
T.L. Forrest, Real Estate Editor for The Weekly Review
Birmingham, Alabama · Friday, June 17, 1949 (Colored newspaper):

*Question: Why is it so different for a Negro GI to get a 100 percent loan on a home in Birmingham?*

*Answer: There have been several reasons in addition to the usual one. The requirements are very high for this particular loan. "The government has certain specifications laid down covering land sights." "In meeting specifications, we find ourselves in the inevitable corner that the Negroes live in Birmingham. It is almost impossible to find a sizable plot of land that can be used exclusively for high-grade residential purposes. As before stated, the same home in different residential zones and industrious encroach will be to create rigid residential sections some distances from the city." "The best subdivision in our city is Ellsberry Park located in Acipco. Last week 100 percent GI loans were approved for these homes." In veteran interested should act at once as there are only about two dozen left."*

History has proven that black GIs across the country did not get much access to these loans while white GIs were going to college and securing housing off the same GI Bill during the Jim Crow era. Now, we look back at history; there was a heavy polluter around Ellsberry Park, one of the few areas that approved GI loans for blacks in Birmingham.

Redlining maps and racial zoning denied black GIs nationwide, which continued even when the maps were removed.

**What happened after 1970?**

Article titled: 'Anti-redlining measure dies but city realizes problem' (Birmingham Post-Herald: Birmingham, Alabama · Wednesday, August 09, 1978)

*The Birmingham City Council yesterday refused to adopt a resolution that the city will not place its money in banks that are redlining neighborhoods but indicated it is sensitive to the problem and will take steps to end the practice.*

*Councilman Larry Langford was unable to get anyone to second his motion to withdraw city money from banks, which evidence shows are redlining. Langford argued that the resolution is needed if local banks are ever to stop discriminating against certain neighborhoods in making loans.*

*Langford asked city economic development director Joe Knight if there was evidence of "overt" redlining by area banks and other lending institutions, and Knight said "there was."*

Birmingham Post-Herald; Birmingham, Alabama: Mon, Oct 6, 1997. Article title: 'Wealth Gap keeps penalizing blacks.'

*The unequal results are caused by an unbroken 132-year legacy of government affirmative action in asset building for white Americans. White Americans received far more land for homesteading at the end of the Civil War than blacks did. In the 1930s, federal programs and tax policies promoted housing and business expansion in the suburbs for white Americans while the Federal Housing Authority denied loans to black neighborhoods.*

*Bank redlining lasting into this decade. The damage done was tremendous. The wealth of white families, enhanced by a rise in home equity twice that of blacks from 1967 to 1997, are in a far better position to transfer wealth to kin, start-up businesses and make other long-term investments.*

*Blacks, with much less upfront money, continue to be punished today in the home purchase market." In all, Oliver and Shapiro estimate that institutional biases in real estate have cost the current generation of blacks 83 billion in assets. They say if nothing is done, the next generation will lose $103 billion.*

It is critical that if you are interested in the economic conditions in Black communities you must be familiar with critical books all published in 2017 that focus on the conditions of intentionally deprived communities

(1) **Color of Law:** A Forgotten History of How our Government Segregated America by Richard Rothstein which is a deep dive into redlining, highway removal act and other laws that destroyed our communities under the color of law and created wealth for others.

(2) **The Color of Money:** Black Banks and the Racial Wealth Gap by Mehrsa Baradaran is a must read on economic policies stretching back the founding of the country to the first black banking system in this country up to the present. The most profound quote from her book is "When the Emancipation Proclamation was signed in 1863, the black community owned a total of 0.5% of the total wealth in the U.S."

(3) **How to Kill a City:** Gentrification, Inequality, and the Fight for the Neighborhood by Peter Moskowitz is a must read for how cities are using policies and deliberate indifference to allow certain communities to fall apart. This book was on the mayor of Birmingham and the economic development director of Birmingham must read list.

The only concern with How to Kill a City, is what do you do when you are in one of those communities and "The System" is allowing your community to be killed?

Injustice is widespread, and my fight for justice in Alabama is federal, so my fight may be similar to your battle in another intentionally targeted and underserved community. I am sharing my letters with you because there are laws I learned, and I started reciting them in the letters as I learned more and more. If you face similar economic injustice in your city, I want you to use my files to help you stand up for your or your client's rights.

I invested in the Ensley historic business district in the city limits of Birmingham, AL. We face multiple devastating economic enemies, all occurring under the color of law involving intentional public disinvestment across the commercial community. We are faced with redlining on all fronts. We are dealing with the economic enemies of unfair banking, unfair appraisals, federal program fraud, redlining, reverse redlining, and municipal disinvestment. Last but not least, we are located in an economic sacrifice zone.

Downtown Ensley in Birmingham is the largest underdeveloped commercial district in the city, and not a single realtor, banker, corporate leader, or political leader has spoken up for undeniable economic injustice in a city that brands itself as a bedrock city for Civil Rights in the U.S. The spirit in the 1963 pictures and videos has been carefully trapped over time, and black Birmingham has remained deprived and concealed by the images of the same repeated few blacks who protect the status quo.

I unknowingly stepped into the worst examples of systemic economic suppression I could imagine. There were some aspects of injustice I expected, but not the scale of the matter and coverups involving nearly a dozen government agencies. You must know the damage redlining has done to underserved communities across the country, so I open with statements from the Department of Justice.

What does the Department of Justice say about modern-day redlining?

Department of Justice and Mayor of Newark, NJ statements – April 2023

*Mayor Baraka, Newark NJ. "Redlining has been historically pervasive and deliberate in this country, and cities like Newark have been at the front end of the abuse. While redlining is illegal, we know that this ugly form of racism is still widely practiced,"*

*"To deny people, specifically in black and Latino neighborhoods in Newark, mortgage-lending services, based strictly on their race, robs and makes the American dream of homeownership unattainable. It impedes families from building generational wealth and widens the racial wealth gap. We must hold lenders accountable for their illegal and racist policies and behaviors and take deliberate action to reverse the effects of redlining and stop it."*

U.S. Civil Rights Division / Combating Redlining Initiative: Assistant Attorney General Kristen Clarke: *"Ending redlining is a critical step in closing the widening gaps in wealth between communities of color and others. We have a duty to act now. Persisting racial inequality and widening wealth gaps makes clear that simply staying the course is not enough. We must take bold, new action if we are ever going to eradicate redlining, and achieve the goal of equal opportunity in our country*

*U.S. Attorney Sellinger: "Part of the promise of America is equal opportunity." "Achieving that dream should be color blind – whether you get a home loan should not depend on the color of your skin or national origin. Redlining is racist, pure and simple. This type of systemic and intentional discrimination cannot – and will not – be tolerated."*

*"In October 2021, Attorney General Merrick B. Garland launched the Justice Department's Combating Redlining Initiative, a coordinated enforcement effort to address this persistent form of discrimination against communities of color." "Since the initiative was launched, the department has announced six redlining cases and settlements and nearly $85 million in relief for communities of color that have been victims of lending discrimination across the country."*
**https://www.justice.gov/opa/pr/justice-department-hosts-forum-newark-new-jersey-highlight-nationwide-effort-combat-modern**

What is redlining, and how did it affect America?

*Federal Reserve (compliance handbook)*

*"Redlining is the practice of denying a creditworthy applicant a loan for housing in a certain neighborhood even though the applicant may otherwise be eligible for the loan. The term refers to the presumed practice of mortgage lenders of drawing red lines around portions of a map to indicate areas or neighborhoods in which they do not want to make loans."*

*"Redlining on a racial basis has been held by the courts to be an illegal practice. It is unlawful under the [Fair Housing Act] only when done on a prohibited basis. Redlining an area on the basis of such considerations as the fact that the area lies on a fault line, or a flood plain is not prohibited."*

*"The prohibition against redlining does not mean that a lending institution is expected to approve all housing loan applications or to make all loans on identical terms. Denying loans or granting loans on more-stringent terms and conditions, however, must be justified on the basis of economic factors and without regard to the race, color, religion, national origin, sex, or marital status of the prospective borrowers or the residents of the neighborhood in which the property is located. For example, a bank may consider such economic factors as • An applicant's income or credit history • The condition, use, or design of the proposed security property (or of those nearby properties that clearly affect the value of the proposed security property), provided that such determinants are strictly economic or physical in nature • The availability of neighborhood amenities or city services • The need of the lender to hold a balanced real estate loan portfolio, with a reasonable distribution of loans among various neighborhoods, types of property, and loan amounts Each of the factors must be applied without regard to any of the prohibited bases."*

https://www.federalreserve.gov/boarddocs/supmanual/cch/fair_lend_fhact.pdf

**According to the Department of Justice:**

*"The majority of pattern or practice cases involve claims of race discrimination."*

*The Fair Housing Act of 1968 prohibits discrimination by direct providers of housing, such as landlords and real estate companies as well as other entities, such as municipalities, banks or other lending institutions and homeowners insurance companies whose discriminatory practices make housing unavailable to persons because of: race or color, religion, sex, national origin, familial status, or disability.*

But what do we do when race and other protected classes are covert, and they no longer use race or a protected class explicitly? We must get to the core of civil rights for all citizens, and then we have a chance.

# CHAPTER 10: THE $0.00 APPRAISAL

When I received a $0.00 appraisal for my commercial buildings and only $45,000 for my land, the unlawful action halted everything remotely close to equal rights in my head and in reality.

This book would not have been created if there were a small semblance of equal rights. I would have been distracted by the positive, constructive spaces I planned to develop. There are no equal rights in a $0.00 appraisal. It always amazed me how people would try to justify the $0.00. The moment a person starts down the road to try to figure out a $0.00 appraisal, it tells me they are either so indoctrinated to injustice that it is normal to them or they are supporters of injustice towards people like me. The only justification for buildings appraised at $0.00 with tenants paying rent is fraud, ethics violation of United States Professional Appraisal Practices (USPAP), modern-day redlining, unfair lending, economic injustice and public agencies turning a blind eye to the rights of the deprived. The only justification for comparing inner city urban multi-story historic buildings to rural farmland and an abandoned car wash is fraud. The distance chosen to find unjust comps is proof to more fraud when many comps exist under 10 miles and several just a mile or 2 away. There is no justification for gross misapplication and covering up their acts other than fraud.

I have filed several hundred pages with state and federal agencies regarding the $0.00 appraisal, and several have taken extreme action to cover up the actions. When state and federal agencies, one after another, turned a blind eye, their actions caused me to dig deep and research everything possible to stand up for my rights taken from me and my community. A $0.00 value for my buildings has to be the worst appraisal in the U.S. A $0.00 value for my active renters has to be the worst income approach to value appraisal in the U.S. The local county not allowing me to protest my taxes as other citizens have caused me to realize that layers of systemic economic injustice are attacking me all at once. Now, I'm dealing with taxation without representation.

What has also been sad in my hometown is the attorneys who will not touch my case. It's as if they are afraid to stand against a known injustice in our communities. Zero lawyers willing to stand up has caused me to educate myself on the law as much as possible. Zero public agencies standing for my undeniable property rights have caused me to lose years preparing for federal court. Zero local black leaders blaming the bank or appraisal company for undeniable fraud and choosing to attack me has made me realize why our communities have not progressed. Too many have a vested interest in our deprivation.

I am like many people across the country. I have heard many express dreams of moving back to their hometowns with a desire to make a difference. I made that move, and over time, I realized that I was standing alone, faced with the weight of undeniable economic injustice committed by the largest appraisal company in the U.S. and a regional bank.

I sought help through my First Amendment right, and I was met with willful blindness, conscious disregard, and deliberate indifference by public officials at the local City government, County government, multiple State governmental agencies, and multiple Federal governmental agencies where all entities chose to turn a blind eye to my undeniable property rights.

Imagine you go to your local convenience store when filling your car up, and you walk in and purchase a single "blow pop" for 25 to 55 cents. Just imagine knowing you purchased 8 commercial buildings with tenants in 5 units, and the appraiser omits 100% of your rent roll and says your buildings have a $0.00 value in the income approach to value. Just imagine the appraiser comparing your urban inner city multi-story 100-year-old historic properties to rural farmland, and more concerning, comps involving a vacant car wash. Then, the appraiser writes that the comps used are superior to your buildings, so there should be a deduction of the value of your buildings to $0.00 in the as-is appraisal approach and only giving you value for your land. Remember, you bought the blow pop for 25 cents, and the appraiser writes out a formal appraisal where the blow pop is more than 25 times the value of your buildings.

You seek help; every governmental agency turns a blind eye and conceals the fraud. You reach out to lawyers and learn that none will stand with you in your so-called civil rights city. You reach out to other banks and they say we are not touching that with very vague responses. You reach out to anyone you can, and they start ghosting you. You are now trapped under the weight of true economic injustice. "They" bankrupted you without bankrupting you as you have no access to 100% of your equity to improve your buildings to increase your rent roll. You have no access to your equity to manage any deferred maintenance, and you are all alone trying to figure out what the hell just happened and how many people and entities are involved. You say to yourself, **"What underworld did I invest in?"**

From 2018 to 2023, I went from being a friend and associate of many local leaders to announcing my purchase of a block of commercial buildings in Ensley. I then announced my dreams of turning these spaces into different versions of creative co-working spaces. I put plans together for an art studio and gallery to bring positive energy to the area. I drew up plans for tech spaces, conference rooms, office spaces, dance and yoga studios, photography studios, lofts, workforce development spaces, and various other spaces to create a needed, positive environment in a shunned, underserved, recklessly neglected community. News agencies across the City interviewed me left and right. City officials, city employees, and non-profit leaders met with me regularly, but I noticed that nothing ever came of their meetings. I lost 6 months, then another 6 months, then another 6 months, and then another. When all the time had passed, I realized "They" didn't come to help; they came to learn me. I wasn't in their plans for Ensley. I wasn't supposed to buy a block of commercial buildings in the heart of Downtown Ensley.

When the $0.00 appraisal was released, it locked me out of 100% of my equity from my buildings. I sought help and was labeled controversial by black leader after black leader. One city executive previously had written a letter of support for all the community work I was involved in, but I was now controversial. I started seeing those I supported 100% turn against me, one by one.

I eventually learned that Downtown Ensley met all the characteristics of an "Economic Sacrifice Zone." There are local, state and federal property rights violations everywhere, and the local government has accepted it as normal. Most local property owners have become numb to the persistent economic injustice and municipal investment. I didn't know the majority black community I invested in was shunned and targeted until I stepped inside the economic sacrifice zone.

What is a Sacrifice Zone?

*In land use planning, the terms sacrifice zones, sacrifice area, and 'locally unwanted land use' (LULU) describe these areas. A sacrifice zone is an area damaged by heavy environmental pollution or economic disinvestment. On June 7th, 2004, in a letter to the US Environmental Protection Agency and the Office of the Inspector General, there is one of the first known mentions of the term 'sacrifice zone.' Professor Robert D. Bullard of Clark Atlanta University says: "The solution to unequal protection lies in the realm of environmental justice for all Americans. No community, rich or poor, black or white, should be allowed to become a 'sacrifice zone.'"*

What is Municipal Disinvestment?

*"Municipal disinvestment is the process by which public jurisdictions decide to target neighborhoods through strategies sometimes known as benign neglect, planned shrinkage, or slum clearance. The purpose is to encourage so-called "undesirable populations" to leave an area to make land available for "best use" applications. Euphemisms such as (re)development, urban renewal, revitalization, and triage are often red flags indicating targeted neighborhoods." (As quoted by Phillip J. Obermiller & Thomas E. Wagner in 'Meeting the Challenge of Municipal Disinvestment')*

This business district had the highest percentage increase of property taxes anywhere in the county, with increases up to 535% in 2020. Neighbors were paying $1100 in taxes in 1 year and then the next year paying over $7500 while there was no new development in the area.

This business district unlawfully recorded the lowest possible appraised value in the country in 2019: my $0.00 appraisal on all 8 of my building structures. This business district is a 2018 – 2028 victim of a 10-year Department of the Treasury and IRS tax fraud scheme through a manipulated federal census robbing us of needed federal, state, and local incentives, programs, resources, and services, and all in local leadership have turned a blind eye. I thought that were enough obstacles in 1 business district. Then I protested my property taxes using the $0.00 approved appraisal, and the county board of equalization denied me my right to protest my taxes, which all property owners have in this country. I thought that was the worst of my experiences until I sought help from state and federal agencies, and every public entity turned a blind eye to undeniable property rights violations.

In American slavery, the enslaved had no rights to property written into the laws of the land in overt legal injustice. Still, my community and I are being injured through covert injustice, and everyone is silent about it in my hometown. I have been a single squeaking wheel with no allies, just associates who whisper in my ear where many work in the same entities of those depriving me, and they say I love what you are standing up for.

Today, no government entity has recognized my rights to property. Maybe I need a clever lawyer to argue my 13th Amendment rights violations, as I'm sure I'm dealing with the existence of badges and incidents of slavery that were supposedly abolished under the 13th Amendment. Finding a lawyer has been almost impossible in this redlined environment. It's like the lawyers have accepted this condition for our communities.

No equal protection of the law has reached this community, and this was confirmed when I asked my neighbors if they had received loans to develop their commercial properties over the last 30-plus years. I learned that in the last 30 years, I could locate 1 black property owner who received a loan from a local bank to properly develop their properties when blacks owned over 50 commercial buildings. The powers to be in the City have proven they have no interest in altering this reality. It's sad because entire commercial districts and adjacent neighborhoods are completely underdeveloped and blighted.

I quickly learned that black and white public officials and private corporate leaders were all knowingly turning a blind eye and intentionally taking actions to deprive me and this community. It did not matter that black leaders had led the local government for 40-plus years. It did not matter that the Ensley business district is now one of the country's largest black-majority commercial property-owned areas. The product of economic suppression was the same, and the local government by skin color is the opposite of 1963 in 2023. Birmingham has been operating under a black-led local government from 1979 to 2023 and counting. The county and state have always been led by a majority white government where almost every major decision that reaches the black community is based on race and economics. It appears that economic opportunity is always hindered by race. In Birmingham, I have witnessed and recorded nearly a 4-decade history led by black-on-black economic discrimination on the face.

It has been a mind-boggling 5 years in what I truly believe is Birmingham's most shunned and targeted majority black community. I am committed to fighting for my stolen dreams. Unfortunately, those close to me are on the other side.

I will not create a contest of what area is more impoverished, shunned, or targeted because when policies, disinvestment, neglect, and other circumstances crush a community economically and environmentally, they are all at the bottom; some are just larger or smaller. Now, we have crabs in human form that were never meant to be in the bucket they were placed in when their natural response is to use their claws, and unfortunately, they pull on everyone trying to escape the bottom. I have seen the bottom in Baltimore, Knoxville, Milwaukee, Richmond, Cincinnati, Jackson, Montgomery, Mobile, Memphis, Savannah, San Francisco, Chicago and many more cities. The first thing I do when I travel is to find America's bottom. It Is an area of purpose for me, and I will fight to improve the conditions of people at the bottom.

**I never knew so many local black leaders were involved in being roadblocks for other black professionals until I came back to Birmingham in 2013.** In Martin Luther King, Jr.'s letter from a Birmingham Jail, King addressed two opposing forces within the black community. I am showing you, with concern, how those 2 opposing forces have compounded with concern 60-plus years after 2020. I have faced every bit of this since moving back to Birmingham while trying to find a way to improve the conditions of one of the most deprived and shunned underserved communities in Birmingham.

1963 Martin Luther King, Jr. 'Letter from a Birmingham Jail':

*"I started thinking about the fact that I stand in the middle of two opposing forces in the Negro community. One is a force of complacency made up of Negroes who, as a result of long years of oppression, have been so completely drained of self-respect and a sense of "somebodyness" that they have adjusted to segregation, and, on the other hand, of a few Negroes in the middle class who, because of a degree of academic and economic security and*

*because at points they profit by segregation, have unconsciously become insensitive to the problems of the masses. The other force is one of bitterness and hatred and comes perilously close to advocating violence."*

*"Oppressed people cannot remain oppressed forever. The urge for freedom will eventually come. This is what has happened to the American Negro. Something within has reminded him of his birthright of freedom; something without has reminded him that he can gain it."*

I remember when I arrived in this majority-black community and started investing. Many former friends and associates were there with me step by step, but the hateful ones were in the background. When I hit my first roadblock and what appeared to be a normal bank delay, the former friends and associates of goodwill were supposedly still with me. A few months passed; I remember asking for help from the City of Birmingham in the Mayor's conference room with 10 or more staff and partners present. I stated that the biggest concern in Ensley is that my neighbors can't get bank financing. I then said I had been met with some concerns with Synovus Bank and needed help. I remember the facial expressions and the loudest silence I ever heard. No one uttered a word. I didn't think much of it because I was unaware of the coming economic fight.

I remember the attack and withdrawals of other blacks in the City who were not directly involved. I asked for help publicly on social media in 2019, and about a week later, this is when the 1963 opposing force MLK spoke of in his letter from a Birmingham Jail appeared to me when he wrote:

*"Of a few Negroes in the middle class who, because of a degree of academic and economic security and because at points they profit by segregation, have unconsciously become insensitive to the problems of the masses"* **began to attack me in 2019.**

**This group, "Of a Few Negroes" began to attack and exile me in 2019 and they never stopped. I kept saying, "What the hell is going on in my hometown?"**

I never knew so many in the black middle class wanted others to fail, and that other was me. It didn't matter that I invested in a truly underserved and deprived community. The street-level crime we see is one thing, but the white-collar black gatekeepers come from those deprived communities. They may not be killing each other, but they are killing opportunities. The end effect for the community is deprivation.

Less than a week later, an extremely popular black TV news anchor approached me and said I will reach out to see if they can help. A city executive responded, "We can't help him." Shortly after, a leading black female realtor I went to high school with criticized me for speaking up about the appraisal. And she is someone who knows what redlining is, but it's better to hope I remain quiet somehow.

Over the next several months, I would see more and more black leaders distance themselves from me. It was amazingly obvious at the coffeehouse I attended. A black radio show host who always spoke to me would order coffee, walk outside and then wave through the window. One other person who is well-known but connected to the power structure wouldn't even walk across the same crosswalk. I saw him approach the crosswalk, turn left, cross the street, and then go across the next crosswalk and walk behind me. I said wow, that is a very controlled Negro. I remember meeting with that same Negro to help me raise funds after he contacted me. He sat down with me and never connected ever again. I now realized he never had any intention of helping but to gather information. I learned he was extremely close to my biggest opposition. I never had a negative conversation with him before.

I came across several black city leaders, non-profit leaders, corporate leaders, and entrepreneurs who would walk up to me and whisper in my ear, "I love what you are standing for in Ensley." Whispers were all I got that was positive from the successful black middle class.

I noted everything and remembered why the children marched in 1963 in this same City of Birmingham against white Jim Crow leaders. The adults had to keep their jobs so that fear was always there, and most never mumbled a word or stood up. Today, black Birmingham is living out the reality of not standing up for nearly 40 to 60 years, but this time, black leaders run the City. Birmingham ranked last in the country for black businesses in 1982 and last for business ownership rates in 2018. Poverty is widely spread throughout the black community, but some have jobs, and some have found success, just as MLK stated when referring to two opposing forces in 1963. The part that concerns me is those blacks who want underserved blacks to stay in their place. As MLK stated, "We must remember that oppressed people cannot remain oppressed forever, as the urge for freedom will eventually come."

A black bank president who I also knew would share statements with a mutual friend; How do we get Brian to shut up about his appraisal? The black bank president met me in my buildings soon after, and we discussed the appraisal, my current tenants, my pro forma, my business plan and my construction plan. He said they didn't even include your rent in your appraisal, which I didn't notice initially because the sales comparisons were so egregious and unethical, causing a 100% devaluation of my equity. When we started discussing how to get me funded, the next statement was not surprising, but it let me know that it didn't matter that the bank president was black and he represented a black bank. He is from the Birmingham area, and the first question was, "What are the demographics of Ensley?". Regardless of our previous association, I saw the same pattern repeat when he made that statement. I responded immediately, "Ensley had the same demographics as Avondale before Avondale was gentrified. I then stated that the demographics are the same as every other gentrified area in Birmingham and every City I have lived in before they were developed." Some may call this tough talk, but I knew he knew our economic obstacles' area and state.

I thought to myself and said this is what training has gotten our black bank leaders because they have been trained knowingly or unknowingly to find a reason not to loan in our communities based on guidelines that have historically deprived our communities. They didn't make the guidelines, but they operate within them while our communities continue to be deprived under their watch. The demographics question is typical, but I knew he knew the area well. The demographics, which would include the average income levels of the underserved residents, would be more than enough reason to decline any loan for commercial development.

There are always other factors, but, in this case, he probably knew the area better than I, as he had been the president for some time and had already given at least one loan in the area for commercial development. I eventually learned that the only loan that ever came from a local bank, which is not a traditional local bank for a black property owner to develop their commercial properties in Downtown Ensley when blacks own over 50 commercial buildings, came from his bank. Now, that one loan went to an attorney who already had a track record of suing the City and U.S. Steel regarding commercial development. The one loan came from a black bank, and Birmingham has many large national and regional banks, but for some reason, redlining is never brought up regarding Ensley.

I remember reaching out to one of the black doctors in Downtown Ensley, and his wife said to me they had to get their loan out of state from a guy in Pennsylvania or New Jersey, and then once we got up and going, we were able to refinance from a regular bank. Let's think about that: a doctor must go across the country post-2000 to get a loan, so what does a regular black person have to do?

I remember contacting another black doctor in Downtown Ensley and asking how she got her building and a loan from a local bank. She looked at me, paused and confirmed what I always believed. I got my building from a non-profit called B.E.A.T. No, I didn't get a bank loan to develop my property. I then said to myself, the setup is real. I am thankful she and others stayed committed to Ensley as they have learned to succeed despite the modern-day redlining.

Now, back to the black bank president: The black bank president eventually said, "This is easy; we can get you financed." I saw him a month or so later, and we shook hands like normal, but this time, he didn't make any eye contact, and he looked down and walked away. I said to myself, did he get bought off too? In my mind, I was determined to move forward legally either way; so I stayed on my path.

During this same period, I wrote the "Bold" grant and secured the grant from the City of Birmingham for my buildings and Downtown Ensley. I selected Urban Impact, a 501I(3), as my fiscal agent because I knew the City would not fund me directly. We won the grant, and the project manager from Urban Impact came to me one day and said "Brian, the Mayor, instructed us to **make sure none of the money goes to your buildings.**"

Around the same time, the mayor and the head of economic development met me in my buildings on October 13th, 2019. October 13th was the day and night that altered everything I believed in about the current Mayor. The mayor interrogated me for 45 minutes on and off about why I kept bringing up the appraisal during this multi-hour conversation with three of my neighbors, two public officials, one city director, and two support staff. The mayor was angry over my asking for help about the $0.00 appraisal. When he could not find any holes in my concerns about the unfair appraisal, he kept asking me, "Brian, what do you want that is tangible?"

I would respond every time the same way. I just want you to go before the community before you approve the city development one block away from me. He would ask, again and again, Brian, what do you want that is tangible? I was unaware that the mayor was trying to bait me. Still, the more I thought about it, I realized a few nights later that if I had said I wanted one dollar or several hundred thousand dollars, that would have likely been the beginning of a bribe to get me tangled in public corruption. The mayor was trying to use his influence to get me to support the Ramsay McCormack redevelopment, a city-owned property and court-ordered development one block away from my buildings, without going before the community. My concern never changed, and that angered the mayor more and more. I wanted the mayor to go before the community and allow more in the community to be involved in the development, which is based on clearly established laws for historic properties that would potentially be demolished. It bothered me when I had time to reflect on the mayor's actions, and I realized his actions could have trapped me into a bribery like so many past black leaders who have fallen for kickbacks.

I am sharing this because I want you, as the reader, to know that you cannot accept any kickbacks or potential kickbacks. We are in the age of social media, cameras, tapped lines, and cell phone recorders everywhere. You can't do it unless you want to be bought, compromised, and controlled. Stay true to your principles that you know are right, your conscience will never bother you, and you will have all you need to stand against injustice.

Back to the Mayor, the Mayor kept asking why you keep bringing this appraisal up. Did you meet with any bank president like he is playing a power play? Why didn't you come to me before? Why didn't you come to someone in the City before about the appraisal? I knew that I had gone to him and the City multiple times, but he was a different man to me at this point. I just didn't know why yet. I eventually discovered the corruption and connections. I will stand on my truth; it took thousands of hours of due diligence.

Later that night, I kept asking myself, "Why was the mayor angry about me asking for help with the appraisal?" This question stomped me many days and nights, but there was one thing he and the head of economic development confirmed in that meeting that caused me to search for evidence 16 plus hours a day for a year. The economic development director stated he and the mayor had a great relationship with Synovus Bank's president. I thought, Wow, I have been asking for help for over 10 months, and now you tell me you all have a great relationship." Between the confirmed great relationship and the angry Mayor when it came to me asking for help for my appraisal, within a week and for over a year straight, I started searching for any connections between the Synovus Bank, Ensley, the Mayor and the economic development director. Roughly, a year later, I found the smoking gun, which was the Federal Opportunity

Zone letter the mayor mailed to the Governor of Alabama, which included the bank, the Mayor, the economic development director, and several others that unlawfully excluded Ensley, where my buildings were located from federal incentives for 10 years.

It took me months to cross reference all included in the letter, and then I started sending hundreds of pages of evidence in formal complaints to state and federal agencies. I hoped for help, and the agencies ignored me or covered up the fraudulent actions of those involved. The inaction by state and federal agencies caused me to start preparing for federal litigation against a stacked deck called, **"The System."** Now, I knew what systemic injustice was. It was no longer a single public actor but many across different offices, agencies, and levels of government.

I was committed at this point, and in my head, I have prepared my mind to be ready to fight for the Supreme Court.

Soon after, one of my friends spoke to the head of economic development for me, saying he didn't know how to help me. I said OKAY because, at this time, I thought a regulatory agency would have helped.

I downloaded every City of Birmingham economic development committee meeting that was still online. I watched every meeting I could find over a 3-to-4-year period, and "Black Ensley Attorney #1" was involved in 2 of those meetings. The city treated him with complete disrespect. He showed up to present. He was on the schedule to present, and they dismissed him, and the meeting was adjourned. I said wow because in every meeting I watched over this 3-to-4-year period, "Black Ensley Attorney #1" was the only black person or, at most, only the 2nd black person. I saw that he presented before the majority black city in the economic development committee, and he was treated like it was Jim Crow, but this time, only the black leaders did it. Meeting after meeting, black leaders approved almost everything with minimum questioning whenever a White business owner presented. I also saw an additional Black lawyer representing most of the White businesses. The next meeting, "Black Ensley Attorney #1" selected one Black lawyer to represent him in the next meeting as he did not attend. Over time, I didn't hear or see anything until "Black Ensley Attorney #1" made nearly $3.5 million off an opportunity zone $4.25 million deal.

Soon, "Black Ensley Attorney #1" announced he had bought several more properties from the City of Birmingham in federal opportunity zones, and the 2250 Bessemer Rd. property was one of those properties. He played cool and won. I admired his wins, but why did he attack me the night of the mayor's re-election and not the mayor?

I studied the deal, and Rev Birmingham, Opportunity Alabama and the first opportunity zone developer in Birmingham were involved in the deal and bought his property to redevelop his former building. I knew Rev Birmingham was one of the twenty-eight companies that co-created the 3/6/18 fraudulent document that excluded Downtown Ensley from opportunity zones. The 3/6/18 letter steered federal resources from Downtown Ensley, Wylam, Pratt City, and half of the 5 Points West commercial district to benefit the men who co-created the letter. No known city councils were involved in the planning as the legislative body for the city. It is sad because the city council has access to the letter, and they never questioned not being the legislative body for the city on the 10-year incentive zone program that locked out most black commercial districts on the city's western side.

I also knew "Black Ensley Attorney #1" graduated from Ensley High School just blocks away from the unlawful fraud that robbed me and my neighbors, but this portion of Ensley didn't matter. I have seen a trend with many professionals in Birmingham where they move away and watch their childhood neighborhoods decay or face obstruction of commerce and intentional municipal disinvestment while they win. I was the new foe either way because I spoke up, and it didn't matter that I was fighting for the place he grew up in after sharing the undeniable fraud that halted my development.

I have nothing against "Black Ensley Attorney #1," but who is building capacity in the intentionally deprived area? Who is addressing the double standard of behaviors in the city that they put on Black businesses versus White? I want you to win, but it is not success if the vast majority is left out.

The few black business people across the city who are successful are treated like celebrities when there still needs to be a focus on building local capacity so more local businesses from the always deprived grow to the extent that they can hire more from the communities they are from. Now, when nothing happens, unemployment and underemployment are never properly addressed.

I have realized I got too close to the cookie jar where "Black Ensley Attorney #1" directly benefited from the sale of the former Red Cross building due to federal opportunity zones. The response against me was swift, and the deliberate indifference to his frat brother's actions has remained.

His new property is also in a federal opportunity zone, but just across the street where the grocery store sits; the fraud caused the entire commercial shopping center to be excluded from federal opportunity zones. Just half a block up on the next street called Warrior Rd, all are excluded across the street going all the way to the freeway covering 94.9 radio station and most, if not all, the Fairview and Bush Hills neighborhood are excluded. Just a mile further, Downtown Ensley is excluded.

No one has spoken up for Fairview, Bush Hills, Ensley Highlands, Belview Heights, and Central Park neighborhoods. The same fraud that excluded Downtown Ensley cut off majority black commercial areas that could have benefitted more easily. Bush Hills, a residential area, for example, has become a majority Black middle-class gentrifying neighborhood with several big-time investors with a lot of capital gains. None of them could use their capital gains through opportunity zones to focus on their developments in Bush Hills. Homes that were not in the best condition, 10 or more years ago were selling for $5000, $10,000, $30,000, and $50,000 on the high end. Investors were buying these properties, putting $75,000 in them, and then selling the same homes north of $200,000 and $300,000 in some cases, and they were making bank, which translates to capital gains. Federal Opportunity Zone legislation said you could write off investing 100% of your capital gains if you invested in an opportunity zone. Then, you can reap all the profit on the exit when you sell in 10 years. That is money on top of money stolen through fraud for the self-developing majority Black middle-class neighborhood. Nobody has spoken for them.

There are two former associates that I became disappointed in because they were at the table of opportunity, and both of their areas where they either live or do business are excluded. The former Black University Professor, now a Diversity and Inclusion manager for a major bank, was appointed as the District 8 representative on the Community Investment Board (CIB) for the Birmingham Inclusive Growth Partnership, created by the City of Birmingham for federal opportunity zones with the Black Ensley Financial Planner led by the former city economic development director.

In addition to the Black University Professor and the Black Ensley Financial Planner, they have placed themselves in the middle of matters of public concern involving a 10-year federal incentive zoning exclusion. Neither one has ever spoken up about the injustice that excludes them and their neighbors.

Even Charles Barkley was part of the public-private partnership with Opportunity Alabama president and more with the Public Benefits Corporation, so now all are connected to matters of public concern.

I intentionally created a 2-hour video on my website from my 8/14/2021 press conference the day after I filed a Department of Justice complaint with the Department of the Treasury Inspector General because I knew investigators would watch the video. Hopefully, regular people from the public would if they had an interest in local misuse of office and modern-day redlining in Downtown Ensley.

Many members of the Black middle class made significant capital gains in his neighborhood that could not use the 10-year federal incentive. I encourage those members to prepare a lawsuit against those involved in your exclusion once you read the facts. I have published my initial federal lawsuit on my website for anyone interested in standing up for property rights in deprived black communities.

It is easy to blame the system and look the other way until you find the evidence, and then you can focus on the actions of those involved.

I'm convinced when the conflict of interest runs too deep, people protect one side of the conflict at the expense of the other side. I'm extremely concerned, and the public should be extremely concerned over a regular pattern of playing musical chairs where the same professionals are placed on multiple key boards of quasi-government agencies. If they turn a blind eye to 1 public board, they will likely turn a blind eye to another public board. Those in power know how to use people willing to be used and rotate them around amidst very serious matters of public concern and interest. We have seen hundreds of millions and billions affected by federal opportunity zones in the local market. The Black University Professor and the Black Ensley Financial Advisor are listed as witnesses, at a minimum, in my federal lawsuit involving multiple public entities affecting the entire western side of Birmingham. I do not think they played a large role in this matter of public concern. Still, silence is compliance, and they played a role that caused a continuation of concealment attached to 2 or more persons that deprived me, my community and even their communities of their U.S. Constitutional rights.

The smallest light in the middle of darkness shines brightly, as most know. Marianne Williams: "Light is to darkness what love is to fear; in the presence of one, the other disappears." When no one chooses to speak up in positions of influence, the journey for the injured continues through deprivation of rights and due diligence until the truth is found.

Many across the City of Birmingham are very aware of the 15-year-plus lawsuit in Downtown Ensley that is forcing the City of Birmingham through court order to stop intentionally depriving Downtown Ensley of equal protection of the law related to economic development.

I'm convinced that when fraud excludes or cuts historic commercial districts and business districts, it affects every business and property owner there. Some may not know the depth of their economic injuries from the rigging and steering of federal resources away through fraud, but I hope they learn before it is too late. There is no equal protection of the law in fraud. Somebody's life, liberty, or property is injured, and I was one of the injured.

I wish many local black attorneys and others with legal backgrounds would help us fight for our economic rights because this fight affects the core of our family providers. Suppose the head of household cannot provide because there are limited to no jobs in their communities due to intentional economic suppression. In that case, their families will continue to be injured. The house becomes increasingly imbalanced, and when it reaches a certain level, those kids who can't afford after-school participation programs or find any that work for them because all the buildings are unusable tend to find their mentors in the streets. When family heads of households have a better income, life choices often change for the entire family. Please help us, wherever you are, to fight for families and communities.

In Ensley, darkness is everywhere, and buildings are not lit up with businesses, so the buildings become places for other activities. Wherever you are, if you are an attorney or in a position of influence or work for a public entity and your role is to protect our rights, please protect our rights.

Black Ensley Attorney #1 performed a legal analysis on Federal Opportunity Zones on June 11th, 2019, called 'Separating Fact From Fiction" on his Facebook page and stated, "The map encompasses most of Downtown, pretty much, all of Downtown Birmingham. It goes over to Ensley (Then his face cringes, his words merge), and it stops right at part of Downtown Ensley is not in the opportunity zone, which is nuts to me."

He confirmed what I was experiencing. It's nuts to me as well and then compounded with my $0.00 appraisal.

So, let's get this straight. For the first time in history, investors get this huge, unprecedented tax break, and they get to stack the capital on top of other state and federal incentives. Our country is built on capitalism. I have nothing against capitalism. I want capitalism all around me winning and incentivized just like other areas so I can win when my property value increases. I want my neighbors to win. I don't want my neighbors crushed because of systemic economic injustice when barrier after barrier stops them from developing so they can get started in the game and prepare for their families and futures.

Suppose a capitalist is federally and locally encouraged to invest their 100% capital gains in the most affluent areas of a city based on a known false report. In that case, the capitalist has been steered, and the monopoly game is played in real life. Let's say you get to invest next to a diamond mine or gold mine, which is the largest employer in the state. Let's say you get to invest next to a diamond mine or gold mine, which is the largest employer in the state. Let's say you get to invest next to the largest funded university in the state, next to the most developed central city area in the state for commercial buildings, next to the highest rent in the city, next to student scholarship-funded housing, federally funded tuition next to a minor league baseball stadium, why would you invest in a truly deprived area in the state when the local, state, and federal incentives have been removed if you are a true capitalist?

Let's say you get to invest immediately adjacent to one of the most affluent areas in the state when you get an extra 100% capital gains right off on the entry and the exit of the investment stacked on the capital stack created by a double agent who worked for both the city and in the office of the president of the largest employer in the state at the same time he excluded truly deprived areas to benefit the employer then you are not concerned about those left out. You follow the flow of incentives and money based on the public maps that say you can invest in this area and get 100% capital gain write-offs.

I have nothing against anyone who won off the selected opportunity zone census tracts in Birmingham that weren't part of the agreement or weren't involved in covering up the agreement where the agreement is the heart of the conspiracy. I found the written document on the official letterhead full of false statements about our Black neighborhoods on the west side of Birmingham.

Now, back to the City of Birmingham and when the mayor met me in my buildings on 10/13/2019:

About a year after the meeting with the mayor in my buildings, the City and a member of the National Community Reinvestment Coalition (NCRC), a national non-profit founded to fight redlining, started planning the federal banking summit in Ensley. This act was to please me as my $0.00 appraisal had become a nuisance. The meeting came, and it was during the first COVID year, so it was an online meeting. The agenda included one of my neighbors, NCRC rep Scarlett Duplechain of the federal Office of the Comptroller of the Currency and David Jackson, a senior adviser with the Federal Reserve Bank of Atlanta. I was completely excluded from the agenda, and I waited until I had a chance to ask one question with a statement during the meeting. I brought up that my buildings were appraised at $0.00, and I stated that the meeting was good to let us know where we could go for help. Duplechain emailed me the next day from my memory, and she sent me a link to file a federal complaint, which will be disseminated to the appropriate agency. I filed 2 formal complaints, 1 regarding the bank and 1 regarding the appraisal company. The Federal Reserve Board of Governors said they didn't see anything wrong with my $0.00 appraisal after their review. The Federal Trade Commission took over 2 years to respond, and they said they don't communicate with individuals but follow up with the State of Alabama. I eventually filed a complaint to protest my taxes, requesting my property taxes to be lowered to $0.00 to match the fraudulent appraisal approved by the Federal Reserve Board of Governors and backed by the Alabama State Appraisal Board later that year and the Jefferson County Board of Equalization would not let me have a hearing to protest my taxes, so the injustice continue. We will talk about taxation without representation in its chapter.

I remember when I went to a major bank in 2020, and I wish I had evidence other than hearsay. I sat with the black lady over Community Reinvestment Act (CRA) funding, and she said with a straight face, "Your problem, you made a mistake. You went to the wrong door. You went through the bank's front door when you should have gone to the back door." She then walked me down the hall and introduced me to her co-worker, who was also black, and she repeated the same statement in front of him. The black banker was sending me to the colored back door because that is how she was trained and how so many others still operate in this covert world of racism and discrimination. All I could think about after the meeting was Carter G. Woodson's words from his famous 1933 book, "The Miseducation of the Negro" when he wrote:

The Miseducation of the Negro by Carter G. Woodson, 1933

"If you can control a man's thinking, you do not have to worry about his action. When you determine what a man shall think, you do not have to concern yourself about what he will do. If you make a man feel that he is inferior, you do not have to compel him to accept an inferior status, for he will seek it himself. If you make a man think that he is justly an outcast, you do not have to order him to the back door. He will go without being told, and if there is no back door, his very nature will demand one."

Those I thought would help me chose a dark alternative where they took actions to injure me intentionally. They have succeeded thus far in stopping me from developing my commercial properties in Birmingham's most underserved and shunned community. I do not know for what gain. I believe at least three critical concerns are taking place.

## Concern #1:

Concern # 1 is the spirit of Negro slave driver I did an earlier chapter on. Rufus Dirt did not have the choice to be a Negro slave driver. Still, the mentality Rufus discussed during his interview on his

experience as a former enslaved person is the same mentality I am
dealing with. I covered my main concern in the chapter on Rufus
Dirt, and my earlier statement was as follows:

It was May 14th, 1937, and Rufus Dirt was being interviewed by
Woodrow Hand of the Federal Writers Project. Rufus, now elderly
and like many former slaves, had no idea how old he was. The part
of the transcript that interests me is how he enjoyed being a black
slave driver and how similar that was to how black leaders operate
today. In the movie Django, the main character was so determined to
get his wife back that he was willing to play the role of the slave
driver. When the white bounty hunter in the movie mentions what
Django's role should be, he says "slave driver," and Django bucked.
No!!!!!! I can't be a slave driver. That is the worst kind of slave. It
was a hated role by some, but it was on many plantations across
America. Let me stop here and let Rufus's own words speak in his
best pronunciation of the English language.

Rufus Dirt 5/14/1937, Birmingham, AL:

"Boss, I dons rightly know Jes how old I is. I was a driver (Negro
boss of other slaves) during slavery and I reckons I was about twenty
sompin'. I don' remember nothin' in particular that caused me to get
dat drivin' job, ceptin' hard work, but I knows dat I was proud of it '
cause I didn' have to work so hard no mo. An' den it sorta' made de
other nigeers look up to me, an' you knows us niggers, boss. Nothin'
makes us happier dan' to strut in front of other niggers. Dere ain't
nothin' much to tell about. We jes' moved one crop after de other till
layin' by time come and den we'd start in on other winter work."

I think of the words of Rufus Dirt every time I see black leaders in
Birmingham abuse their leadership roles and decide to abuse
individuals from their community. It pops up in the form of
gatekeepers, mini dictators, little kings and worse; it shows up in a
double caste system black leaders have created in Birmingham and
across America. It's amazing how proud many black leaders are to
show their power or at least perceived power when dealing with
their own.

## Concern #2:

There is a plan for Ensley, and I was not supposed to be in it. As black people, we often say, "They" got plans for Ensley, but we don't know what they are. We often blame the "System," but we don't know who violated what law. We just know we are always robbed of opportunity and deprived. We guess what is happening locally from time to time, but all black leaders continue with the same actions. Turn a blind eye. Ignore Ensley. Ignore Brian. Ignore, Ignore, Ignore. Neglect, Neglect, Neglect. It doesn't help at any cost, but fortunately, the attorney one block away from me sued the City and has a 15-year lawsuit going that originally started in 2008. He has been on the winning side of forcing the City with a court order to invest some tax dollars here. The City of Birmingham has already set precedence proven in court, depriving Downtown Ensley. The actions of the City confirm there is no real intention to help the majority black business district and community without court orders.

## Concern #3: The willingness to crush your own.

In Brazil, between 1967 and 1968, local educator Paulo Freire wrote Pedagogy of the Oppressed in Portuguese, and the book was first published in Spanish in 1968 by Bloomsbury Publishing. Freire breaks down the minds of those who have been oppressed. The quotes that stick out to me the most from his book show how the former oppressed tend to oppress themselves, which I'm dealing with in my hometown. The other major quote from this book reminds me of how politicians and major corporations use false charity without properly helping us get our votes or getting us distracted. Here are those quotes:

Freire, Paulo. Pedagogy of the Oppressed. Bloomsbury Publishing.

"Almost always, during the initial stage of the struggle, the oppressed, instead of striving for liberation, tend themselves to become oppressors, or 'suboppressors.'"

"In order for this struggle to have meaning, the oppressed must not, in seeking to regain their humanity (which is a way to create it), become in turn oppressors of the oppressors, but rather restorers of the humanity of both."

"True generosity consists precisely in fighting to destroy the causes which nourish false charity. False charity constrains the fearful and subdued, the "rejects of life" to extend their trembling hands. True generosity lies in striving so that these hands—whether of individuals or entire peoples—need be extended less and less in supplication, so that more and more they become human hands which work and, working, transform the world."

"Only power that springs from the weakness of the oppressed will be sufficiently strong to free both. Any attempt to "soften" the power of the oppressor in deference to the weakness of the oppressed almost always manifests itself in the form of false generosity; indeed, the attempt never goes beyond this."

"Dehumanization, which marks not only those whose humanity has been stolen, but also (though in a different way) those who have stolen it, is a distortion of the vocation of becoming more fully human. This distortion occurs within history; but it is not an historical vocation. Indeed, to admit of dehumanization as an historical vocation would lead either to cynicism or total despair. The struggle for humanization, for the emancipation of labor, for the overcoming of alienation, for the affirmation of men and women as persons would be meaningless. This struggle is possible only because dehumanization, although a concrete historical fact, is not a given destiny but the result of an unjust order that engenders violence in the oppressors, which in turn dehumanizes the oppressed."

"The more completely they accept the passive role imposed on them, the more they tend simply to adapt to the world as it is and to the fragmented view of reality deposited in them."

I first learned of sacrifice zones when I was studying the environmental pollution of Cancer Alley in Louisiana, an 85-mile stretch along Interstate 10 between New Orleans and Baton Rouge containing hundreds of petrochemical plants and refineries. Cancer

Alley is an environmental or pollution sacrifice zone, but people live there, and the majority of those people are poor black Americans. There are versions of Cancer Alley and environmental sacrifice zones across the country in neighborhoods where the majority are poor black Americans. These areas are well known. The government, private industry, and residents know that the injured or killed are sacrifices for the industry to succeed. That part of "life, liberty, or property" under both the $5^{th}$ and $14^{th}$ Amendments in the U.S. Constitution has been breached, and you, as the citizen, must figure out the state and federal rules of procedure and other relevant laws to stand for all of your rights.

I've realized that American civil courtrooms are based on proving the injury to you or your entity. Blight, underdeveloped buildings, abandoned buildings, urban decay, and municipal disinvestment became the norm, but what about the legal rights of those business owners and property owners left to fend for themselves when actions can be proven intentional or, at a bare minimum, negligent? Ensley in Birmingham, AL is a perfect case study for municipal disinvestment or the national term many hate to hear again called benign neglect and how it affects the livelihood of so many still living and investing in these communities. Benign neglect was popular in 1970 as portrayed in Patrick Moynihan's memo to President Nixon, where he stated: "The time may have come when the issue of race could benefit from a period of 'benign neglect'." Let's use today's most popular term: outsiders can benefit from the long-standing practice or custom of forced property value depreciation through gentrification. Gentrification is not wrong or unlawful, but the intentional deprivation of rights for those who live in those communities is.

So, let's think about that: the government intentionally neglects an area based on race. The same government should implement plans to take advantage of that known neglect. But who addresses the conscious disregard for the targeted community's people, businesses, and property owners in a country where due process of law and equal protection of the law are your go-to U.S. Constitutional violations under the 5th and 14th Amendments for actions caused by federal or state actors?

Merriam-Webster defines benign neglect as "an attitude or policy of ignoring an often delicate or undesirable situation that one is held to be responsible for dealing with." Black communities nationwide have become true national examples of municipal economic disinvestment.

Now, let me step back to how I discovered the fraudulent letter that Woodfin and his head of economic development wrote that unlawfully excluded Ensley from federal resources.

I would not have discovered the Department of the Treasury / IRS 10-year fraud that unlawfully removed from Ensley and the associated letter written to the Governor of Alabama if the open abuse had not happened to me. I kept seeking help and was met with red flags of intentional economic injustice in every direction. I would not have seen the additional political and campaign schemes and abuse of public tax dollars involving the mayor and his beloved Birmingham Promise non-profit violations. Birmingham Promise is a local scholarship program created by the mayor's administration with local tax dollars. The mayor's anger from 10/13/2019, when I was still seeking help for my unfair $0.00 appraisal, was the red flag of potential official misconduct, but I didn't know what it was then.

On Oct 13th, 2019, just 1 day before the City approved $4,000,000 for the Ramsay McCormack court-ordered development 1 block away from my $0.00 buildings and 1 day before the City approved the $10 million for Birmingham Promise in their budget and finance, the mayor and the head of economic development and a few others met me in my building. When the Mayor first addressed me, he was angry with my appraisal, but he was not angry with what Synovus Bank and CBRE appraisal company, who approved the $0.00 appraisal, did to me. CBRE is the largest appraisal company in the U.S. and the world, and they know it is a hard fight to fight giants from underserved communities.

During this Ensley meeting, the economic development director who was sitting to my left stated that the City has a great relationship with Synovus Bank CEO. I was in awe as I had been asking the mayor, economic development director, and the City for help for over 10 months now. All I wanted them to do at this time was advocate for me regarding my undeniably fraudulent $0.00 appraisal that robbed me of my livelihood, as I knew nothing of Amendment 772 then. I left that meeting saying what had just happened. Why did a black mayor get mad at me for asking for help regarding my appraisal? I started searching every city file I could find over the next 2 plus years to understand the public-private connection to economic barriers and obstruction of commerce in Ensley. I eventually found the 3/6/2018 Federal Opportunity Zone fraudulent "false letter to influence legislation" that was sent to the Governor of Alabama that excluded Downtown Ensley of federal resources prepared by the economic development director, signed by black mayor #5, signed by Synovus Birmingham division CEO, signed by UAB President and others. Then I realized where the anger of black mayor #5 came from.

I eventually uncovered many violations with the current administration, involving Birmingham Promise and Prosper Birmingham. I wrote the details in the chapter titled Actual Letters to the FBI.

I wasn't looking for it, but when I started searching for the root of the mayor's anger, I searched and watched everything I could find to fight for my stolen dreams.

I filed complaints with the State of Alabama Office of Public Examiners of Public Accounts. I filed complaints with the FBI, SEC, FTC, ASC, U.S. DOJ Civil Rights Division, Department of the Treasury, and DOJ Criminal Division. 100% of my equity was stolen through fraud, and every agency I have approached thus far has taken no action.

To understand systemic economic injustice, you must understand what it is like when 7 or more public agencies fail to act to protect your rights and choose to act with deliberate indifference to undeniable injustice. People like me have no Liberty when agencies at so many levels allow your rights to be removed. When you have no Liberty with your commercial property, you can't use the property to provide for your life and the lives it will support through public facilities and public accommodations through leases, housing and the services businesses provide to the community.

Now, I understand why there are so many blighted buildings in Downtown Ensley and every other majority-black commercial district I have visited nationwide, where crumbling buildings and underdeveloped buildings are the norm.

I thought my $0.00 unconscionable appraisal on 8 commercial buildings with tenants still in several of them was my main legal concern in this underserved majority-black commercial district until I uncovered the intentional injuries to businesses, Life, Liberty, and Property happening all around me in this community.

One day, I looked down 19th St. Ensley while standing on the only completely renovated block, and I looked in 1 direction for 3 blocks. I saw at least 19 boarded-up storefronts, windows covered with plastic bags, severely broken windows and several with active businesses. I looked to the west, and I saw even more. I increasingly realized how conditioned people were to the economic suppression and fires in vacant buildings.

As suppressed as Ensley is, there is still value in our communities, and the capitalists, Mayor, city employees, county staff, state representatives and federal representatives know it. The county tax assessor knows this as they keep charging me taxes on my building's improved value but won't let me protest my taxes to prove that my buildings can't be worth $0.00.

In the chapter titled "Federal Reserve, Racism and the Economy" and Amendment 772 chapter, I pointed out several million in grants given out by the same city leaders from underserved communities who would go above and beyond to accommodate white property owners and businesses while at the same time turning a blind eye to known economic injustice, deferred economic development for the oppressed who looked like them. It's mind-boggling to believe you have a chance for help from those who know you, who choose to oppress you instead.

I must repeat Neel Kashkari's (President of the Federal Reserve Bank of Minneapolis) statement he made during the Federal Reserve series on Racism and the Economy in 2022 with a focus on the wealth divide:

I must repeat Neel Kashkari, President of the Federal Reserve Bank of Minneapolis statement he made during the Federal Reserve series on Racism and the Economy in 2022 with a focus on the wealth divide, made the following statement:

"Its [Racism and the Economy is] only invisible because we haven't been looking. Since my eyes were opened, everywhere I look I see. And it's impossible not to see it... Once my eyes were open, I could see so many examples where wealth has been given to whites by the government"

I've had to sit still again to think about all this economic injustice happening to me and around me and what to do with it. Almost 2 years later, after uncovering so many constitutional, federal, state and local violations while searching for the why, sitting in Applebee's one night, I made a list of 30 or more specific concerns, all injuring this majority black community and the majority black population in the City of Birmingham. I then drew a small circle and placed the words "$0.00 appraisal" in the middle. I then drew 4 larger circles and wrote all 30 plus known injuries I knew of happening around me from the concentration of poverty, forced court-ordered city investment, environmental injustice, commercial redlining, historic redlining, demolition of historic properties, government and nearly 25 other inequality concerns.

I realized these injuries to the local black community were obvious in every U.S. city I have traveled to over the last 20 years with any sizable black population.

I don't know as many deep details and sources in other cities, but I am convinced that when I see blight and vacant buildings on Sweet

Auburn Ave in Atlanta, it's very concerning post-2020. It is concerning when I see Avondale / North Avondale, where Fred Shuttlesworth left Birmingham when he moved his family to Cincinnati in the 1960s. When I visit Lockland, OH, vs. Wyoming, OH and Over the Rhine in the greater Cincinnati area, it is concerning. It is concerning when I see Baltimore the moment I leave the Harbor. It is concerning to see the level of gentrification that has consumed Charlotte, NC. It is concerning to see the South Side of Chicago or North Milwaukee, WI or Rosa Parks Drive in Montgomery, AL, and so many other places resembling Birmingham's underserved communities. With these concerns, I will dive deeply into this document.

When I started this journey, I only read but never used the word deprivation in context. I didn't understand systemic injustice or even the systems at play depriving many of us of our legal rights where we can legally sue. I didn't understand systemic vs. institutional injustice, racism vs. discrimination, good faith vs. bad faith, governmental immunity, lawful vs. unlawful, racketeering vs. conspiracy or color of law, and many other relevant words.

I couldn't deny the present conditions even when my peers were involved. My economic rights were wiped off the table as if I had no right to develop.

I've experienced 5 years of deprivation of rights in this majority-black community today. Still, blacks in Ensley have experienced 120+ years of deprivation of rights in the same community for black property owners throughout other chapters previously discussed. Our economic fight is too important to walk away when public officials and employees openly violate our rights under the Color of Law.

I ask this question again: if our economic development leaders are planning out personal gain and campaign schemes with public dollars through education schemes and local leaders are turning a blind eye to open corruption, then who is putting the citizens first and planning out the economic development needs of underserved businesses and business districts in Birmingham?

A Tale of Two Cities Is a statement often used In Birmingham to describe the West Side primarily vs. Downtown.

Below are quotes that concerned me and were merely false charity, just as described in Pedagogy of the Oppressed:

On 3/16/2018, just 10 days later, the economic development director's false report locked out federal resources from underserved areas. The new director stated during Mayor's first 100 days event:

*"Tracey, Sarena, and I have spent the last 4 months diving deep into what makes up the economic landscape in this city." "Putting People First is more than a slogan, it's an economic strategy." "We believe that the growth, the momentum the city has seen is important,* **there are too many people that are still hurting, there are too many people who haven't felt the opportunity in their neighborhoods."** *"We believe Birmingham is experiencing a tale of two cities." "While we have had incredible wins... despite all of this growth, despite all the momentum we have seen, Birmingham still has a 30% poverty rate, 42% poverty rate for women and children. Over 60% of the households in this City make less than $40,000 a year and that is less than the living wage." "Even though our unemployment rate remains fairly low, it is still one of the hardest places in the country to find a job if you don't have one. Too many people in this room, too many people we have encountered are living that experience. So that is the challenge you (Mayor) and I find ourselves in. That is the opportunity that we also find ourselves in. And we know from research that inclusion really is the other side of the coin to innovation.* **Every day that we aren't inclusive, every moment, every strategy, every tactic, everyone that doesn't include all of us, we all lose.** *So we firmly believe that Birmingham can be the best place in the world to change the world because it already has been. But in order to do that we have to lay the groundwork for your (Mayor) vision. We have to lay the groundwork for ourselves as a community to be a hub, a national hub for qualified and diverse talent that fuels prosperity through inclusion, inclusive growth, and innovation."*

UAB President was quoted on 10/29/19:

*"Mayor often says as goes Birmingham or as goes UAB goes Birmingham. He and I and his administration and our employees work like this together(as the president visibly put his 10 fingers together)* **to do all we can to fight poverty and to improve the quality of life of those that live in Birmingham** *and we are going to continue to have a bigger economic impact because we know it's so important so thank you for all that you do, thank you for being here today."*

Economic Development Director 5/25/20:

*"If you ever want to know if you are doing the right thing, ask yourself is it helping the poorest person."*

**Birmingham is a tale of two cities where one side benefits from a "partial" government and the other is harmed economically by a "partial" government.** I'm asking for help at the state and federal level for our underserved communities in Birmingham and undeniable ethics violations. **To manipulate federal programs with a false report that is still causing economic injuries designed to help the underserved for the most affluent is a true example of a "partial" government that ignore ethics laws. These unlawful and unequal acts, add another layer of systemic economic injustice caused by the present-day leaders of Birmingham.**

I had no idea of present-day economic suppression's real and accustomed conditions until I chose Ensley. The conditions I have experienced in Ensley since the city economic development director excluded Ensley from resources are as follows:

I have been in Ensley for 5 years, and it has been a form of ethnographic research. I didn't realize the true reality of the conditions inside communities like Ensley until I was there every day.

**In a deprived community, poverty becomes your friend and your enemy.** Many are conditioned to the environment, whether they are well paid professionals, successful entrepreneurs, underpaid workers, or the unemployed. To be locked out of resources is just a way of life because it has always been that way, from banks to the government.

**In a deprived community**, you see men searching for opportunity every day. Every day, if you stand outside your building, I guarantee several men will walk up to you of all ages and ask you if you have any work. If you have any work, you let them perform the work.

It became normal to see people pick through trash illegally dumped behind buildings and walk away with shoes, jackets and shirts. **In a deprived community**, you look at those struggling with addictions differently, as many become your friends and your trusted helpers. These helpers teach you about life in so many ways, and you learn never to call them a wino because you don't see a person addicted to alcohol. You see a person.

**In a deprived community**, you speak to people with severe speech impediments, but these speech impediments are caused by true poverty. Teeth may be completely gone, and when they speak, you must concentrate as their words are mumbled together, but when they see you, their spirit and your spirit lights up.

**In a deprived community**, you see men from all types of broken backgrounds gifted with various forms of visual art. You see men not for their past choices but as men and friends and workers. You don't see women strolling like the men. You don't see kids playing, but when you see kids walk through the alleys on their way to school, you are disappointed because they must walk by so much blight every day.

It is common to cross paths with many entrepreneurs without resources, but they dream of someday launching their business or growing their business. **In a deprived community**, you learn what survival is as you see men miss meals for days until you can give them work, as there are no homeless programs nearby.

**In a deprived community**, you will not see any metal of any kind on the ground as the metal is lunch money. Recycling metal, aluminum, copper, and any larger appliances full of mixed metal are hot commodities.

Politics with resources never reach them, and they know the local leaders.

It bothers me daily when men ask for work, and I have to tell them I don't have any work because I have been locked out, but I'm fighting for resources daily. I'm studying the law. I'm writing state and federal complaints daily. I'm studying the law more. I am standing up to banks and studying the law more because **the barriers I face are not just my barriers but the barriers to men looking for work.**

**We spend years fighting for our property rights or become accustomed to the conditions of not having true liberty.** We need help here. We need resources. We don't just need community-based intervention. We need government-based intervention. I hope I have explained some economic concerns and how we need an "impartial government" working for our rights.

I'm thankful for Andre Perry, but after a while, **I felt more like an economic injustice lab rat**, and I had to figure out how to get out of this case study test lab and maze when those studying me had the contacts and resources to pull me out of containment.

In Perry's Bloomberg article titled, "This is how hard it is to invest in black neighborhoods'. (5/13/2020 https://www.bloomberg.com/news/articles/2020-05-13/why-it-s-so-hard-to-invest-in-black-neighborhoods )

*Rice pointed to the history of redlining in Ensley. "We're in an area where banks have chosen not to invest"; "Brian Rice's development is exactly the kind of endeavor that another type of federal funding — the Opportunity Zone provision is supposed to support." "Rice's projects fell outside of the opportunity zone"; "Real estate developers like Rice need support from government agencies. Council members and mayors sit on a perch where they can see the overall economic landscape beyond the city limits. Local elected officials control federal, state, and local resources."*

Brian K. Rice quotes from BBC World News titled: The Frustration of Trying to Invest in my Hometown link by Ivana Davidovic July 26th, 2020.

When I was featured in this international article, and the black leaders saw the article, I was hated and exiled even more. To the world, it seemed good, but oppression kept coming from the opposing forces. He said he was fighting here 60 years ago, just as MLK described in his letter from a Birmingham Jail.

*"I thought it was the worst appraisal in the United States," he says, recalling the moment he opened the valuation the bank had given him for his properties and read its justification.*

*"They compared my eight historic properties to farmland 14 or so miles away, and they compared my buildings to an abandoned car wash. Nothing about my properties resembles those."*

*"It's one thing to do this with one building," he says, "if it is small and falling apart. It's another thing to do it with eight buildings with sitting tenants. So I said, 'It's my time to speak up and stand up.' This shouldn't happen to the next person."*

Perry was invited to speak at the A.G. Gaston Conference for small businesses in 2022. It was a unique day when Andre made me the feature of his speech. Andre brought me back into the limelight for 1 day as I had already started my isolation to study law. Several in the room didn't like that I was featured, as my story was supposed to be silenced in my hometown. I had a chance to speak, and people could hear my cries for help, but no help came. One entity expressed interest, but one of the guys who has tried to harm me economically as part of the inner circle of black dynamiters of economic injustice was on the board of that entity, and he was not in the room that day, so I never went through the run around with them. The representative doesn't know of the internal issue as other forms of corruption are occurring near me, and I have been the light sharing the truth. Darkness doesn't like light. Lies don't like truth. I've been through too much run around only to be sabotaged from the inside again in my hometown.

Every agency assigned to protect our equal rights and due process under the law, that I have thus filed formal complaints with regarding my $0.00 appraisal and modern redlining when they know there are undeniable violations has turned a blind eye and acted with deliberate indifference. I am like many who have been economically oppressed and abused. I must prepare for the next level of equal protection under the law. I must bring civil action to the American justice courtrooms the best way I can.

**We must fight for our stolen dreams.**

## CHAPTER 11: LETTERS TO DOJ, FBI, DEPT OF TREASURY, STATE OF ALABAMA

I sent this actual letter to the Department of Justice on 8/29/2022 requesting help. I hoped the concerns would have been addressed by stated public entities, officials, and employees listed in the letter before now. I feel it is a major matter of public concern when agencies will not respond or choose to conceal the gross mismanagement of public funds for the benefit of personal and or private gain of another unlawfully.

### Section 1: Letter to DOJ, FBI, Dept of the Treasury 8/29/2022:

To the United States Department of Justice, Criminal Division, Fraud Section and to the Federal Bureau of Investigation Public Corruption, Civil Rights, Color of Law, White Collar Crime divisions and to the Department of the Treasury Inspector General:

This document covers criminal level organized white collar [unlawful activity], public corruption, local to federal fraud, color of law violations and election schemes taking place in the City of Birmingham, AL. Laws have been ignored at every level of government as if laws don't exist. We have no equal rights here if all the abuses continue without accountability.

On FBI.gov the following statement is written, and this letter covers these violations and others in the City of Birmingham, Jefferson County Alabama, the State of Alabama, and several federal agencies.

1.      Government Program Fraud: "Are you aware of any individuals or groups receiving government program benefits by providing false information?"

2.      Contracting Fraud: "Are you aware of any scheme that enables any individuals (including public officials) or businesses to take advantage of program intricacies to defraud the government?"

3.      Color of Law Violations: "It's a federal crime for anyone to use their position to willfully deprive or conspire to deprive a person of a right protected by the Constitution or U.S. law." "Failure to keep from harm: The public counts on its law enforcement officials to protect local communities. If it's shown that an official willfully failed to keep an individual from harm, that official could be in violation of the color of law statute."

4.      Examples of White-Collar Crime / Corporate Fraud: the FBI focuses its efforts on cases that involve accounting schemes and self-dealing by corporate executives, as well as obstruction of justice (activities designed to conceal this type of criminal conduct); False accounting and/or misrepresentations of financial conditions

5.      The FBI works with partners to investigate mortgage and financial institution fraud cases.

On the Public Integrity Section, the following is stated:

1.      The Public Integrity Section oversees the federal effort to combat corruption through the prosecution of elected and appointed public officials at all levels of government.

2.      The section has exclusive jurisdiction over allegations of criminal misconduct on the part of federal judges and also monitors the investigation and prosecution of election and conflict of interest crimes.

My name is Brian K. Rice and I live in the city of Birmingham, AL where I have witnessed no government accountability in this democracy for African American underserved communities and businesses who reside here. Local public corruption led by majority African American political leadership and white corporate leadership is run without the accountability of public oaths of office or local laws or the laws and Constitution of the United States of America. We are not just dealing with traditional discrimination or racism of the past that Birmingham is known for, we are dealing with a double caste system here in Birmingham where African American political leaders are conspiring with corporate entities depriving African American communities of equal protection of the law. The depths of systemic institutional public and corporate economic injustice are extensive here when public agencies of accountability also turn a blind eye to economic injustice, financial fraud, ethics laws, non-profit schemes, election schemes, federal program fraud, revolving doors, organized sophisticated white collar crimes, racketeering (RICO), IRS tax schemes, and color of law violations from local government to federal entities all affecting Ensley and other underserved communities in Birmingham, AL. I am asking the DOJ Criminal Division and FBI Public Corruption, Civil Rights, Color of Law divisions and the Department of the Treasury OIG to thoroughly investigate the actions of associated public agencies, public officials, public employees, public agents, public boards responsible for upholding the law who also turned a blind eye against the law and thereby approving public corruption. The actions of the AL Ethics Commission, AL Real Estate Appraisal Board, the Federal Appraisal Subcommittee, the Federal Reserve Board of Governors, the City of Birmingham, the Jefferson County Board of Equalization, the University of Alabama at Birmingham, Southern Research Institute and the 2 private corporate entities who fraudulently deprived me of 100% of my equity by redlining me in a federal related transaction by appraising my buildings at $0.00 must be investigated because every level of government I sought help from turned a blind eye to injustice and thereby deprived me of equal protection of the law. The City of Birmingham former Economic Development Director, Josh Carpenter, and Mayor Randall Woodfin we are at the center of all attached City of Birmingham fraud. The Alabama Real Estate Appraisal Board is at the center of the appraisal fraud that started with FIRREA violations with Synovus Bank and CBRE appraisers, Harvill and Neyhart. If the state'appraisal r'gulatory board would have done their job per the law to protect the public interest, appropriate actions could have taken place in 2019 or 2020 or even 2021 but they continued to cover up fraudulent appraisal and banking practices.

Systemic Economic Injustice is what I have experienced which are color of law violations at every level:

On 8/13/21 I filed a formal complaint with the Department of the Treasury Inspector General and I received an email receipt immediately afterward and nothing else in over 365 days.

The Office of the Inspector General (OIG [for the Department of the Treasury] have had supporting documents with attached "false letters to influence legislation" recreating redlining in 2018 through 2028+ in Birmingham, AL in the Ensley census tracts that knowingly defraud the government in other census tracts that would not have been approved without known false reports. I also sent the same documents I sent to the AL Ethics Commission on 2/22/22 to the OIG because new evidence was attached associated with revolving doors, color of law violations, and misuse of office violations for the city economic development director, mayor of Birmingham, and president of UAB. The formal complaints connected federal laws 18 USC 666 Federal Program Fraud, 18 USC 371 Conspiracy to Defraud the US Government, 18 USC 1341/1343 mail/wire fraud, 31 USC 3279 False Claims that are directly related to AL Ethics Laws 36-25-26 False Reports to Influence Legislation, 36-25-5 Misuse of Office for Personal or Private Gain, 36-25-6 Candidate Contributions and more. Official documents were sent confirming the "false report" that deprived Ensley of federal incentives and resources with a known false report prepared by Josh Carpenter and signed by Mayor Randall Woodfin and concealed by both which is another violation of ethics law 36-25-17 for reports of violations by the Governmental Agency Head. The actions clearly involve more than 2 or more entities and persons regarding deprivation of rights, and we are also dealing with 18 U.S. Code § 241 – Conspiracy against rights. I am asking the attached federal offices to thoroughly investigate each complaint submitted and the associated color of law violations for the agencies and agency representatives who chose to deprive me and my neighbors of our rights for choosing to turn a blind eye to justice and equal protection of the law.

On 2/22/22 I filed an ethics complaint with the Alabama Ethics Commission with 240+ supporting pages of evidence covering 4 public officials and employees that involve felony level violations and misuse of office or position. Here are the links and follow up links to responses from the AL Ethics Commission which you can reference later in your review of evidence:

a.      2/22/22 Ethics letter #1:

b.      The 8/13/21 letter sent to DOJ Department of the Treasury from above was sent as well

c.      3/19/22: Ethics response to questions regarding Josh Carpenter and Ray Watts

d.      4/6/22: Ethics and Alabama Attorney General Letter expressing concerns as a whistleblower and that all city councilors at the City of Birmingham could be charged with felonies specifically concerning Birmingham Promise and the revolving door actions of Josh Carpenter primarily

e.      7/1/22: Ethics response to AL Ethics Commission saying they didn't see any evidence on the face when the evidence is overwhelming

I submitted City of Birmingham, University of Alabama at Birmingham, Southern Research Institute, and Birmingham Promise, official letters, official minutes, official press releases, news articles, official videos, official budgets, official financial reports, timelines, social media screenshots, policies, related laws and other supporting documents to confirm multiple violations by several of the same elected and appointed public officials and employees and the ethics representatives reviewing the files turned a blind eye to justice.

1.      The evidence confirmed $10 million dollars in associated "revolving door" violations with city tax dollars and an additional $8 million in IRS write offs which are federal write offs with Birmingham Promise that was also illegally tied to a local election campaign scheme. The mayor (Randall Woodfin), the city economic development director (Josh Carpenter, who was also still employed

at UAB), and the city economic development employee (Rachel Harmon) all were present when they presented the $10 million plan at city hall on 7/16/2019. The local city council approved the $10 million in funding with $2 million allocated each year for 5 years and then 6 months later not 2 years for revolving door requirements, the city employee responsible for creating the private 501c3 resigned from city hall was now the executive director of the 501c3. All 9 city councilors and the mayor turned a blind eye to misuse of public funds and associated revolving doors. The city council has approved $2 million each year since for this felony level scheme and misuse of tax dollars. The 501c3 promoted the mayor during his election campaign which is a 501c3 violation as well. UAB President (Ray Watts) and UAB was the first public school to support this fraudulently created 501c3. The AL Ethics Commission turned a blind eye to this injustice. Per the Al Ethics Commission policy, it states they have 180 days to complete their investigation, 180 days was 8/22/22.

A.      City of Birmingham public officials and employees showed that they are not willing to following their own local ordinance which means they have shown they are not willing to follow state or federal laws for misuse of office for personal or private gain as well.) The City Council and Mayor and public attorneys ignored the City of Birmingham own ordinances which state:

i.      A.      Mayor Council Act: "Sec. 8.06. Officers and employees not to be privately interested in city's contracts: No member of the council, officer or employee elected or appointed shall be interested, directly or indirectly, in any contract for work or material, or the profits thereof, or services to be furnished or performed for the city, and no such member of the council, officer or employee shall be interested, directly or indirectly, in any contract for work or material, or the profits thereof, or services to be furnished…" "Every such contract or agreement shall be voidable by the mayor or the council."

2.      If Birmingham Promise is created out of a known "revolving door" and "inside deal" with city tax dollars from the highest official

and $10 Million has already been approved illegally where the 501c3 was created under Mayor Woodfin and Josh Carpenter, the city economic development director, and Carpenter's direct report Rachel Harmon, then what is created out of fraud / corruption is bound to be connected to more fraud and public corruption.

When Prosper Birmingham, another 501c3 was announced with over $50 Million from local corporations which was an initiative planned out of city hall public and private partnerships by the same people who setup Birmingham Promise immediately after Birmingham Promise was fraudulently launched with revolving door inside deal violations and campaign schemes, it was bound to me more corruption as corruption was and still is the culture.

501c3's was the cover to move money around. Both money moves put helping black kids or businesses on the front line and this was a great tactic to get a poor community and the local enforcement or federal enforcement to turn and look the other way with all the money and how the deals were set up. The DOJ Criminal Division and FBI need to investigate the flow of money and the change of hands.

Prosper Birmingham first money move was $8 million given to Birmingham Promise where Mayor Woodfin was the presenter of the additional "revolving door" check to his former employee Rachel Harmon and now executive director of Birmingham Promise. Mayor Woodfin also serves on the board of Prosper Birmingham. This is a serious $18+ multi-million-dollar minimum scheme now for Birmingham Promise which was created out of a known misuse of office scheme. Mayor Woodfin and Josh Carpenter, city economic development director presented the $10 million request to Birmingham city council with city employee Rachel Harmon who was responsible for creating Birmingham Promise in her Talent and Workforce development role under Josh Carpenter seated immediately behind them in the official City of Birmingham city council meeting video on 7/16/2019 which the council approved 10/15/2019. A visual chart is attached later in this letter.

Woodfin as the City of Birmingham Governmental Agency Head who was a former City Prosecutor, is very familiar with ethics law turned a blind eye because it was part of a fraudulent public corruption scheme from the beginning. Woodfin nor his campaign team never said anything about Birmingham Promise promoting Woodfin election page on their website during campaign season either. Woodfin political and campaign schemes used Birmingham Promise and the amount of funding that has gone to them over and over and over throughout his 2021 campaign even when the funding is created out of local, state, and federal violations.

There are clear local, state, and federal violations and there are likely several more with the associated 501c3's and I'm asking the FBI and DOJ Criminal Division to investigate as these are all our tax dollars and misuse of office and positions for personal and or private gain and election campaign schemes.

3.      Also in the AL Ethics Commission complaint were undeniable revolving door violations and misuse of office or position for personal and / or private gain by the former city of Birmingham economic development director, Josh Carpenter who also worked for UAB, a state school directly in the office of the president of UAB, Ray Watts where "conflict of interest" was ignored by both the city of Birmingham and UAB. The violations directly affect federal resources allocated by the Department of the Treasury / IRS. The violations directly affect city, county, and state tax dollars as well.

A.      On 3/6/2018 Josh Carpenter – City Economic Director and Mayor Randall Woodfin sent an official city letter with known "false report to influence legislation" to Governor Kay Ivey. Governor Ivey at the state executive branch level approved the nominated census tracts in the fraudulent prepared report as submitted and then The Department of the Treasury / IRS along with President Trump approved the fraud from the local level immediately causing present day redlining and a redirection of federal resources from underserved census tracts based on known false information that defrauded the federal government. In Birmingham, AL the fraudulent preparers went above and beyond, and they boldly submitted a written "false report to influence legislation" where the material facts are recorded evidence that deprived Downtown Ensley of federal incentives and resources. Josh, other employer which is UAB benefitted more than any other area in the city of Birmingham with over $600 million in adjacent developments supported by a known false letter sent to influence legislation. Josh newest employer, benefitted by the same false letter with over $300 million in adjacent developments while Downtown Ensley has received $0.00 in adjacent developments due to the same false letter. Josh blamed a "clerical error" for several years regarding why Ensley was left out until I found the official letter which showed there were no clerical errors. Downtown Ensley census tracts were fraudulently affected more than any other underserved census tracts in the city. Downtown Ensley is the largest majority own African American commercial district in the city and state of Alabama, and it was no clerical error which is an admission to negligence at a minimum but no correction that excluded Ensley of needed federal incentives and resources. The AL Ethics Commission has all of the felony level undeniable evidence, and they said there is no evidence on the face playing it politically correct to protect their fellow state employees and that is why I am reaching out to the Department of Justice and FBI to review the submissions and to investigate Color of Law violations.

b.      Just imagine you were able to assume the City of Birmingham highest economic development position and you were allowed to write out your own economic plans as if misuse of office laws and public corruption don't exist supporting an $84 million development and you walk back into city hall as the president of the $84 million development and you are approved violating revolving door laws less than 1 year later by all city councilors, attorneys, and mayor of the city. We'll that is exactly what the city of Birmingham former economic development director did in 2020 and in 2021. Official documents were sent to the AL Ethics Commission, and they turned a blind eye to abuse of power and misuse of office from public officials and employees.

c.      The City Council and Mayor and public attorneys ignored the City of Birmingham own ordinances which state:

i.      A.      Mayor Council Act: "Sec. 8.06. Officers and employees not to be privately interested in city's contracts: No member of the council, officer or employee elected or appointed shall be interested, directly or indirectly, in any contract for work or material, or the profits thereof, or services to be furnished or performed for the city, and no such member of the council, officer or employee shall be interested, directly or indirectly, in any contract for work or material, or the profits thereof, or services to be furnished…" "Every such contract or agreement shall be voidable by the mayor or the council."

**On June 20th, 2019**, the same day there was a Congressional hearing on the Appraisal Industry on Capitol Hill in the White House, CBRE the largest appraisal company in the country and world completed the most fraudulent appraisal performed by [CBRE Appraisers] that I could have ever expected. On June 21st, 2019, Synovus Bank performed an internal appraisal review. On June 24th, 2019, the retail banker, Bill Inabinet called me and said the bank had completed the internal review and immediately before hanging phone up, he stated "You are not going to like it". I received the email moments later and I went to the valuation page and there was $45,000 allotted for my land and $0.00 allotted for my 8 multi story building structures in the sales comparison approach. All rental income at the time was omitted from the income approach to appraisal value. I filed a formal complaint with state appraisal regulatory agency, the Alabama Real Estate Appraisal Board (AREAB) whose mission is to protect the public from unscrupulous appraisers under the FIRREA Act (The Financial Institutions Reform, Recovery, and Enforcement Act of 1989). I was deprived of my rights and have been dealing with accruing injury daily since that day being locked out of 100% of my equity to improve my real property to increase commerce through the property. It took AREAB over 12 months on 9/25/2020 to respond when the federal policy state less than 1 year and their response was the vaguest response you could imagine protecting the violations of CBRE appraisers and

Synovus Bank. AREAB total response: "In accordance with your complaint filed with the Board, the complaint has been reviewed and investigated by the Board. Action as deemed appropriate by the Board has been taken. We appreciate you bringing this matter to our attention." So now I have a state agency who has conspired with 2 or more to deprive me of my rights to real property and to equal protection under the law. We are not just dealing with FIRREA Act violations we are dealing with antitrust violations, 18 U.S. Code § 241 – Conspiracy against rights as well as other laws. I contacted AREAB immediately after receiving their vague response and the attorney stated she was not aware if they looked at unfair comps or if they looked at the omission of rental income and she would follow up. To this day of this letter her follow up has never happened and has been left open, ongoing, and incomplete.

a.      1/10/22: This is my last joint letter with the Federal Appraisal Subcommittee, Jefferson County Board of Equalization, AL Real Estate Appraisal Board showing the USPAP violations, FIRREA Act violations, the over Taxation of fraudulent appraised $0.00 buildings and cover ups on a federal related transaction.

b.      I filed a complaint with the Federal Reserve Board of Governors, and they turned a blind eye to the fact that my buildings were appraised less than a single U.S. penny regarding the internal approval of Synovus Bank.

c.      I filed a formal tax protest to my real property ad valorem taxes from Jefferson County which fall under the Alabama Department of Revenue and the deprivation of rights continue with these entities and employees operating in their official capacity. The Jefferson County Property Appraiser who assessed my properties stated in my pre-hearing to protest my property taxes that Jefferson County have known for a while that there are bad appraisals taking place in Ensley. The Property Appraiser, The Chair of the Board of Equalization and a 3rd Party appraiser met me at my buildings on 8/13/2021 the same day I submitted my complaint to the DOJ Department of the Treasury Inspector General and they all stated, there is no way my buildings could be worth $0.00, and they would have to charge me taxes. They stated they would lower the taxes to help me on my upcoming bill, but they could not lower it to $0.00 and if I didn't approve of the new value I could protest, and I would be assigned a hearing with the Board of Equalization. I protested the new value and was denied the hearing and now I'm being taxed for buildings by Jefferson County and Alabama Department of Revenue and being denied 100% of my equity at the same by the Alabama Real Estate Appraisal Board, CBRE appraisers and Synovus Bank. This is taxation without representation and unequal protection of the law.

D.      I filed a formal complaint with the Federal Appraisal Subcommittee (ASC) who is the federal regulatory agency for the Alabama Real Estate Appraisal Board under the FIRREA Act and they said they have no jurisdiction to help me or communicate to me and for me to go back to the Alabama Real Estate Appraisal Board. I sent a response to the ASC which stated "I'm concerned with federal policy associated with ASC if there is no ability to utilize section 1118 [12 USC 3347] regarding the actions that can be taken against a state licensed or certified appraiser who willfully violates professional code of conduct of USPAP and FIRREA. I'm concerned that the section regarding imposing sanctions against a state agency that fails to have an effective appraiser regulatory program and imposing interim actions as describe in ASC policy and statues below really don't protect the public if they can't be used. If real property owners can be abused at will to deprive them of 100% of equity and value by a state regulatory agency, then who can the public victims reach out to for help and how can ASC correct true violations? I don't know what to do but if there is no public agency to help above the state agency then policy is missing a key safeguard for the public who must use appraisers, banks, and go to the state appraisal regulatory agency for help and if all three are involved with unethical actions, then there is no checks and balances. If section 1118 exists as shown below from your policy and it can't be used, then the law must be abandoned, or it must be revised to ensure ASC truly has federal oversite over state regulatory agencies if the letter Jim Park prepared is true. From a public point we need to push for a change of the law because we have public accountability to depriving African Americans of real property rights. I truly believe ASC has the ability to make a difference per the law. I want ASC to know that my buildings reside in a commercial district with over 100 buildings and over the last 40+ years African American commercial property owners have only been able to get 1 commercial loan from a local bank. We are redlined and we have no help."

e.      I filed a 2nd complaint with the Alabama Real Estate Appraisal Board after I was denied of my real property ad valorem tax protest, and I used the new assessed value assigned by the Jefferson County to file the 2nd complaint on 11/22 2021 and on 12/2/2021 AREAB Attorney responded saying "I will take this complaint back to the Board". "The Board will only consider the complaint you have in connection to Harvill and Neyhart." The Board has no jurisdiction over CBRE or any other appraisal company.

f.      We need equal protection of the law. I am asking federal agencies to investigate public agencies and the associated bank and appraisal company as systemic institutional public and corporate economic injustice is depriving me and my neighbors of our equal rights. It is no coincidence this community has led the city in death by homicide as there is no public help to secure resources to create alternatives, jobs, businesses, and constructive spaces in our properties. We need help here; we have no equal rights unless one public agency stand up to the constitution and the laws of the United States of America to help us.

**The next section is a visual overview of the summary from 8/13/21 to 2/22/22 and 6/20/19.**

The first section is the 8/13/21 Department of Justice Department of Treasury Inspector General Complaint where Josh Carpenter, City Economic Director economic interest with UAB and Southern Research become more obvious and they cause "economic personal injury" through public fraud to Ensley real property owners and other underserved areas that overwhelmingly benefit Carpenter, UAB, and SRI and others to be discovered who were apart of the scheme

# Josh Carpenter: UAB, Southern Research, and City of Birmingham AL Ethics Violations and Federal Program Fraud

Prepared by Brian K. Rice
www.briankrice.com

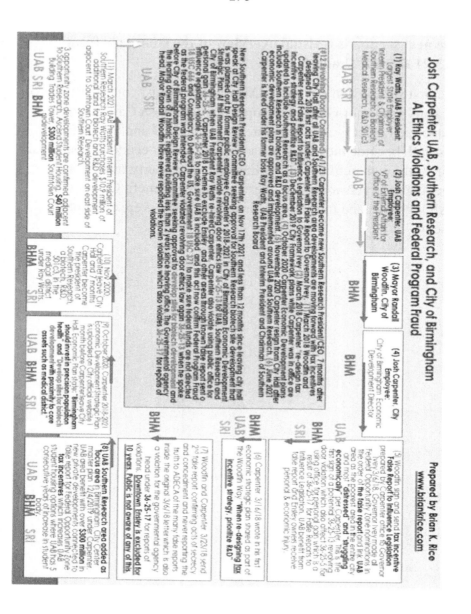

**(1) Ray Watts, UAB President.** Interim President & Chairman of Southern Research, a biotech, Medical Research. R&D 501c3

UAB SRI

**(2) Josh Carpenter, UAB Employee.** VP of External Affairs for Office of the President

UAB

**(3) Mayor Randall Woodfin, City of Birmingham**

BHM

**(4) Josh Carpenter, City Employee.** City of Birmingham: Economic Development Director

BHM

**(5)** Woodfin sign and send tax incentive **False Report to influence Legislation** prepared by Carpenter once to Governor Ivey 3/6/18. Governor Ivey made all the order of the **false report** and link UAB area as the poorest area in the entire city and most "**distressed**" and "**struggling economically**" per Capacity. This is the first sign of a bona fide 36-25-1 revolving door violation which also affect 36-25-5 for using office for approval plan which is a violation to Legislation. UAB benefit from false report and Briley owned receive personal & economic injury.

BHM UAB SRI

**[#12 Revolving Door(s) Continued] 6/1/21 Carpenter become new Southern Research area President/CEO** 7 months after leaving City Hall after all UAB and Southern Research area developments are moving forward with tax incentives designed in 2018 first acts under Carpenter with False Report to Governor Ivey. (1) March 2018 Woodfin and Carpenter send false report to influence Legislation to Governor Ivey (2) March 2018 Carpenter re-design tax incentive strategy and prioritize R&D (3) December 2019 City Framework plans while Carpenter was in office are updated to include Southern Research as a focus area (4) October 2020 Birmingham Economic Development plans include Southern Research in biotech and R&D development (5) November 2020 Carpenter resign from City Hall after economic development plans are approved and implemented around UAB and Southern Research. (6) June 2021 Carpenter is hired under his former boss Ray Watts, UAB President and Interim President and Chairman of Southern Research Board.

UAB SRI

**New Southern Research President/CEO** Carpenter on Nov 17th 2021 and less than 12 months since leaving city hall speak at City Hall Design Review Committee seeking approval for Southern Research area development that is was planned out by former public employee Carpenter 2018-2021 in City of Birmingham Economic Development Strategic Plan. At this moment Carpenter violate revolving door ethics law 36-25-13 for UAB, Southern Research and City of Birmingham when UAB President Ray Watts re-hired Carpenter. Carpenter also violate using public office for personal gain 36-25-5. Carpenter 2018 scheme to exclude Briley and other areas through known false report sent a influence Legislation 18 USC 371. Carpenter violate 36-25-5 to make sure UAB is included as the federal program 18 USC 371 to defraud the US Government. Carpenter violate 18 USC 371 and Conspiracy to Defraud the US Government and intended Carpenter seeking approval to develop plan for biotech development and before City of Birmingham Design Review Committee violated revolving door ethics law again 36-25-13 for reports of the leaving down of a historic registered building less than 2 year since leaving office. The Government agency head, Mayor Randall Woodfin have never reported the known violation which also violates 36-25-17 for reports of violations.

BHM UAB SRI

**[10] Nov 2020** Carpenter leave City Hall and 7 months before Carpenter become the president of Southern Research, a biotech, R&D 501c3 in the medical district under Ray Watts.

BHM SRI

**[9] October 2020** Carpenter 2018-2021 Economic Development strategic Plan a updated on City office website a 1 month before Carpenter leave City Hall Economic Plan state: "**Birmingham should invest in precision population health**" and "**Develop sites for biotech development with proximity to core assets such as medical district**".

UAB BHM SRI

**[6]** Carpenter 3/16/18 wrote in his first economic strategic plan shared as part of the Woodfin Way "**When re-designing tax incentive strategy, prioritize R&D**"

BHM UAB SRI

**[7]** Woodfin and Carpenter 3/23/18 send 2nd false report confirming acts of secrecy and concealment and never reporting the truth to ADECA of the many false reports made the original 3/6/18 letter which is also a violation for the governmental agency head under 36-25-17 for reports of violations. **Downtown Entity is excluded for 10 years. Public is not aware of any of this.**

UAB BHM SRI

**[8] UAB Southern Research area added as focus area** in Birmingham City Center master plan 12/4/2019 under Carpenter. UAB area beatpath with over $300 million in new private developments connected to new tax incentives which increases UAB student housing options where UAB has 5 consecutive years of increase in student body.

UAB BHM SRI

**[11]** March 2021 UAB President/Interim President of Southern Research, Ray Watts purchases $109 million of additional land for biotech and R&D development adjacent to Southtown Court Development on east side of Southern Research.

UAB SRI BHM

3 opportunity zone developments are confirmed adjacent to Southern Research. Ascend Student Housing, **$40 million** Building Trades Tower **$300 million** Southtown Court redevelopment

3 opportunity zone developments are confirmed adjacent to Southern Research and R&D development adjacent to Southtown Court Development on east side of Southern Research.

UAB SRI BHM

(100) Open Public Corruption involving Governor Ivey, Mayor Woodfin, City of Economic Director, UAB, SRI regarding Federal Program Fraud and local leaders turn a blind eye

Just imagine, Birmingham's largest employer which happen to the State of Alabama largest employer who is also one of the largest real property owners in the city and the institution is allowed to have one of their highest officials placed over the highest position of economic development for all citizens and companies in Birmingham and that official was allowed to create tailor made economic plans for his already established economic interest and at the exact same time fraudulently exclude federal resources from smaller business districts and all city leaders turn a blind eye. Insider dealing is bad but what is worse is everyone turned a blind eye to undeniable "false report to influence legislation" where 1 abused his position for financial gain and at the same provided false information causing more structural disadvantages for the underserved. 10 of 10 City of Birmingham elected officials are affected as all turned a blind eye when they had a duty to report local, state and federal violations.

## UAB area is labeled "struggling economically" in public statements:

Carpenter created the perfect biased economic development environment for UAB and its affiliate SRI. Carpenter was allowed to manipulate free and open market openly and then labeled the UAB area as struggling economically but the Birmingham Business Journal Crane Watch show Ensley and the entire western side of Birmingham as struggling economically. Birmingham Business Journal Crane Watch map show major construction projects in Birmingham over a 4-year period from 2017-2022. Also adjacent to SRI, Carpenter played a significant role in the city economic plans for Southtown Projects as Economic Development Director and then he leaves the City of Birmingham and go and work with UAB affiliate SRI next door.

**3/6/2018 Opportunity Zone False Report to Influence Legislation is sent to Governor Ivey with original letter prepared by Woodfin and Carpenter and others to be discovered during the ethics investigation:**

Note in zip code 35233 which is the area immediately around UAB encompasses Railroad Park and several hundred million in new student housing for UAB. This zip code is key because it is a part of Census Tract 45 where Southern Research and UAB reside. This area is ranked number 1 in Carpenters' market manipulated "data driven" "false report". False data is omitted more than once for Ensley and other west Birmingham majority black areas which lets me know there was no "clerical error" as stated by Carpenter that excluded Ensley under the "Color of Law". 28 corporations were a part of the planning and the 28 supporting letters and not a single city councilor statement or review appeared to be included. When tracts were selected there were concerns regarding Downtown Ensley and everyone turned a blind eye.

# City Scoring Chart sent to the Governor shows that Ensley has "0" City Assets and "1" Brownfield Site

Table 1: Community & Economic Development Assets Located in Birmingham by Zip Code and Enumeration of Zip Codes*

| Zip Codes | Brownfield Sites | City Assets | Co-Working Spaces | Commercial District | Education Institution | Foreign Trade Zones | Incubator / Accelerator | Transit Nodes | Overall Ranking |
|---|---|---|---|---|---|---|---|---|---|
| 35233 | 21 | | | | | | | | 88 |
| 35203 | 11 | | 2 | 2 | 3 | | 1 | 1 | 68 |
| 35222 | 10 | 3 | | | | | | | 51 |
| 35204 | 4 | 6 | | 2 | | | | | 36 |
| 35212 | 6 | 1 | | 1 | | | | | 24 |
| 35205 | 1 | 7 | 2 | 1 | 2 | | 1 | | 24 |
| 35254 | 1 | | | | | | | | 22 |
| 35229 | 1 | 3 | | 2 | | | 1 | | 16 |
| 35217 | 5 | 1 | | | | | | | 16 |
| 35234 | 9 | | | | | | | | 16 |
| 35207 | 2 | | | | | | | | 11 |
| 35218 | 2 | | | | | | | | 10 |
| 35208 | 3 | 1 | | 1 | | | | | 9 |
| 35216 | | | | | | | | | 6 |
| 35214 | 2 | | | | | | | | 6 |
| 35206 | 2 | 1 | | | | | | | 6 |
| 35215 | | | | | | | | | 6 |
| 35218 | | 2 | | | | | | | 12 |
| 35217 | | | | | | | | | 13 |
| Ensley 35208 | | | | | | | | | 15 |
| 35044 | | | | 1 | 1 | | 1 | 1 | 16 |
| 35203 | | 1 | | | | | | | 22 |
| 35224 | | | 1 | 1 | | | | | 24 |
| 35294 | NOT IN A BIRMINGHAM TRACTS | | | | | | | | 51 |
| 35244 | NOT IN A BIRMINGHAM TRACTS | | | | | | | | 51 |
| 35242 | NOT IN A BIRMINGHAM TRACTS | | | | | | | | 51 |
| 35223 | NOT IN A BIRMINGHAM TRACTS | | | | | | | | 51 |

This slide is content from Brian K. Rice, www.briankrice.com, federal complaint against the City of Birmingham for Obstruction of Commerce in majority Black Communities in Birmingham

The City Scoring Chart omitted 5 City Assets in Downtown Ensley which "would have been reasonably known by the city" an increased Ensley zip code score alone by ?? points and increasing its ranking from #10 to being ranked #5

This slide is content from Brian K. Rice, www.briankrice.com, federal complaint against the City of Birmingham for Obstruction of Commerce in majority Black Communities in Birmingham

Carpenter was working under the office of UAB President Ray Watts (and Chairman of SRI board) as the UAB Director of External Affairs when this document was being created but submitted 3/6/2018 when he was employed at the city over the highest economic position under Woodfin. UAB is also a public institution that fall under the same ethics laws as the city of Birmingham so there were immediate violations associated with personal gain where Carpenter continued to be employed at UAB for several more years while working as city director. Carpenter left City Hall after all surrounding development plans were implemented. Behind Southern Research on the adjacent block, the Building Trades Development benefitted from known opportunity zone "false report" sent to Governor Ivey to influence legislation. Adjacent to Southern Research on the eastern side is the Southtown Development that benefits from the known opportunity zone "false letter" sent to the Governor. UAB adjacent student housing and apartments benefited from the known false opportunity zone letter sent to Governor Kay Ivey. The Marshall $55 Million development and the 20 Midtown $110 million developments are just 2 of several developments that benefited from Woodfin and Carpenter false reports and signed letter sent to falsely influence legislation for private development for student housing adjacent to UAB medical district. 7 months before Carpenter leave City Hall, UAB purchase $10.9 million property for Southern Research adjacent developments. Carpenter prepares City strategic plan to include biotech site development and Carpenter resign and go work for biotech research institution and benefit from his actions immediately violated 36-25-5 and 36-25-13 and other laws. Woodfin is the city governmental agency head who move at the will of UAB and it is proven over and over throughout this document. Below are just some of the developments that sped up or just benefitted from the false report. It is always nice to have 100% capital gain write offs as additional incentives to invest in areas "struggling economically" adjacent to the largest employer in the state, largest funded University in the state, where students can easily pay for luxury student housing with federal financial aid when there is already several years straight of record student enrollment.

Carpenter plans served his known economic interest and local public officials, and attorneys turn a blind eye.

New UAB Student Housing that benefitted developers from Woodfin and Carpenter Federal Opportunity Zone False Letter that was signed and sent to Governor Ivey to influence legislation: violating AL Ethics Law Section 36-25-26 False Reports to Influence Legislation

Apartments completed or under construction since FOZ approval that are immediately adjacent to UAB and Southern Research Institute

1. Ascend

2. The Palmer

3. The Marshall

4. Lumen in Birmingham

5. Lumen Above Railroad Park

6. Foundry Yards

7. Alight

Some Additional FOZ Developments:

8. Denham Building

9. Building Trades Tower

10. Southtown Development

11. 20 Midtown development

Turning a blind eye to the UAB Director of External Affairs assuming the City Economic Director position and all the associated plans that benefitted his former and current employer.

City Councilman Darrell O'Quinn knew in 2020 that it wasn't right but just asking a question is not helping the situation. Every city council has the ability to investigate any departments at the city of Birmingham especially when fraud may be at play where citizen tax dollars are affected. I honestly still believe in O'Quinn but what I see is a pattern where city leaders have become lax several years. I strongly recommend that the city council secure their own attorney separate from close friends and associates hired for the mayor's office to protect the citizens by having a second non-biased eye.

## FBI 8/29/22 Letter Continued:

At no point in recent history has the Economic Development Director of the City of Birmingham been involved in writing himself or herself into personal developments and violating ethics laws, associated state laws and federal laws. (1) The last major Birmingham situation was when former State Rep. Oliver Robinson received payments to mislead the citizens of North Birmingham. (2) The time before in Birmingham was when Mayor Larry Langford was sentenced for accepting more than $156,000 in payments in exchange for "bond swaps" before becoming Mayor as a County Commissioner that benefitted banks by $120 million that resulted in a $3.2 billion bond debt contributing to the Jefferson County bankruptcy. (3) Langford allowed for "bond swaps" and Carpenter "swapped truly distressed census tracts with the most affluent tracts" in an undeniable "false report" where the data was manipulated to affect the free and open market to ensure federal resources went to support development around UAB and SRI area and fraudulently rob federal resources from Downtown Ensley. Over $600 in new development have started or has completed around UAB / SRI benefitting from Carpenter's false report. (4) Carpenter continues and one month before Carpenter resign from the City of Birmingham Economic Development Director position, Carpenter revised and uploaded city plans that specifically benefit himself at SRI where he would be the president less than 7 months later where Carpenter former boss UAB President Ray Watts served as Interim President / CEO and Chairman of the board of SRI. Carpenter boldly moved without law as he continued to violate ethic laws for personal gain.

(5) In November 2021 Carpenter as CEO of SRI receive approvals from City for his City biotech development plans, he wrote out as a City director barely a year earlier and to date no public official, public employee, has brought this before the public as these acts are truly violations of ethic laws, state laws and federals laws.

Downtown Ensley is suffering from economic barriers caused by Carpenter where UAB and SRI area experienced $300+ million in record breaking luxury student housing developments from the same false reports produced by Carpenter. Carpenter was allowed to manipulate free and open market without accountability as if he and others are above the law. Please stand up for economic justice. Brian K. Rice

## **Birmingham Economic Director Write Himself into $84+ Million Deal**

Public Officials Turning a Blind Eye, Brian K. Rice

In Birmingham, AL we have a local government run without ethics and conflict of interest laws. Misuse of office for personal or private gain is the rule of law and oaths of office for associated "public official surety bonds" are statements on paper as those not in the inner circle of cliques are left out of an impartial government. In 2021 Dr. Josh Carpenter, recent UAB Director of External Affairs, recent City of Birmingham Economic Development Director, and current President of Southern Research Institute (SRI) (UAB Affiliate) wrote himself, UAB, and SRI into an $84+ million development through city economic plans from 2018- 2020 that he created and then walk back in city hall, less than 1 year later and secure approval and the design review committee, mayor, attorneys, public officials and employees turn a blind eye. Over $300 million in SRI surrounding developments magically move forward while he was in charge of city economic plans. Once inside deals were set up, he resigns and magically assumed the President position of SRI where his former boss and current UAB President was also the Interim President and Chairman of SRI. (link to key city file, last modified 10/12/2020, 1 month before Carpenter resign;

https://www.birminghamal.gov/wp-content/uploads/2020/10/IEO-Strategic-Plan_2018-to-2021.pdf )

The 35+ year historic fight to save the façade of Birmingham's only castle that was placed on the National Historic Register ended with a "revolving door" violation especially for a former director for AL Ethics Law 36-25-13 and of other state and federal violations for manipulated city plans related to conflict of interest. (Historical Context) In 1993, the city purchased the castle. In 1999 in City Councilman Jimmy Blake asked for an investigation of the Quinlan Castle deal in which the city originally sold to Southern Research Institute. Blake said he recognizes SRIs importance to the city but said the council was misinformed about the deal. In 2021 either the council was misinformed or complicit with the inside deal, pushed forward by Carpenter, the new CEO and most recent economic director of the city. Jimmy Blake in 1999 said "The city bought the facility in the first place to save the historical structure." In 2008, City Councilor Valerie Abbott, the only remaining city councilor today was the only "no vote" on the sale to SRI because there was no language in the sale protecting the historic façade. Carpenter also used the same language he used as the city economic director in April 2020 for the Historic Ramsay McCormack building in Downtown Ensley where the city violated its own historic ordinances for razing the building.

UAB and Southern Research related images showing Southern Research added as focus area shaded in blue in 2019 under Carpenter.

In 2020 before Carpenter left there were other approvals to be uncovered in trial. In 2021 the current city council approved the open ethics violations, and all turned a blind eye

Links: https://www.downtownbhamplan.com/

See page 3 of Birmingham Post link: https://www.downtownbhamplan.com/uploads/4/8/0/4/48049787/birmingham_poster_ch_12092019.pdf

UAB and Southern Research "Revolving Doors" #1

October 12th, 2020, City Economic Strategic Plan is completed and uploaded on City Website 1 month before Carpenter resign

1.      This direct evidence of what Carpenter SRI President/ CEO was planning while still employed at City Hall and what the City approved violated revolving doors ethics law and many other laws:

2.      Link to pdf file, last modified 10/12/2020; https://www.birminghamal.gov/wp-content/uploads/2020/10/IEO-Strategic-Plan_2018-to-2021.pdf

Just imagine you were able to assume the City of Birmingham highest economic development position and you were allowed to write out your own economic plans and walk back into city hall and you are approved less than 1 year later.

Carpenter and the City allowed this to happen with a former direct report in 2020 as if he was testing the political waters. (This will be the focus of part 2). In 2022, Carpenter openly solicits $10 million from the city and county to support his SRI developments violating ethics laws again.

It is of utmost importance that citizens of Birmingham, city employees, city officials, city attorneys, UAB, SRI, the Department of Justice, AL Ethics Commission, and AL Attorney General investigate the UAB / SRI land purchase just 3 months after Carpenter resign and 2 months before Carpenter was announced as CEO of SRI (UAB Affiliate). It is of utmost importance to review city approvals of Southtown Housing Projects and the $300+ million development next door where land deals and city approvals took place under Carpenter that now involve another current City Councilor who has not recused herself of votes associated with Southtown and SRI where she has financial gain. The $40+ million Ascend Luxury Apartments and the $40+ million Building Trades Tower Development immediately next door were able to benefit from Carpenter's 2018 "false report to influence legislation" AL Ethics Law violation 36-25-26 to be discussed later in this document that robbed resources from the underserved communities in the name of redirecting resources to areas in Birmingham that were "struggling economically". UAB area was labeled "struggling economically" and Downtown Ensley was left out over a "clerical error" in public statements by Carpenter and local officials turned blind eye. (Image below will be discussed in part 3)

Everyone so far has turned a blind eye so were they participants or they just didn't know City Ordinances, Mayor Council Act, Ethics Laws, State Laws and Federal Laws were being violated where a public employee entrusted with the highest city economic position was allowed to create tailor made city economic plans for himself, UAB, and SRI and walk back in city hall and secure all approvals.

Affected City of Birmingham Ordinance, City Mayor Council Act, AL Ethics Law

The General Code or the City of Birmingham also state:

A.      Sec. 2-4-2. – Interest in contracts, etc.—Generally; No officer or employee elected or appointed in the city shall be interested, directly or indirectly, in any contract for work or material, or the profits thereof or services to be furnished or performed for the city. No such officer or employee shall be interested, directly or indirectly, in any contract for work or materials, or the profits thereof, or services to be furnished or performed for any person, firm or corporation.

B.      Sec. 2-4-3. – Same—Violation renders contract void; Every contract, express or implied, hereafter made in violation of any of the provisions of or contained in section 2-4-2 shall be absolutely void and of no effect.

C.      Sec. 2-4-4. – Same—Penalty; Any person soliciting, procuring, entering into, participating in or performing any express or implied contract, or any work or business, knowing that any officer or employee of the city is interested in the same in any manner hereinbefore described, or any person who shall in any other manner violate any provision contained in section 2-4-2 shall be punished for each offense as provided in section 1-1-6.

Mayor Council Act state:

D.　　Sec. 8.06. – Officers and employees not to be privately interested in city's contracts; No member of the council, officer or employee elected or appointed shall be interested, directly or indirectly, in any contract for work or material, or the profits thereof, or services to be furnished or performed for the city…

AL Ethics Commission: AL Ethics Law 36-25-13 and 36-25-5

E.　　Alabama Code 36-25-13. Actions of former public officials or public employees prohibited for two years after departure; (f) No public official or public employee who personally participates in the direct regulation, audit, or investigation of a private business, corporation, partnership, or individual shall within two years of his or her departure from such employment solicit or accept employment with such private business, corporation, partnership, or individual.

F.　　Alabama Code 36-25-5 — Use of official position or office for personal gain; (a) No public official or public employee shall use or cause to be used his or her official position or office to obtain personal gain for himself or herself, or family member of the public employee or family member of the public official, or any business with which the person is associated unless the use and gain are otherwise specifically authorized by law. Personal gain is achieved when the public official, public employee, or a family member thereof receives, obtains, exerts control over, or otherwise converts to personal use the object constituting such personal gain.

G.　　Alabama Code 36-25-26. False reporting for purpose of influencing legislation; No person, for the purpose of influencing legislation, may do either of the following: (1) Knowingly or willfully make any false statement or misrepresentation of the facts to a member of the Legislative or Executive Branch. (2) Knowing a document to contain a false statement, cause a copy of the document to be received by a member of the Legislative or Executive Branch without notifying the member in writing of the truth.

UAB Ethics Policy

H.     UAB employees (faculty, staff, and student workers) are subject to the State of Alabama's ethics laws, the intent of which is to prevent public employees from using their positions to reap private gains and to prevent conflicts of interest between the employees' private interests and the duties of their public position. The 'ethics law' was passed in 1975 under the heading of "Code of Ethics for Public Officials, Employees, Etc.", Chapter 25 of Title 36 of the Code of Alabama 1975. Copies of the actual law and of an associated handbook are available free of charge from the Alabama Ethics Commission (334-242-2997). The Alabama Ethics Commission maintains a website at Alabama Ethics Commission.

I.     UAB Duty to Report and Non Retaliation Policy for Wrongful Conduct: Examples include, but are not limited to: https://secure2.compliancebridge.com/uab/portal/getdoc.php?file=97

a.     Illegal or fraudulent activity;

b.     False claims, financial misstatements, or accounting or auditing irregularities;

c.     Undisclosed or unmanaged conflicts of interests;

d.     Violations of the UAB Enterprise Code of Conduct;

e.     Back to the UAB Policies and Procedures Library

f.     Physical, sexual, verbal, and mental abuse;

g.     Gross mismanagement of a contract or grant;

h.     Gross waste of funds and other resources;

i.      Abuse of authority, including that relating to a contract or grant;

j.      Giving false information, knowingly making false statements, or failing to cooperate in an investigation;

k.      A substantial and specific danger to public health or safety;

l.      A violation of law, regulation, UAB policy, contractual obligation, or grant;

m.      A supervisor or UAB official compelling a UAB Member to violate a law, regulation, UAB policy, contractual obligation, or grant;

n.      Falsification, fabrication, or plagiarism of research or scholarly activities or the pressure or demand to do the same or,

o.      Retaliation, as that term is defined above.

J.      UAB Enterprise Conflict of Interest, Conflict of Commitment state: This policy describes the UAB Enterprise's commitment to conducting its activities in ways that promote and maintain public trust and sets forth requirements for employees and other designated individuals in identifying and managing conflicts of interest and conflict of commitment.

K.      Southern Research Conflict of Interest Policy: The Southern Research conflict of interest policy state: "Southern Research has entered into an agreement with its affiliate, The University of Alabama at Birmingham (hereinafter "UAB"), under which the UAB Conflict of Interest Review board (hereinafter "CIRB") will work with Southern Research to ensure compliance with federal regulations related to financial conflict of interest."

## Section 3 FBI Letter: Birmingham Promise:

2/22/22 Ethics Complaint also confirmed revolving door and election scheme violations with 501c3 Birmingham Promise created inside City Hall at the City of Birmingham under the Mayor,

Economic Development Director, Economic Development
Employee

## BHM Promise Part 1: 501c3, Ethics, Campaign Violations

To Birmingham citizens and to city, county, state, federal officials,
and employees, if our economic development leaders are planning
out personal gain and campaign schemes with public dollars through
education schemes and local leaders are turning a blind eye to open
corruption then who is putting the citizens first and planning out the
economic development needs of underserved businesses and
business districts in Birmingham? We need state and federal oversite
in Birmingham immediately as no one at the city will stand up to the
open corruption even when City of Birmingham ordinance 2-4-3
state every contract, express or implied, hereafter made in violation
of any of the provisions of or contained in section 2-4-2 shall be
absolutely void and of no effect.  Brian K. Rice

I listed all known affected local and state ordinances and laws first in
the first box covering City of Birmingham multiple ethics violations,
501c3 violations, and campaign violations with the misuse of public
dollars for personal gain associated Birmingham Promise, Prosper
Birmingham, Brookings, UAB, Woodfin, Carpenter, and Harmon:

- Affected City and State Laws:
- City of Birmingham Mayor Council Act: Sec 8.06
- City of Birmingham Ordinance: Sec 2-4-2, 2-4-3, 2-4-4
- AL Ethics Laws: 36-25-5, 36-25-6, 36-25-11, 36-25-13, 36-25-17, 36-25-27
- AL Fair Campaign Practice Laws: AL Code 36-14-18, 17-17-5, 17-17-4, 17-5-12, 17-5-19, 17-5-15, 17-17-3
- Box #1: 7/16/19 Josh Carpenter, Rachel Harmon & Mayor present BHM Promise at City Council Meeting. Public servants planning out how to pay self and promote self with city dollars.
- Box #2: City approve $10 million over 5 years on 10/15/19. Funding was submitted by City Attorney and recommended by Mayor to be placed on consent agenda which all City

192

Councilman approved.

> **ITEM 23.**
> A Resolution approving and authorizing the Mayor to execute a Project Agreement between the City of Birmingham and **Birmingham Promise, Inc.**, under which (1) Birmingham Promise will implement and administer a program to, among other things, increase post-secondary opportunities and increase economic prosperity for Birmingham City School graduates, thus developing a pipeline of talent for regional employers, and (2) the City of Birmingham will provide funding to Birmingham Promise, Inc. in the amount of $2,000,000.00 per year for five (5) years, subject to extension in accordance with the terms of the Agreement. **[Funding Source: 001_400_96200_96216.550-003 – General Fund Boards and Agencies]** (Submitted by the City Attorney) (Recommended by the Mayor) **

- Box #3: Harmon leave City to become Executive Director 4/29/20 violating Mayor Council Act and Ethics laws 36-25-13 and 36-25-5 of program she created with public dollars under Carpenter and Woodfin
- Box #4: City send $2 million in FY20 + $2 million in FY21 of public dollars to BHM Promise with known "revolving door" 36-25-13 ethics violation after Harmon arrive after Harmon planned her own job with city dollars. Carpenter become board member. City economic development department employees planning out personal gain through education scheme while underserved businesses districts need economic development.
- Box #5: Harmon and Woodfin in interview 5/24/21 during campaign season openly talk about BHM Promise ethics violations. BHM Promise openly to violate 501c3 IRS campaign laws after receiving $4 million of tax payer dollars and promote Woodfin multiple times in official press conferences and promoting "The Committee to Re-Elect Woodfin" Facebook page during campaign season and executive director, public officials, public employees, and city attorneys turn blind eye with multiple state & federal violations and misuse of public dollars

•

## Section 4 FBI Letter: Part #2: Birmingham Promise and Prosper BHM violations:

City of Birmingham Ordinance 2-4-3 "Every contract, express or implied, hereafter made in violation of any of the provisions of or contained in section 2-4-2 shall be absolutely void and of no effect."

I listed all known affected local and state ordinances and laws first in the first box covering City of Birmingham multiple ethics violations, 501c3 violations, and campaign violations with the misuse of public dollars for personal gain associated Birmingham Promise, Prosper Birmingham, Brookings, UAB, Woodfin, Carpenter, and Harmon:

- Affected City and State Laws:
- City of Birmingham Mayor Council Act: Sec 8.06
- City of Birmingham Ordinance: Sec 2-4-2, 2-4-3, 2-4-4
- AL Ethics Laws: 36-25-5, 36-25-6, 36-25-11, 36-25-13, 36-25-17, 36-25-27
- AL Fair Campaign Practice Laws: AL Code 36-14-18, 17-17-5, 17-17-4, 17-5-12, 17-5-19, 17-5-15, 17-17-3
  Box #1: Woodfin and Carpenter setup public private partnership with Brookings while Harmon still works in City Economic Development Department (IEO) Brookings pic below is 12/5/18 with initiative to create Prosper BHM and funding source for BHM Promise

Box #2: UAB President Watts make UAB 1st university to partner with BHM Promise 1/29/20. Carpenter who was the recent UAB former Director of External Affairs under Watts and now City Economic Development Director is responsible for the creation of BHM Promise with Harmon all under Woodfin

Box #3: Carpenter work for Brookings Institute as a Sr Non Resident Fellow violating 36-25-5, 36-25-13 and Mayor Council Act.

Box #4: (1) Prosper approve $8 million for BHM Promise where (2) Woodfin and Watts are Prosper board members; (3) BHM Promise is already openly promoting Woodfin as a 501c3 violating IRS and State Fair Campaign Practices. (4) Carpenter is BHM Promise board member, (5) Harmon is Executive Director of BHM Promise that she created under Woodfin and Carpenter as city employee violating ethics laws, mayor council act, and city ordinances for misuse of office for personal gain. Public Officials, Public Employees, City Attorney, Non-Profit all turn blind eye to city, state, and federal violations

Inside Box 4: 7/16/19 City Economic Development Employees & Mayor present BHM Promise education program at City Council Meeting. Council approves $10 million on 10/15/19. 6 months later, Harmon is the Executive Director of program she created violating ethics laws, mayor council act, and city ordinances. 2 Years later BHM Promise is promoting Woodfin campaign violating 501c3 Fair Campaign Practice Laws.

Summary: BHM Promise and Prosper BHM violations: To Birmingham citizens and to city, county, state, federal officials, and employees, if our economic development leaders are planning out personal gain and campaign schemes with public dollars through education schemes and local leaders are turning a blind eye to corruption then who is putting the citizens first and planning out the economic development needs of underserved businesses and business districts in Birmingham?

## Section 5: This is where I came into the picture where I was unaware of all the active systems of economic injustice taking place in Ensley:

It was at the entry of investing in Ensley that I was met with economic barrier after economic barrier.

Public Officials Turning a Blind Eye, Brian K. Rice 5/16/2022.

In 2018 is where I came into the picture very unaware of the level of present day "systemic injustice" in Birmingham and 40+ years of "municipal disinvestment", "benign neglect", and "redlining" beyond UAB and Downtown. When we asked what happened to Ensley being excluded of federal incentives, Carpenter blamed a "clerical error". I'm not sure if in other cities and states if they left the data vague but here Carpenter admitted to negligence and provided and "false report" that sped up the existing economic boom already taking place near UAB, Lakeview, Avondale, Downtown, Midtown and economic starvation for Downtown Ensley. Public officials turned a blind eye to continued economic injustice in Ensley.

I want to thank ADECA representative Mike Presley and the leadership of Ken Boswell for standing up to the truth and disagreeing with City of Birmingham economic director Josh Carpenter who blamed a "clerical error" in the August 5th, 2018, Route Fifty Article, "Figuring Out If 'Opportunity Zones' Can Revitalize Struggling Neighborhoods". The article stated "Mike Presley, a spokesman for the Alabama Department of Economic and Community Affairs, the lead agency in the state for Opportunity Zones, said after looking into what happened with Ensley over the course of a day last week, he was "not aware" of any error." This statement which is 4 months after the initial letter also confirm that the truth was never updated and sent back to ADECA who then would send an update regarding the truth to Governor Ivey which continues to violate Alabama Ethics Law when learning of the truth. I believe there are many within the Woodfin Administration that were aware of the false statements regarding Ensley that Carpenter state were "clerical" errors and Woodfin state the Governor did it but chose to conceal which will be uncovered in a full investigation. The false statements and misrepresentations that influenced legislation by the city have caused ongoing benefit for selected areas, associated investors, real property owners and hundreds of millions in capital gains write offs through the present day of this letter and through 2028 which is great for them and the developments taking place but the false statement that have influenced legislation have caused ongoing personal injury and economic injury to other real property owners in Ensley and myself that should have been included through 2028. The false statements have caused ongoing injury to myself and neighbors within my associated census tracts through 2028. I have watched the City of Birmingham and the unethical actions of several of their leaders deny their own citizens constitutional rights and cause a "deprivation of rights" while acting under the color of law when public trust was given to them by the same citizens.

Every investor, banker, real estate agent I met asked me for 2+ years is Downtown Ensley in an Opportunity Zone and then several said, we have OZ investors and they are only looking for OZ properties. "I responded every time saying, the OZ stopped 2 blocks from my properties at the entrance of the Ensley commercial district". All communication stopped after they learned Ensley was not apart of opportunity zones.

I tried to sell my properties and even my agent stated he had investors that were looking for OZ properties. I tried to get traditional lending and was faced with historic levels of redlining by receiving a $0 appraisal on my 8 structures of 33,000sf. I spoke with a billion dollar finance group out of New York as well and the first question they asked me was about opportunity zones.

One of many text messages I received from 2018-2020 investors, bankers, realtors

Is Ensley designated an "Opportunity Zone"?

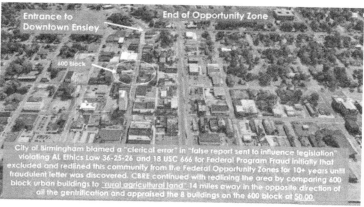

Entrance to Downtown Ensley

End of Opportunity Zone

600 block

City of Birmingham blamed a "clerical error" in "false report sent to influence legislation" violating AL Ethics Law 36-25-26 and 18 USC 666 for Federal Program Fraud initially that excluded and redlined this community from the Federal Opportunity Zones for 10+ years until fraudulent letter was discovered. CBRE continued with redlining the area by comparing 600 block urban buildings to "rural agricultural land" 14 miles away in the opposite direction of all the gentrification and appraised the 8 buildings on the 600 block at $0.00.

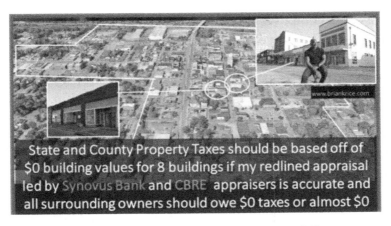

State and County Property Taxes should be based off of $0 building values for 8 buildings if my redlined appraisal led by Synovus Bank and CBRE appraisers is accurate and all surrounding owners should owe $0 taxes or almost $0

Woodfin anger after I sought help was the red flag.

I honestly would not have discovered the violations in this letter if the open abuse had not happened to me when I sought help for my buildings being fraudulently appraised at $0.00. I honestly would not have seen the Birmingham Promise violations with our tax dollars if it wasn't for the Oct 13th, 2019, meeting.

On Oct 13th, 2019, just 2 days before the City Council approve $10,000,000 million for Birmingham Promise as I was seeking help for Downtown Ensley, Woodfin and Carpenter met me in my building and when Woodfin first addressed me he was angry with my appraisal but not Synovus Bank or CBRE who approved the $0.00 appraisal. (Birmingham Promise is another inside scheme, ethics violations, and fair campaign practice violations to be discussed in the Birmingham Promise section involving Carpenter and Woodfin.)

During this Ensley meeting, Carpenter who was sitting to my left stated that the city has a great relationship with Synovus Bank CEO Bean. I was in awe as I had been asking Woodfin and Carpenter and the city for help for over 10 months now. All I wanted them to do at this time was advocate for me regarding my undeniable fraudulent $0.00 appraisal that have robbed me of my livelihood. I left that meeting saying what just happened, why did a black mayor get mad at me for asking for help regarding my appraisal. I started searching every city file I could find over the next 2+ years to understand the public private connection to economic barriers and obstruction of commerce in Ensley. I eventually find the 3/6/2018 Federal Opportunity Zone fraudulent "false letter to influence legislation" that was sent to Governor Kay Ivey that excluded Downtown Ensley of federal resources prepared by Carpenter, signed by Woodfin, signed by Synovus CEO Bean, signed by UAB President Watts and others and then I realize where the anger of Woodfin came from. I filed a federal complaint on 8/13/2021 regarding the false letter and intentionally put a 2 hour plus interview on website https://www.briankrice.com/doj-federal-complaint because federal officials, attorneys, citizens who care, and social justice groups need to see the evidence of present-day redlining in Birmingham under Woodfin. Woodfin anger confirmed that Ensley was not supposed to develop. Ensley was not supposed to have resources. Ensley was supposed to be locked out and me asking for help was a problem. Helping me and those in Ensley was not a solution.

I eventually uncover many violations with Woodfin and Carpenter involving Birmingham Promise, Prosper Birmingham, Southern Research Institute, UAB and others. This Birmingham Promise snapshot is just 1 category of multiple felony level violations taking place under the Color of Law.

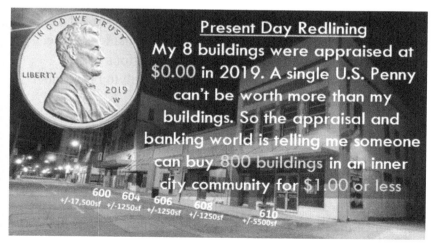

1.  My 8 Commercial Buildings/ Structures in Downtown Ensley located at 600, 604, 606, 608, 610, 615, 617, and 619 19th St Ensley Birmingham AL 35218 (Yes, 3 of my buildings needed more repair than others but they still had value, my tenants had value, my other buildings had value)

2.  The entire value of my structures was erased by omission or commission and valued at $0.00 and all entities who I have sent letters of help to have delayed their decision, concealed the facts, or remained silent regarding the undeniable errors of omission and commission and undeniable USPAP violations by CBRE appraisers Harvill and Neyhart

3.  CBRE $0.00 appraisal cannot equal $229,790 JCBOE Assessed Value for 2019 Ad Valorem Taxes

4.  CBRE $0.00 appraisal cannot equal $122,800 JCBOE Assessed Value for 2021 Ad Valorem Taxes

5.  Any Value Greater than Zero cannot equal Zero Value at the same time

6.  Rural Land cannot equal Urban Land as similar appraisal comps

7.  Rural Rock Creek, AL 1456-person unincorporated rural city cannot equal urban Birmingham, AL 212,237 incorporated city (per 2010 US Census) unless the aggregate of USPAP errors are ignored

8.  CBRE As Is Active Rental Income cannot equal $0.00 unless 100% of As Is Rent Roll is omitted from the appraisal in an act of omission or commission

9.  CBRE Car Wash comparison cannot equal 8 Multi-Story Office / Mixed Use Commercial Buildings

10. Masonry Steel Frame Partition Car Wash cannot equal 8 Mediterranean Revival Style/ Art Deco Historic Multi-Story Commercial Buildings with pent tile roofs, corbelled cornice contributing Early 20th Century Commercial historic architecture

11.     Synovus Bank $0.00 federal related transaction internal bank approval cannot equal $0.00 unless the illegal practices of redlining are legal and has been the center of many Department of Justice cases from traditional redlining and reverse redlining.

12.     The $0.00 approved appraisal was allowed to remain without any corrective actions from Alabama Real Estate Appraisal Board (AREAB) headed by executive director Lisa Brooks and they are the state regulatory agency for appraisers and if they believe the buildings are worth $0.00 then I'm experiencing redlining and my ad valorem taxes should be appraised at $0.00 for my structures otherwise any amount over $0.00 is over taxation and reverse redlining for taxes.

13.     I also filed a complaint with the Federal Reserve Board of Governors, and they took no action to correct the $0.00 approved appraisal and they are the federal oversite agency of Synovus Bank.

It was unknown to me when I approached Synovus Bank for a loan, Synovus Bank was a part of the fraudulent letter prepared by City Economic Director Josh Carpenter and signed by the Mayor Randall Woodfin of Birmingham targeting Ensley and redlining and excluding Ensley of federal resources until I found the letter. I did not know I was caught in the middle of public and private corruption, redlining and obstruction of commerce in Downtown Ensley until I was met with obstruction and deprivation of rights in every direction.

When a community is locked out of opportunities to restore buildings then the community is locked out of the ability to create new spaces for new businesses. When a community can't create new businesses then they can't create jobs and if they can't create jobs then families can't provide and when families can't provide then there is an imbalance and we have seen the imbalance in underserved across the country. In Birmingham, the Ensley imbalance has led the City in Homicides for decades. Economic Injustice is a direct link to social injustice and the unhealthy environment that consume underserved communities. On the Department of Justice building in Washington D.C. inscribed are the word "Where Law Ends, Tyranny Begins". The law has ended in Ensley and that tyranny has led the city of Birmingham in homicides for decades, blighted structures, unemployment and more. Help us by standing up for equal protection of the law and investigate and hold accountable the city, county, state and federal offices, agencies, and boards who deprived me and the citizens of the Ensley neighborhood of our Constitutional, local, state, and federal rights.

## Ensley Reverse Redlining and Over Taxation

Ensley is also the only place in in America where we have $0.00 appraised building and real property ad valorem taxes increasing up to 535+% in the same period.

In 2020, the Ensley Business District had the highest increase of commercial property taxes than anywhere in the city where mom and pop business taxes were doubling, tripling, quadrupling, and increasing from 49% to 535% so we have present day "Reverse Redlining" at the same time we have present day "Redlining" and all local leaders have turned a blind eye. The Jefferson County public property appraiser who interviewed me stated during an Ensley property protest hearing, we have been aware of bad appraisals in the Ensley area and other areas on the west side of Birmingham for some time.

Ensley is the only place in Birmingham or America where there are buildings appraised at $0.00 and surrounding mom and pop small business owners property taxes see uneven Inflated Property Tax Spikes between 100% to 535% when sales have been flat for years and no completed developments but the only Fortune 500 company in Birmingham values has the lowest increase at only 15% or just $432. Contact the Board of Directors of Synovus Bank & CBRE. Contact the Board of Equalizations and City of Birmingham on our behalf. Visit www.briankrice.com for info. Complaint filed against Birmingham for Federal

The 8 $0.00 Appraised Buildings.

Lower my property taxes to $0.00 or stand up for equal protection of the law for my equity. THIS IS TAXATION WITHOUT REPRESENTATION.

Brian K. Rice study over 40 surrounding small business owners property taxes in Ensley and there were uneven Inflated Property Tax Spikes between 100% to 535%? This is 2017-2021 Economic Injustice in Birmingham.

| Address | 2016 Baseline Value | 2016 Appraised Value | 2016 Taxes | Year | Cummulative Percentage Change Since 2016 | Appraised Value | County Appraised Value difference against 2016 | Taxes | Tax payment difference against 2016 |
|---|---|---|---|---|---|---|---|---|---|
| 411 19th St Ensley | 2016 | $82,300 | $1,193 | 2016 | 535% | $622,200 | $499,900 | $7,972 | $6,379 |
| 1234 Ave F | 2016 | $54,100 | $784 | 2020 | 424% | $283,500 | $229,400 | $4,111 | $3,326 |
| 1608 Ave E | 2016 | $48,200 | $699 | 2020 | 422% | $251,600 | $203,400 | $3,644 | $2,949 |
| THIS IS TAXATION WITHOUT REPRESENTATION | | | | | | | | | |
| 630 19th St Ensley | 2016 | $39,500 | $573 | 2020 | 390% | $193,600 | $154,100 | $2,807 | $2,234 |
| 626 19th St Ensley | 2016 | $138,400 | $2,007 | 2020 | 377% | $660,200 | $521,800 | $9,573 | $7,566 |
| 1911 Ave F | 2016 | $13,500 | $225 | 2020 | 365% | $72,100 | $56,600 | $1,045 | $821 |
| 1800 Ave E | 2016 | $80,800 | $1,164 | 2020 | 331% | $346,100 | $265,800 | $6,018 | $3,854 |
| 611 19th St Ensley | 2016 | $46,000 | $667 | 2020 | 182% | $129,800 | $83,800 | $1,882 | $1,215 |
| 601 19th St Ensley | 2016 | $161,000 | $2,335 | 2020 | 145% | $394,300 | $233,300 | $5,717 | $3,383 |
| THIS IS TAXATION WITHOUT REPRESENTATION | | | | | | | | | |
| 615 19th St Ensley | 2016 | $39,300 | $526 | 2020 | 139% | $0.00 $86,700 | $50,400 | $1,257 | $731 |
| 700 19th St Ensley | 2016 | $88,700 | $1,286 | 2020 | 117% | $192,400 | $103,700 | $2,790 | $1,504 |
| 704 19th St Ensley | 2016 | $48,609 | $705 | 2020 | 93% | $93,900 | $45,300 | $1,362 | $657 |
| 626 20th St Ensley | 2016 | $140,000 | $2,080 | 2020 | 86% | $260,300 | $120,300 | $3,774 | $1,744 |
| 417 19th St Ensley | 2016 | $214,100 | $3,104 | 2020 | 76% | $376,800 | $162,700 | $5,464 | $2,359 |
| 525 19th St Ensley | 2016 | $187,100 | $1,356 | 2020 | 67% | $312,400 | $125,300 | $2,265 | $908 |
| 1821 Ave G | 2016 | $85,900 | $1,246 | 2020 | 49% | $128,200 | $42,300 | $1,859 | $613 |
| 1801 Ave E | 2016 | $386,600 | $2,803 | 2020 | 15% | $446,000 | $59,500 | $3,235 | $432 |

We need the state or federal government to help in Ensley regarding present day redlining and reverse redlining.

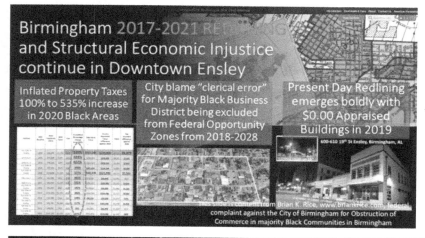

Downtown Ensley has been faced with Federal Opportunity Zone Redlining through discovered "false report to influence legislation", Appraisal Redlining through $0.00 confirmed appraisal, Reverse Redlining with Ad Valorem Taxes for small mom and pop businesses, and Taxation Without Representation and all local officials have turned a blind eye.

We need the help of the Department of Justice. We have no help locally from the City of Birmingham.

I had no idea of the real and accustomed conditions of present-day economic suppression until I chose Ensley

The conditions I have experienced in Ensley since Carpenter excluded Ensley of resources are as follows: I have been in Ensley for 4 years and it has been a form of ethnographic research and today I will speak about a snapshot into some of the conditions I see daily. I didn't realize the true reality of the conditions inside of communities like Ensley until I was there every day.

Poverty become your friend and your enemy. Many are conditioned to the environment whether they are the professionals or those with very little. To be locked out of resources is just a way of life because it has always been that way from banks to government.

You see men searching for opportunity every day. Every day, if you stand outside your building, I guarantee several men a day are going to walk up to you of all ages and ask you if you have any work. If you have any work, you let them perform the work.

It became normal to see people pick through trash illegally dumped behind buildings and walk away with shoes and jackets and shirts. You look at those struggling with addictions differently as many become your friends and your trusted helpers. These helpers teach you about life in so many ways and you learn to never call them a wino because you don't see a person addicted to alcohol, you see a person.

You speak to people with severe speech impediments, but these speech impediments are caused by true poverty. Teeth may be completely gone and when they speak, you must concentrate as their words are mumbled together but when they see you, their spirit light up and your spirit light up.

You see men from all types of broken backgrounds gifted with various forms of visual art. You see men not for their past choices but as men and friends and workers. You don't see women strolling like the men. You don't see kids playing but when you see kids walk through the alleys on their way to school, you are disappointed because they must walk by so much blight every day.

You cross paths with many entrepreneurs with no resources but they have the dream to launch their business one day. You learn what survival is as you see men miss meals for days until you can give them work as there are no homeless programs nearby.

You will not see any metal of any kind on the ground as the metal is lunch money. Recycling metal, aluminum, copper, and any larger appliances full of mixed metal are hot commodities.

Politics and resources never reach them, and they are definitely aware of the local leaders.

This is just a tiny snapshot. The one question that bother me daily is when men ask for work, and I must tell them I don't have any work because I have been locked out but I'm fighting for resources daily. I'm studying the law. I'm writing state and federal complaints daily. I'm studying the law more. I am standing up to banks and I'm studying the law more because the barriers I faced are not just my barriers but the barriers to men who are looking for work.

"We either spend years fighting for our economic real property rights or we become accustomed to the conditions. We need help here. We need resources. We don't just need community-based intervention, we need government based intervention. I hope I have been able to explain some of the economic concerns, needs, and how we need an "impartial government" working for our rights.

I am asking for the Department of Justice Criminal Division and the FBI White Collar Organized Crimes, Civil Rights, Color of Law divisions and the department of the Treasury Inspector General to launch a full investigation into the public corruption in this letter taking place from the local level to the federal agency level. We have no equal rights here in Ensley in Birmingham, AL and because we have no equal rights, we cannot restore our buildings and blight is normalized. We cannot update spaces for new business that ultimately can create jobs or create constructive options for our community. We cannot improve the value of our properties because people like me have been locked out of 100% of equity based on fraud and color of law violations from corporate entities and the public agencies who are there to protect the public. Ensley has led the city in Death by Homicide for decades because street life is the best option when resources are locked out from small businesses. We need 1 public agency, entity, or office to stand up for our rights under the Constitution and under the laws of the United States of America and against the Color of Law violations that are depriving us here.

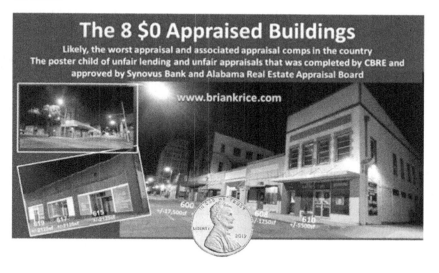

# CHAPTER 12: STANDING FOR YOUR RIGHTS OR THE RIGHTS OF OTHERS.

I share what I have learned because I had so little help. I hope this short collection of laws helps you, especially if you are dealing with violations from public officials.

Now, if your rights have been breached and you have no idea what to do, there are a few key areas I recommend you review to give you a baseline. Don't be afraid of legal language. Relax, you are more than capable. Hopefully, you will find good legal help regardless of your financial condition.

The first baseline of information has already been set by local, state, and federal courts near you to help you with some of your fears of potentially standing alone or as a family or at least giving you a guideline of parameters for the attorney that may represent you. I have learned of too many unethical stories of lawyers skirting their professional code of ethics and duties required of them by the state bar that injure their clients. I have learned of too many examples where backroom deals have been cut for the attorney, and the injured have been even more deprived of their legal rights. I have learned of the many examples where the plaintiff or defendant has filed bar complaints or had to sue their lawyer and has won.

I strongly recommend that everyone purchase a Black's Law Dictionary, and your understanding of your rights will immediately change. You will have the baseline of the legal definition of each word and not how we may use the word in our everyday lives. Yes, if you can afford it, it will be like the price of a university textbook and worth every bit of it. If you can't afford it, the most important resource every citizen has outside the internet is your local courthouse.

I have had my rights breached like many others. I want my rights to be honored and protected, and I want your rights to be honored and protected. It is heartbreaking to write and send several thousand pages of formal complaints to state and federal government agencies and to see a complete dismissal of the ideals placed inside of the

U.S. Constitution regarding my rights and the rights of my neighbors.

Color of Statute (Law):

42 U.S. Code § 1983 is one of the most important laws when dealing with cities, counties, towns, and state public officials and employees regarding standing up for your rights at the federal level. Regardless of race, this is likely the most used law in the country's history. However, too many black citizens have been so deprived of true education that they have not learned the importance of this law while the violations crush their communities. I repeat with emphasis, every citizen whom their local and state government has injured must understand the importance of this law especially if those public servants have breached the U.S. Constitution or a federal law.

On many occasions, local public servants (public officials and public employees) have abused the doctrine of "Willful Blindness" so much that the only likely solution is federal intervention through courts using 42 U.S. Code § 1983, which mirrors the reason the Ku Klux Klan Enforcement Act(s) of 1870 and 1871 was created that was centered around the deprivation of rights of black citizens at the local and state level. The Federal government needed a federal statute to be created to bring criminal and civil action into federal courts. 42 U.S. Code § 1983 was birthed out of the 41st and 42nd Congress, and this Civil Rights statute is the only statute linked to every federal case involving color of law violations at the local and state levels. You can't sue local governments in federal courts for deprivation of rights unless you use this statute.

Today's unfortunate part is that black political leaders are also leading the efforts to deprive black citizens of their local, state, federal and Constitutional rights when they are sitting at the table of opportunity. The "conscious disregard" one constant in a vast number of cities is the routine "customs or practices" of intentional, willful, reckless, malicious deprivation of rights to majority black communities, businesses, and citizens under the color of statute(s). Note: There are many critical legal words, laws, codes of federal regulations, ordinances, and policies. I am not a lawyer, so I'm just sharing what has helped me, but if you learn the baseline of certain critical words in advance, you will be far better prepared than me.

The law as written:

*42 U.S. Code § 1983 – Civil action for deprivation of rights Every person who, under color of any statute, ordinance, regulation, custom, or usage, of any State or Territory or the District of Columbia, subjects, or causes to be subjected, any citizen of the United States or other person within the jurisdiction thereof to the deprivation of any rights, privileges, or immunities secured by the Constitution and laws, shall be liable to the party injured in an action at law, suit in equity, or other proper proceeding for redress, except that in any action brought against a judicial officer for an act or omission taken in such officer's judicial capacity, injunctive relief shall not be granted unless a declaratory decree was violated or declaratory relief was unavailable. For the purposes of this section, any Act of Congress applicable exclusively to the District of Columbia shall be considered to be a statute of the District of Columbia.*

Now, remember this is just the baseline and you must adjoin this federal law with the other federal (s) law that was taken from you.

The U.S. Constitution you learned that you probably have not looked at since k-12 schooling is the ideal for your rights when dealing with local, state and federal governments. We petition the government for redress of grievances under our First Amendment right with the hope that our petition will redress the grievance (violation) and nudge the public actions of the public servants or servants or entities back within the ideals of this country.

It is critical that you know how to search for laws. Don't be fearful of legal language as it is written. Don't rush through your reading. Take your time and find the word or statement in the law that has been breached that took your right away. As you are more intrigued, especially if you do not have any help, secure a copy of Federal or State Rules of Civil Procedure Federal or State Rules of Evidence as an introduction to courtroom procedure. You are only seeking a baseline of information, and as you learn more, you will be more equipped to help you make the best decision while seeking legal help or standing up for yourself.

Remember, if you have one, your lawyer is your practitioner of choice, and they don't know all of what you have experienced. You don't even know all you have experienced but when you start learning legal words and laws, you will realize more of what you have experienced and more opportunities to stand for your rights. I have learned that many lawyers are so focused on their area of focus that they may not be aware of the laws you researched, which is okay. Now, for those who can express their concerns clearly enough and have a lawyer specializing in that area, use them if you can afford them.

Now, I am concerned about the people who can't afford the several hundred dollars and nearly a thousand dollars an hour for some lawyers.

You know your injury; you just don't know the law yet that has been violated. Just a few decades ago, we did not have access to the internet, so use it and search until you find your answer. Make sure you use the local courthouse, as there is a free legal library, which is required by law, available to the public across the country. I have found it helpful to use Justia and Law Cornell to look up different laws on the internet. Lexis Nexus is extremely popular if you can afford it. If you can't afford it, you can get access at the local courthouse in the legal library. For example, when I use Law Cornell or Justia, I will type "bid law, Justia, Alabama code" into the search engine to see what comes up. Title 41 State Government, Chapter 16 – Public Contracts pops up as my first search item. I now have the law I need to review to see if there has been a violation of the associated state laws. Now, I can be more specific and focused when I go to a lawyer. I must still consider other violations and keywords until I find enough to stand on. I know this is just a start, but this start is the key to knowing there is a violation of a law.

I have devoted thousands of hours performing legal research because I had no help with finding a remedy for the undeniable economic justice in the majority black commercial district I invested in. One lawyer, like a friend of mine, told me locally that we are like a fraternity, and we are not going against the local establishment with the local leader as he is a lawyer, too. In my eyes, that friend was no longer a friend to me. Right did not matter. The local BAR association was placed above the right. I approached over 20 different lawyers, some would give advice, but it was all at a whisper level. None would stand next to me. I knew I was alone. I spent 2 plus years searching laws, writing state complaints, writing federal complaints and finally preparing my case with a whisper from a lawyer every once and a while.

The other thing that helped me was seeing how local, state, and federal laws were organized. For example, if you just type "Alabama Code, Justia" or "U.S. Code, Law Cornell" or whatever combination you need, all the laws are shown at the state and federal level and then you get to select the sections you think apply to you. It is time-consuming, but losing your rights is losing your liberty, and your rights are worth standing up for because they will affect you, your family, your business, and your community for the rest of your life and beyond.

You have power at your fingertips, but you must know you have power at your fingertips. You have brilliance in you regardless of the education that you have learned thus far. Tap into the importance of your rights, tap into your learning style and you will learn like you have never learned before.

Before I share additional thoughts on this law, what does the Department of Justice say about it and how it connects to their creation and to the torture and deprivation of rights of black citizens?

DOJ Website:
July 1, 1870: Creation of the U.S. Department of Justice and Civil Rights Enforcement, 1870-1872

*In 1870, the amount of litigation involving the post-Civil War United States necessitated the expensive retention of private attorneys, until Congress passed the Act to Establish the Department of Justice, led by the Attorney General, to handle the legal business of the United States. The Act gave the Department control over all federal law enforcement, and all criminal prosecutions and civil suits in which the United States had an interest.*

*Of the many challenges facing a new Department of Justice and its first Attorney General, Amos Akerman, none was more prominent than assuring the civil and voting rights for African Americans during Reconstruction (1865-1877) in the former Confederate states. The adoption of the Thirteenth, Fourteenth, and Fifteenth Amendments to the Constitution extended civil and legal protections to former slaves and prohibited states from disenfranchising voters "on account of race, color, or previous condition of servitude." President Ulysses S. Grant ordered that the new Department of Justice's initial mandate was to counter and subdue those groups in the South who had been using intimidation and violence to oppose the Amendments. No other group was more dangerous than the Ku Klux Klan who often carried out lawless acts of violence and aggression, terrorizing African Americans for exercising their right to vote, running for public office, and serving on juries.*

*In response to the Ku Klux Klan's acts of terror, Congress passed a series of Enforcement Acts in 1870 and 1871 to end such violence and empower the President to use whatever legal and military means necessary to protect African Americans. Amos Akerman would be Grant's choice for his Attorney General to spearhead this enforcement. Amos T. Akerman—a former Confederate Army officer and unlikely choice to head up a new Department of Justice tasked with overseeing Reconstruction— would ultimately prove one of the best choices Grant ever made for his cabinet and administration.*

*Both Attorney General Akerman and the first U.S. Solicitor General, Benjamin Bristow, used the new powers and resources of the Department of Justice to successfully prosecute Ku Klux Klan members in the early 1870s. In the first years of Grant's first term in office as President, there were over 1,000 indictments against Klan members with over 550 convictions won by new Department of Justice lawyers. By late 1871, there were more than 3,000 indictments and 600 more convictions. Due to the initial and highly successful efforts of the new Department of Justice and Attorney General Akerman, there was a dramatic decrease in violence in the South by the time he left office in 1872. This would prove to be just the beginning to a celebrated 150 years of federal law enforcement by the officials and employees of our Department of Justice.*

*The DOJ creation came from the deprivation of rights of black citizens. The DOJ creation came as a way to implement the KKK Enforcement Acts. The most important law inside the KKK Enforcement Acts was R.S. § 1979 which was approved on Apr. 20, 1871 in ch. 22, § 1, 17 Stat. 13. Over time this act has been codified by Congress and it is now identified as 42 U.S. Code § 1983.*

Now, back to 42 USC 1983. It opens with "every person" so that is every person "who, under color of any statute, ordinance, regulation, custom, or usage of any state or Territory or the District of Columbia, subjects, or causes to be subjected, any citizen of the United States or other person within the jurisdiction thereof to the deprivation of any rights, privileges, or immunities secured by the Constitution and laws." 42 USC 1983 describes what every person can do when any violation of "any clearly established law" in this country has taken place injuring every person. The law continues again and says the person or entity that injured you "shall be liable to the party injured in an action at law, suit in equity, or other proper proceeding for redress." This law is the baseline for every person's right when a local or state public servant has breached federal or constitutional laws.

You will start asking yourself, how do I sue in local, state, or federal court, and once you do, you will have a better start than me.

Here is a short list of words, websites, and resources I wished would have been shared with me. I am sharing this short list to help you understand some critical laws and words.

- Black's Law Dictionary
- Your local courthouse and free legal library that is available to all citizens in the country.

- Local, state, and federal court websites. Each have a pro guide that is very helpful.
- Your local Bar website. (I recommend being familiar with it because you must understand the professional code of ethics for the lawyer that may represent you.
- The 5<sup>th</sup> and 14<sup>th</sup> Amendments are the most important U.S. Constitution amendments regarding your rights being breached by the local, state, or federal government.
- What does "due process of law" mean?
- What does it mean when a state or local government violates "equal protection of the laws?
- What websites can I use to find federal, state, and local laws?
- For example, when I use Law Cornell or Justia, I will type "bid law, Justia, Alabama code" into the search engine to see what comes up. Title 41 State Government, Chapter 16 – Public Contracts appears as my first search item. I now have the law I need to review to see if there has been a violation of the associated state laws.
  - Now, I can be more specific and focused when I go to a lawyer. I must still consider other violations and keywords until I find enough to stand on. I understand this is the beginning, but this start is the key to knowing there is a violation of a law.
- How can you sue when the government violates a U.S. Constitutional right?
- What is the Color of Law?
- 42 U.S. Code § 1983 – Civil action for deprivation of rights
- What is Fraudulent Misrepresentation?
- What is Fraudulent Concealment?
- What is Unjust Enrichment?
- What is Unjust Conversion?
- What is Willful blindness, Deliberate Indifference, or Ostrich Instruction, and how is it used in federal courts?
- What are Antitrust laws?
- What is Governmental Immunity or Sovereign Immunity, and how is it breached, which gives you a legal chance to sue for your rights?
- When I think of the fact that people often blame "The System," I think of the following:
  - I guarantee people in a deprived community have blamed "They" or "The System" for something that has happened

against them or their community. The next likely question is, "Who did it specifically in their official capacity?" "What did they do in their official capacity?". "Did they cause a false statement to be sent to the federal agency?" I guarantee if most people in underserved communities paused for a moment and just thought of all the lies they heard about your community, you would probably find a violation, but you can only find it if you know the law. The law on false statements below may be one of those laws.

- Did someone submit a false, fictitious, or fraudulent claim for their gain or the gain of another unlawfully to the federal government? Simultaneously, were your rights violated associated with those same federal government services? Did their actions cause conversion or unjust enrichment?
  - 18 U.S. Code § 1001 – Statements or entries generally
  - 18 U.S.C. § 287 (false claims)
  - 18 U.S.C. § 371 (conspiracy to defraud the government)

Trust me, this is a very limited list, but it gets you thinking. Remember to breathe, relax, and take your time as you read legal language. You have all you need if you cannot find help. I wish it were easier to find legal help, and I hope more and more will help the truly deprived over time. There is a way to do it and be financially successful.

For lawyers who have gone to school, passed the bar and practiced, you know exactly what we need. Many of you are from the same community that is always attacked by **never-ending injustice.** We need you to remember those who paved the way for you. You are their dream, and their dream was not for the majority of black lawyers to sit back and watch their communities be hit with undeniable serial violations where those in the community have been beaten down for so long they have no idea if there is any help for them. We just want help regardless of race, but the reality is that it's always our race.

100 years ago, throughout this country, blacks may have had one practicing courtroom attorney in their states, but there were zero in many states. Today, serially economically injured black citizens have extremely limited options for legal professionals to seek help.

Most walk away from undeniable injustice because they have no help. Many have limited resources and can't afford proper legal help. Many find attorneys who take their cases but do not have the experience, competence, or capacity to help them properly. The result is the same as in Alabama from 1865 to 1949. Through 1938, there were zero black courtroom attorneys and a limited number of others standing for the black citizens. From 1939 to 1949, there was only 1 black practicing attorney in the state of Alabama in the state courts. The result of inaction today with so many legal representatives is extremely similar and heartbreaking. It is hard to watch undeniable constitutional rights be taken away from many black businesses, property owners and those who live in targeted, shunned communities.

Being from Birmingham and exiled for standing up for my economic rights after moving back has been mind-boggling, but it brings up other concerns in this majority-black city. I went to a well-known and outspoken civil rights foot soldier in Birmingham, and the person told me, you will not find a lawyer here in this city and possibly the state, especially not a black one. This statement was repeated everywhere I went. This statement also caused me to think of the days when black Americans had no practicing courtroom attorneys from their community. Today, many are licensed, so why is it so hard for all the people I have come across with various cases beyond the overly glamorized personal injury accident cases? I have come to think of a few concerns I kept running across while searching for legal representation. It is imperative that for major fights you need an attorney(s) with competence, capacity, courage, and integrity.

Historically, people must realize that from 1865 – 1939, there was not 1 black attorney practicing in the state courts. A few black lawyers worked behind the scenes for white lawyers who took their files to court. In 1937, Arthur Shores became licensed and from 1939 – 1949, he was the only black lawyer practicing in Alabama courts.

Now, let's pause history for a moment and think of all the injustice and the trauma being inflicted that has compounded to an already abused people that we have learned of when we had ZERO representation for 70 plus years from our community.

I need you who look the other way when you have the resources or experience to help when you know injustice is taking place to realize that enough trauma has already compounded in our unfortunate communities.

We are in the era of podcasts, talk shows, and social media, where everyone has a statement about everything behind computer screens and cell phones. At the same time, our communities face worse and worse conditions. Some are self-afflicted, and others inflict some. Regardless, we have widespread imbalanced communities. Many have turned a blind eye to what they know is wrong about the conditions many live in that are not self-inflicted.

Unfortunately, throughout the book, I felt I needed to hyper-focus on the opposing forces MLK spoke about in his Letter from a Birmingham Jail. It is critical that we not only know our history but also understand how that history and our actions play into the unfortunate repeated acts or the better acts that improve the situation.

I also covered some aspects of psychological conditioning that have carried over through a longstanding trauma-induced environment where dehumanization has injured many of our ancestors and us presently. Our way of thinking is not always natural because of the unfortunate environment. We must be mindful of what traits we carry that harm us were never removed.

We must do all we can to create positive, constructive opportunities in deprived communities when people are starving because there are no jobs. How do we create jobs in mass when people are locked out of equal protection when applying for funding? We know that more decay, underdevelopment, and vacant buildings will keep increasing until they are torn down unless we do what is right to allow economic development with equality. We also know that if the youth have limited or no role models because the entrepreneurs and professionals that could be in the buildings near their communities are not there, then they are getting their role models from somewhere else. We also know that if a healthy amount of income is not created and excess income is not created, then non-profit, mentoring, workforce development, and entrepreneurship development programs will be limited or non-existent. We must choose to invest in economic development.

We also know that when those so deprived can't find what they need to get by, they will venture into other neighborhoods if they have adopted criminality. Your cars, your homes, your movie theaters, and your pretty parks are going to be visited by people who have been limited by intentional deprivation of rights.

Now, I can keep going on the importance of economic development, but knowing how to stand for your rights and help others stand for their rights is critical. I encourage people to start with the simplest thing they could do: buy a Black's Law dictionary and learn legal terms. This book is our guide to our rights. So many questions will flow through your head once you understand the legal meaning of words that matter to you. The one set of words that I have always heard is "turning a blind eye." Turning a blind eye is not legal when public officials and employees turn a blind eye to your rights. You must learn how the courts use deliberate indifference, conscious disregard, ostrich instruction, and reckless indifference. Then, you will know why the legal words and terms are important to your rights.

**Believe in you.**

**Stand for your family, future, legacy, and community. Fight for your stolen dreams.**

# CHAPTER 13: SHORTLIST OF FEDERAL AND STATE LAWS I WISH I KNEW:

My cases had much to do with fraud, so I have listed several relevant laws. Regardless of your state, these laws, policies, and regulations may be relevant to you. I have added local and state laws for reference in case of a similar law in your state. Many violations occur daily, and many don't know where to start, so we just say "they" or "the system." Find the right law and stand for your rights. Sit down with a lawyer if you can find one, but if finding a lawyer remains elusive, don't walk away from the legal fight you are assigned to, especially if it can improve your life, family, community, and legacy. The following is a small list to review to get you thinking about potential laws that may affect you. I hope you can find the right lawyer, but sometimes you are the right lawyer.

## 5th Amendment of the U.S. Constitution:

*No person shall be held to answer for a capital, or otherwise infamous crime, unless on a presentment or indictment of a grand jury, except in cases arising in the land or naval forces, or in the militia, when in actual service in time of war or public danger; nor shall any person be subject for the same offense to be twice put in jeopardy of life or limb; nor shall be compelled in any criminal case to be a witness against himself, nor be deprived of life, liberty, or property, without due process of law; nor shall private property be taken for public use, without just compensation.*

## 14th Amendment of the U.S. Constitution:

*Section 1.*
*All persons born or naturalized in the United States, and subject to the jurisdiction thereof, are citizens of the United States and of the state wherein they reside. No state shall make or enforce any law which shall abridge the privileges or immunities of citizens of the United States; nor shall any state deprive any person of life, liberty, or property, without due process of law; nor deny to any person within its jurisdiction the equal protection of the laws.*

## 42 U.S. Code § 1983 - Civil action for deprivation of rights

*Every person who, under color of any statute, ordinance, regulation, custom, or usage, of any State or Territory or the District of*

*Columbia, subjects, or causes to be subjected, any citizen of the
United States or other person within the jurisdiction thereof to the
deprivation of any rights, privileges, or immunities secured by the
Constitution and laws, shall be liable to the party injured in an
action at law, suit in equity, or other proper proceeding for redress,
except that in any action brought against a judicial officer for an act
or omission taken in such officer's judicial capacity, injunctive relief
shall not be granted unless a declaratory decree was violated or
declaratory relief was unavailable. For the purposes of this section,
any Act of Congress applicable exclusively to the District of
Columbia shall be considered to be a statute of the District of
Columbia.
(R.S. § 1979; Pub. L. 96–170, § 1, Dec. 29, 1979, 93 Stat. 1284;
Pub. L. 104–317, title III, § 309(c), Oct. 19, 1996, 110 Stat. 3853.)*

**Now that you know you have been injured, what is the checklist
to sue the local or state entity in federal court? What is Monell
Liability? What is failure to train or supervise? What is failure
to correct or discipline? When is a longstanding practice or
custom considered a policy, and why does it matter?**

Monell Liability is your baseline checklist to stand for your rights
deprived of you under the color of law at the state and local levels.
https://supreme.justia.com/cases/federal/us/436/658/

*Monell v. Department of Soc. Svcs., 436 U.S. 658 (1978)*

*To impose Monell Liability on a municipality under Section 1983,
plaintiff must prove*

*(1) plaintiff had a constitutional right of which he was denied;*

*(2) the municipality had a policy;*

*(3) the policy amounts to deliberate indifference to his constitutional
rights;*

*(4) and the policy is the moving force behind the constitutional
violation. Daugherty v City of Covina, 654 F.3d 892, 900 (9th
Circuit) 2011*

Municipal Liability and 42 U.S.C. 1983: Contemporary Decisions

## Monell Liability

*Municipalities are considered "persons" under 42 U.S.C. § 1983
and therefore may be liable for causing a constitutional deprivation.
Monell v. Department of Soc. Servs., 436 U.S. 658, 690, 98 S. Ct.
2018, 56 L. Ed. 2d 611 (1978); Castro v. County of L.A., 797 F.3d
654, 670 (9th Cir. 2015). A municipality, however, "cannot be held
liable solely because it employs a tortfeasor or, in other words, a
municipality cannot be held liable under [42 U.S.C. § 1983] under a
respondeat superior theory." Monell, 436 U.S. at 691; see Castro,
797 F.3d at 670. Liability only attaches where the municipality itself
causes the constitutional violation through "execution of a
government's policy or custom, whether made by its lawmakers or
by those whose edicts or acts may fairly be said to represent official
policy." Monell, 436 U.S. at 694; Price v. Sery, 513 F.3d 962, 966
(9th Cir. 2008). Municipal liability may be premised on: (1) conduct
pursuant to a formal or expressly adopted official policy; (2) a
longstanding practice or custom which constitutes the "standard
operating procedure" of the local government entity; (3) a decision
of a decision-making official who was, as a matter of state law, a
final policymaking authority whose edicts or acts may fairly be said
to represent official policy in the area of decision; or (4) an official
with final policymaking authority either delegating that authority to,
or ratifying the decision of, a subordinate. See Thomas v. County of
Riverside, 763 F.3d 1167, 1170 (9th Cir. 2014); Price, 513 F.3d at
966.*

**So, you can't find the policy, but you know it is a regular
practice or custom of the city. Breathe; you are ahead of the rest
because you see the violations, practices, and customs. You have
the evidence of the longstanding practice or custom, so you must
find the policy. It may be unwritten, but you have the evidence
to prove it is policy. What did the previous paragraph say about
a "Municipal liability may be premised on? "**

*Supreme Court says: "a public entity may be held liable for a
"longstanding practice or custom." See Thomas v. County of
Riverside, 763 F.3d 1167, 1170 (9th Cir. 2014);*

## What do the courts say about failure to train, failure to supervise, and failure to implement procedural safeguards?

*Such circumstances may arise when, for instance, the public entity "fail(s) to implement procedural safeguards to prevent constitutional violations" or, sometimes when it fails to train its employees Tsao v. Desert Palace, Inc., 698 F.3d 1128, 1143 (9th Cir. 2012) (citing Oviatt v. Pearce, 954 F.2d 1470, 1477 (9th Cir. 1992); See also Connick v, Thompson, 563 U.S. 51, 61, 131 S.Ct. 1350, 179 L.Ed.2d 417 (2011) "A municipality's culpability for a deprivation of rights is at its most tenuous where a claim turns on a failure to train." (citation omitted); Flores v. County of Los Angeles, 758 F.3d 1154, 1159 (9th Cir. 2014) (requiring a plaintiff asserting a claim based on a failure to train to allege facts showing defendants "disregarded the known or obvious consequence that a particular omission in their training program would cause municipal employees to violate citizens' constitutional rights. Connick, 563 U.S. at 61, 131 S.Ct. 1350*

*Municipal Liability and 42 U.S.C. 1983: Contemporary Decisions*

## So, let's say you know of a policy that injured you the moment it was signed.

*"A local government may be held liable under section 1983 when 'the individual who committed the constitutional tort was a an official with final policy-making authority' or such an official 'ratified a subordinate's unconstitutional decision or action and the basis for it.'" Clouthier v County of Contra Costa, 591 F.3d 1232, 1250 (9th Cir, 2010) (quoting Gillette v. Delmore, 979 F.2d 1342, 1346-47 (9th Cir. 1992), overruled on other grounds by Castro, 833 F.3d at 1070). ; on separate line at the end of the page) Gordon v. County of Orange, 6, 6 F. 4th 961 (9th Cir 2021)Municipal Liability and 42 U.S.C. 1983: Contemporary Decisions*

A "state action requires both an

*(1) alleged constitutional deprivation caused by the exercise of some right or privilege created by the state or by a rule of conduct*

*imposed by the state or by a person for whom the state is responsible,*

*(2) and that the party charged with the deprivation must be a person who may fairly be said to be a state actor." Am. Mfrs. Mut. Ins. Co. v. Sullivan, 526 U.S. 40, 50, 119 S.Ct. 977, 143 L.Ed.2d 130 (1999) (internal quotation marks and citation omitted). Bourne Valley Court Trust v. Wells Fargo Bank, NA, 832 F. 3d 1154 (9th Cir. 2016).*

*Publications, LandMark. State Actors and 42 USC 1983 (p. 2). LandMark Publications. Kindle Edition.*

*(I strongly recommend you to purchase the LandMark book source of this case law, if you believe your rights have been violated by the state. There is so much more in the book.)*

### To succeed on [a] § 1983 claim, plaintiffs must prove:
*(1) the deprivation of a right secured by the Constitution or federal law*

*(2) and that defendants were acting under color of state law. Armato v. Grounds, 766 F.3d 713, 719-20 (7th Cir. 2014) (citing Parratt v. Taylor, 451 U.S. 527, 535, 101 S.Ct. 1908, 68 L.Ed.2d 420 (1981)). For a private actor to act under color of state law he must have "had a 'meeting of the minds' and thus reached an understanding" with a state actor to deny plaintiffs a constitutional right. Adickes v. S.H. Kress & Co., 398 U.S. 144, 158, 90 S.Ct. 1598, 26 L.Ed.2d 142 (1970); see also Hanania v. Loren-Maltese, 212 F.3d 353, 356 (7th Cir. 2000) (requiring a showing of "a concerted effort between" a private actor and state actor and that a state actor and private actor "reached an understanding to deprive the plaintiff of her constitutional rights"); Cunningham v. Southlake Ctr. for Mental Health, Inc., 924 F.2d 106, 107 (7th Cir. 1991) ("A requirement of the joint action charge ... is that both public and private actors share a common, unconstitutional goal."). Because § 1983 allows a private actor to be sued as if it were the state and makes state actors potentially liable as well, the state actor must share the private actor's unconstitutional goal in order for a state actor to be acting under color of state law. In other words, "[a] private actor ... cannot*

*unilaterally convert a state actor's legitimate activity into an illegal act, conferring both constitutional accountability on itself and liability on the state." Cunningham, 924 F.2d at 108. Wilson v. Warren County, Illinois, 830 F. 3d 464 (7th Cir. 2016).*

*Publications, LandMark. State Actors and 42 USC 1983 (p. 2). LandMark Publications. Kindle Edition.*

(I strongly recommend you to purchase the LandMark book source of this case law, if you believe your rights have been violated by the state. There is so much more in the book.)

## Due-process claims built on the special-relationship doctrine have four elements.

*(1) First, the plaintiff must demonstrate the existence of a special relationship, meaning that the plaintiff completely depended on the state to satisfy basic human needs. DeAnzona v. City & Cty. of Denver, 222 F.3d 1229, 1234 (10th Cir. 2000).*

*(2) Second, the plaintiff must show that the defendant knew that the plaintiff was in danger or failed to exercise professional judgment regarding that danger. Schwartz, 702 F.3d at 583.*

*(3) Third, the plaintiff must show that the defendant's conduct caused the plaintiff's injuries. Id.*

*(4) And finally, fourth, the defendant's actions must shock the conscience. Id. Dahn v. Amedei, ibid.*

*Publications, LandMark. State Actors and 42 USC 1983. LandMark Publications. Kindle Edition. (I strongly recommend you to purchase if you believe your rights have been violated by the state. There is so much more in the book.)*

## Has a special relationship been created between you and the state that has been violated?

*The existence of the special relationship is the pivotal issue. If none exists, a state cannot be held liable for a person's injuries at the hands of a private third party as opposed to a state actor. "A special relationship exists when the state assumes control over an individual sufficient to trigger an affirmative duty to provide protection to that individual . . . ." Uhlrig v. Harder, 64 F.3d 567, 572 (10th Cir. 1995).*

*"Generally, the scope of this relationship has turned on the dependent and involuntary nature of the custodial relationship between the individual and the State." Schwartz, 702 F.3d at 580. Plaintiffs must show that the state has restrained them against their will, because "if there is no custodial relationship there can be no constitutional duty." DeAnzona, 222 F.3d at 1234. And the state has a special custodial relationship only with "individuals [who] depend completely on the state to satisfy their basic human needs." Maldonado v. Josey, 975 F.2d 727, 733 (10th Cir. 1992) (emphasis added). Dahn v. Amedei, ibid.*

*Publications, LandMark. State Actors and 42 USC 1983. LandMark Publications. Kindle Edition. (I strongly recommend you to purchase if you believe your rights have been violated by the state. There is so much more in the book.)*

## **Qualified immunity:**

*The primary purpose of qualified immunity is to shield public officials "from undue interference with their duties and from potentially disabling threats of liability."[9] This immunity can be overcome, however, when public officials violate clearly established constitutional rights of which a reasonable person would have been aware.[10] In the words of the Supreme Court, qualified immunity protects "all but the plainly incompetent or those who knowingly violate the law."*

*[11] To resolve a claim of qualified immunity, courts engage in a two-pronged inquiry:*

*(1) whether the plaintiff sufficiently alleged the violation of a constitutional right, and*

*(2) whether the right was "clearly established" at the time of the official's conduct.[12] "[W]hether a particular complaint sufficiently alleges a clearly established violation of law cannot be decided in isolation from the facts pleaded."*

[13] Thus the sufficiency of L.R.'s pleading is both "inextricably intertwined with" and "directly implicated by" Littlejohn's qualified immunity defense.[14]

Publications, LandMark. State Actors and 42 USC 1983 (p. 127). LandMark Publications. Kindle Edition

(I strongly recommend you to purchase and look into LandMark publications on various topics if you believe your rights have been violated. They have a wealth of books as a starting point to your rights. There is so much more in their books than the little bit I have shared.)

### Do you believe the state actor knew the injury would happen to you?

Foreseeable and Fairly Direct Harm Next, we ask whether "the harm ultimately caused was a foreseeable and a fairly direct result of the state's actions."[37] L.R. alleges that Littlejohn "w[as] aware that releasing pupils to unidentified and otherwise unverified adults would result in harm to those pupils, including but not limited to sexual assault."[38] Defendants counter that the complaint is devoid of any facts that support the inference that Littlejohn could have known of Regusters' intent to harm Jane. That is not the appropriate inquiry. Rather, the plaintiff must only "allege an awareness on the part of the state actors that rises to the level of actual knowledge or an awareness of risk that is sufficiently concrete to put the actors on notice of the harm."[39] We think the risk of harm in releasing a five-year-old child to a complete stranger was obvious.

Publications, LandMark. State Actors and 42 USC 1983 (p. 130). LandMark Publications. Kindle Edition

### Often, local jurisdiction funds are distributed from federal programs. These federal programs may have been manipulated at the local, state or federal level, directly depriving you of equal protection of the law and due process of the law, and you were excluded. The following federal laws may be relevant if you discover unlawful activity.

## 18 U.S. Code § 666 - Theft or bribery concerning programs receiving Federal funds

*(a)Whoever, if the circumstance described in subsection (b) of this section exists—*

*(1)being an agent of an organization, or of a State, local, or Indian tribal government, or any agency thereof—*

*(A)embezzles, steals, obtains by fraud, or otherwise without authority knowingly converts to the use of any person other than the rightful owner or intentionally misapplies, property that—*

*(i)is valued at $5,000 or more, and*

*(ii)is owned by, or is under the care, custody, or control of such organization, government, or agency; or*

*(B)corruptly solicits or demands for the benefit of any person, or accepts or agrees to accept, anything of value from any person, intending to be influenced or rewarded in connection with any business, transaction, or series of transactions of such organization, government, or agency involving any thing of value of $5,000 or more; or*

*(2)corruptly gives, offers, or agrees to give anything of value to any person, with intent to influence or reward an agent of an organization or of a State, local or Indian tribal government, or any agency thereof, in connection with any business, transaction, or series of transactions of such organization, government, or agency involving anything of value of $5,000 or more; shall be fined under this title, imprisoned not more than 10 years, or both.*

*(b)The circumstance referred to in subsection (a) of this section is that the organization, government, or agency receives, in any one year period, benefits in excess of $10,000 under a Federal program involving a grant, contract, subsidy, loan, guarantee, insurance, or other form of Federal assistance.*

*(c)This section does not apply to bona fide salary, wages, fees, or other compensation paid, or expenses paid or reimbursed, in the usual course of business.*

*(d)As used in this section—*

*(1)the term "agent" means a person authorized to act on behalf of another person or a government and, in the case of an organization or government, includes a servant or employee, and a partner, director, officer, manager, and representative;*

*(2)the term "government agency" means a subdivision of the executive, legislative, judicial, or other branch of government, including a department, independent establishment, commission, administration, authority, board, and bureau, and a corporation or other legal entity established, and subject to control, by a government or governments for the execution of a governmental or intergovernmental program;*

*(3)the term "local" means of or pertaining to a political subdivision within a State;*

*(4)the term "State" includes a State of the United States, the District of Columbia, and any commonwealth, territory, or possession of the United States; and*

*(5)the term "in any one-year period" means a continuous period that commences no earlier than twelve months before the commission of the offense or that ends no later than twelve months after the commission of the offense. Such period may include time both before and after the commission of the offense.*

*(Added Pub. L. 98–473, title II, § 1104(a), Oct. 12, 1984, 98 Stat. 2143; amended Pub. L. 99–646, § 59(a), Nov. 10, 1986, 100 Stat. 3612; Pub. L. 101–647, title XII, §§ 1205(d), 1209, Nov. 29, 1990, 104 Stat. 4831, 4832; Pub. L. 103–322, title XXXIII, § 330003(c), Sept. 13, 1994, 108 Stat. 2140.)*

## 18 U.S. Code § 371 - Conspiracy to commit offense or to defraud United States

*If two or more persons conspire either to commit any offense against the United States, or to defraud the United States, or any agency thereof in any manner or for any purpose, and one or more of such persons do any act to effect the object of the conspiracy, each shall be fined under this title or imprisoned not more than five years, or both.*

*If, however, the offense, the commission of which is the object of the conspiracy, is a misdemeanor only, the punishment for such conspiracy shall not exceed the maximum punishment provided for such misdemeanor.*
*(June 25, 1948, ch. 645, 62 Stat. 701; Pub. L. 103–322, title XXXIII, § 330016(1)(L), Sept. 13, 1994, 108 Stat. 2147.)*

## 18 U.S. Code § 1346 - Definition of "scheme or artifice to defraud" (Also referred to as Honest Service Fraud)

*For the purposes of this chapter, the term "scheme or artifice to defraud" includes a scheme or artifice to deprive another of the intangible right of honest services.*

## 18 U.S. Code § 1341 - Frauds and swindles

*Whoever, having devised or intending to devise any scheme or artifice to defraud, or for obtaining money or property by means of false or fraudulent pretenses, representations, or promises, or to sell, dispose of, loan, exchange, alter, give away, distribute, supply, or furnish or procure for unlawful use any counterfeit or spurious coin, obligation, security, or other article, or anything represented to be or intimated or held out to be such counterfeit or spurious article, for the purpose of executing such scheme or artifice or attempting so to do, places in any post office or authorized depository for mail matter, any matter or thing whatever to be sent or delivered by the Postal Service, or deposits or causes to be deposited any matter or thing whatever to be sent or delivered by any private or commercial interstate carrier, or takes or receives therefrom, any such matter or thing, or knowingly causes to be delivered by mail or such carrier according to the direction thereon, or at the place at which it is directed to be delivered by the person to* *whom it is addressed, any such matter or thing, shall be fined under this title or imprisoned not more than 20 years, or both. If the violation occurs in relation to, or involving any benefit authorized, transported, transmitted, transferred, disbursed, or paid in connection with, a presidentially declared major disaster or emergency (as those terms are defined in section 102 of the Robert T. Stafford Disaster Relief and Emergency Assistance Act (42 U.S.C. 5122)), or affects a financial institution, such person shall be fined not more than $1,000,000 or imprisoned not more than 30 years, or both.*

*(June 25, 1948, ch. 645, 62 Stat. 763; May 24, 1949, ch. 139, § 34, 63 Stat. 94; Pub. L. 91–375, § (6)(j)(11), Aug. 12, 1970, 84 Stat. 778; Pub. L. 101–73, title IX, § 961(i), Aug. 9, 1989, 103 Stat. 500; Pub. L. 101–647, title XXV, § 2504(h), Nov. 29, 1990, 104 Stat. 4861; Pub. L. 103–322, title XXV, § 250006, title XXXIII, § 330016(1)(H), Sept. 13, 1994, 108 Stat. 2087, 2147; Pub. L. 107–204, title IX, § 903(a), July 30, 2002, 116 Stat. 805; Pub. L. 110–179, § 4, Jan. 7, 2008, 121 Stat. 2557.)*

## 18 U.S. Code § 1343 - Fraud by wire, radio, or television

*Whoever, having devised or intending to devise any scheme or artifice to defraud, or for obtaining money or property by means of false or fraudulent pretenses, representations, or promises, transmits or causes to be transmitted by means of wire, radio, or television communication in interstate or foreign commerce, any writings, signs, signals, pictures, or sounds for the purpose of executing such scheme or artifice, shall be fined under this title or imprisoned not more than 20 years, or both. If the violation occurs in relation to, or involving any benefit authorized, transported, transmitted, transferred, disbursed, or paid in connection with, a presidentially declared major disaster or emergency (as those terms are defined in section 102 of the Robert T. Stafford Disaster Relief and Emergency Assistance Act (42 U.S.C. 5122)), or affects a financial institution, such person shall be fined not more than $1,000,000 or imprisoned not more than 30 years, or both.*

*(Added July 16, 1952, ch. 879, § 18(a), 66 Stat. 722; amended July 11, 1956, ch. 561, 70 Stat. 523; Pub. L. 101–73, title IX, § 961(j), Aug. 9, 1989, 103 Stat. 500; Pub. L. 101–647, title XXV, § 2504(i),*

*Nov. 29, 1990, 104 Stat. 4861; Pub. L. 103–322, title XXXIII, §
330016(1)(H), Sept. 13, 1994, 108 Stat. 2147; Pub. L. 107–204, title
IX, § 903(b), July 30, 2002, 116 Stat. 805; Pub. L. 110–179, § 3,
Jan. 7, 2008, 121 Stat. 2557.)*

**RICO is more relevant to many of us than we believe. RICO is
not just some cool movie term. Many of us have been victims of
RICO, and as a regular citizen, you can stand for your rights
under Civil RICO. There is also a 4-year statute of limitations
after the last wrongful act. RICO may give you time in case
other statutes of limitations have expired.**

**18 U.S. Code § 1964 - Civil remedies (Civil RICO)**

*(a)The district courts of the United States shall have jurisdiction to
prevent and restrain violations of section 1962 of this chapter by
issuing appropriate orders, including, but not limited to: ordering
any person to divest himself of any interest, direct or indirect, in any
enterprise; imposing reasonable restrictions on the future activities
or investments of any person, including, but not limited to,
prohibiting any person from engaging in the same type of endeavor
as the enterprise engaged in, the activities of which affect interstate
or foreign commerce; or ordering dissolution or reorganization of
any enterprise, making due provision for the rights of innocent
persons.*

*(b)The Attorney General may institute proceedings under this
section. Pending final determination thereof, the court may at any
time enter such restraining orders or prohibitions, or take such
other actions, including the acceptance of satisfactory performance
bonds, as it shall deem proper.*

*(c)Any person injured in his business or property by reason of a
violation of section 1962 of this chapter may sue therefor in any
appropriate United States district court and shall recover threefold
the damages he sustains and the cost of the suit, including a
reasonable attorney's fee, except that no person may rely upon any
conduct that would have been actionable as fraud in the purchase or
sale of securities to establish a violation of section 1962. The
exception contained in the preceding sentence does not apply to an*

*action against any person that is criminally convicted in connection with the fraud, in which case the statute of limitations shall start to run on the date on which the conviction becomes final.*

*(d)A final judgment or decree rendered in favor of the United States in any criminal proceeding brought by the United States under this chapter shall estop the defendant from denying the essential allegations of the criminal offense in any subsequent civil proceeding brought by the United States.*

*(Added Pub. L. 91–452, title IX, § 901(a), Oct. 15, 1970, 84 Stat. 943; amended Pub. L. 98–620, title IV, § 402(24)(A), Nov. 8, 1984, 98 Stat. 3359; Pub. L. 104–67, title I, § 107, Dec. 22, 1995, 109 Stat. 758.)*

## Antitrust Laws and You from: Antitrust Division of the U.S. Department of Justice
https://www.justice.gov/atr/antitrust-laws-and-you

*Many consumers have never heard of antitrust laws, but enforcement of these laws saves consumers millions and even billions of dollars a year. The Federal Government enforces three major Federal antitrust laws, and most states also have their own. Essentially, these laws prohibit business practices that unreasonably deprive consumers of the benefits of competition, resulting in higher prices for products and services.*

*The three major Federal antitrust laws are:*
1. *The Sherman Antitrust Act*
2. *The Clayton Act*
3. *The Federal Trade Commission Act.*

*The Sherman Antitrust Act*

*This Act outlaws all contracts, combinations, and conspiracies that unreasonably restrain interstate and foreign trade. The Sherman Antitrust Act includes agreements among competitors to fix prices, rig bids, and allocate customers, which are punishable as criminal felonies.*

*The Sherman Act also makes it a crime to monopolize any part of interstate commerce. An unlawful monopoly exists when one firm controls the market for a product or service and obtains market power, not because its product or service is superior to others but by suppressing competition with anticompetitive conduct.*
*The Act, however, is not violated simply when one firm's vigorous competition and lower prices take sales from its less efficient competitors; in that case, competition is working properly.*


## The Clayton Act

*This Act is a civil statute (carrying no criminal penalties) prohibiting mergers or acquisitions likely to lessen competition. All persons considering a merger or acquisition above a certain size must notify the Antitrust Division and the Federal Trade Commission. The Act also prohibits other business practices that may harm competition under certain circumstances.*

## The Federal Trade Commission Act
*This Act prohibits unfair methods of competition in interstate commerce but carries no criminal penalties. It also created the Federal Trade Commission to police violations of the Act.*

## Related Offenses
*The Antitrust Division also often uses other laws to fight illegal activities that arise from conduct accompanying antitrust violations, or that otherwise impact the competitive process, as well as offenses that involve the integrity of an antitrust or related investigation, including laws that prohibit false statements to Federal agencies, perjury, obstruction of justice, conspiracies to defraud the United States and mail and wire fraud. Each of these crimes carries its own fine and imprisonment term, which may be added to the fines and imprisonment terms for antitrust law violations.*

*Read more about the activities of the Antitrust Division:*

*Price Fixing, Bid Rigging and Market Allocation Schemes: What They Are and What to Look For*

*Updated August 8, 2023*

## The American Bar Association has created a shortlist of extending the statute of limitations.

https://www.americanbar.org/groups/litigation/committees/consumer/practice/2019/many-ways-to-extend-a-limitations-period/

I believe we all need to look up each word within:
1. Statutory discovery rule
2. Common-law discovery rule
3. Equitable estoppel (Fraudulent Concealment)
4. Equitable tolling

## fraudulent concealment

## U.S. Department of Justice: Office of Justice Programs
*Federal Doctrine of Fraudulent Concealment (From Techniques in the Investigation and Prosecution of Organized Crime - Materials on RICO, P 1096-1144, 1980, G. Robert Blakey, ed. - See NCJ-78839)*

*https://www.ojp.gov/ncjrs/virtual-library/abstracts/federal-doctrine-fraudulent-concealment-techniques-investigation*

*Under the Federal doctrine of fraudulent concealment, the statutory limitations period will begin to run when the cause of action is discovered, or should have been discovered, by the exercise of due diligence. What one must plead and show to establish fraudulent concealment depends on the circumstances of each case. In actions not based on fraud, the plaintiff must plead with particularity and show (1) fraudulent concealment by the defendant; (2) the ignorance of the plaintiff as to the cause of action prior to the running of the limitations period before the commencement of the suit; and (3) that once on notice of the possible cause of action, the plaintiff exercised due diligence in discovering the facts of the claim. In actions based on fraud, the plaintiff need not plead fraudulent concealment if the concealment claim is based on the substantive fraud because the defendant is on notice of the fraud claim. When the defendant claims*

*that the statute of limitations bars the suit, the plaintiff must
establish the last two aforementioned elements. If the concealment
does not involve the substantive fraud, the plaintiff must establish all
three elements. For all types of cases, leave to amend is liberally
granted with few exceptions. A total of 175 footnotes are listed. For
additional material on RICO, see NCJ 78839.*

https://www.law.cornell.edu/wex/fraudulent_concealment
*Under contract law, a plaintiff can recover from a defendant on the
grounds of fraudulent concealment where the defendant:*
1. *concealed or suppressed a material fact;*
2. *had knowledge of this material fact;*
3. *that this material fact was not within reasonably diligent
   attention, observation, and judgment of the plaintiff;*
4. *that the defendant suppressed or concealed this fact with the
   intention that the plaintiff be misled as to the true condition of
   the property;*
5. *that the plaintiff was reasonably so misled; and*
6. *that the plaintiff suffered damages as a result.*
   *[Last updated in January of 2023 by the Wex Definitions
   Team]*

## fraudulent misrepresentation
*Fraudulent misrepresentation is a tort claim, typically arising in the
field of contract law, that occurs when a defendant makes an
intentional or reckless misrepresentation of fact or opinion with the
intention to coerce a party into action or inaction on the basis of
that misrepresentation.*

*To determine whether fraudulent misrepresentation occurred, the
court will look for six factors:*
1. *A representation was made*
2. *The representation was false*
3. *That when made, the defendant knew that the representation
   was false or that the defendant made the statement
   recklessly without knowledge of its truth*
4. *That the fraudulent misrepresentation was made with the
   intention that the plaintiff rely on it*
5. *That the plaintiff did rely on the fraudulent
   misrepresentation*

6. *That the plaintiff suffered harm as a result of the fraudulent misrepresentation*

*Like most claims under contract law, the standard remedy for fraudulent misrepresentation is damages.*
*[Last updated in January of 2023 by the Wex Definitions Team]*

## 42 U.S. Code § 1981 - Equal rights under the law
*(a)Statement of equal rights*

*All persons within the jurisdiction of the United States shall have the same right in every State and Territory to make and enforce contracts, to sue, be parties, give evidence, and to the full and equal benefit of all laws and proceedings for the security of persons and property as is enjoyed by white citizens, and shall be subject to like punishment, pains, penalties, taxes, licenses, and exactions of every kind, and to no other.*

*(b)"Make and enforce contracts" defined*
*For purposes of this section, the term "make and enforce contracts" includes the making, performance, modification, and termination of contracts, and the enjoyment of all benefits, privileges, terms, and conditions of the contractual relationship.*

*(c)Protection against impairment*

*The rights protected by this section are protected against impairment by nongovernmental discrimination and impairment under color of State law.*

*(R.S. § 1977; Pub. L. 102–166, title I, § 101, Nov. 21, 1991, 105 Stat. 1071.)*

## 42 U.S. Code § 1982 - Property rights of citizens
*All citizens of the United States shall have the same right, in every State and Territory, as is enjoyed by white citizens thereof to inherit, purchase, lease, sell, hold, and convey real and personal property.*
*(R.S. § 1978.)*

## Federal Tort Claims Act

https://www.house.gov/doing-business-with-the-house/leases/federal-tort-claims-act

*A. Making a Claim Under the FTCA*

*Individuals who are injured or whose property is damaged by the wrongful or negligent act of a federal employee acting in the scope of his or her official duties may file a claim with the government for reimbursement for that injury or damage. In order to state a valid claim, the claimant must demonstrate that (1) he was injured or his property was damaged by a federal government employee; (2) the employee was acting within the scope of his official duties; (3) the employee was acting negligently or wrongfully; and (4) the negligent or wrongful act proximately caused the injury or damage of which he complains. The claimant must also provide documentation establishing that his claim satisfies all the elements of the FTCA.*
https://www.law.cornell.edu/wex/ftca

*The Federal Tort Claims Act of 1946 (FTCA) is a monumental bill that enabled the Federal government to be sued for tortious activities of its employees within the scope of their employment. Prior to this legislation, sovereign immunity protected the Federal government from essentially all lawsuits. However, the FTCA opened up the doors for the Federal government to be sued similarly to any other employer for negligence of its employees. However, the FTCA limits liability of the government in multiple ways such as not covering most intentional actions of employees and not allowing punitive damages. The laws that apply to an FTCA case often follow the rules and tort laws of the district court where the claim is filed.*

*In practice, the FTCA makes the United States liable for the acts of its employees in a similar manner to any other employer. That said, the FTCA does not grant the United States liability for the majority of intentional actions of its employees and does not allow for punitive damages.*

*[Last updated in January of 2023 by the Wex Definitions Team]*

I mentioned a Voting Rights Act violation earlier in the book, so please be aware of where the law is so you can stand against injustice. It's much longer than the other laws, so I have cited the law for your research if you believe your rights have been violated

*52 U.S. Code § 10101 - Voting rights*

**Know where to find the following state laws, as your answers to your rights are there.**

1. State Ethics Laws
2. State Bid Laws
3. State notice of claim laws (for example, to sue a municipality under state law, a person must file a notice of claim within 6 months.
4. Municide is a great website to look up your city ordinances: https://library.municode.com/

## CLOSING STATEMENT:

There is so much more to learn and so much to know. Now, depending on where you are, don't give up. You may be the one to mount the insurmountable mountain of injustice that others could not. You may be the one who opens the doors to the deprived. You may be the one to change the unfortunate conditions in your community or a community you can reach. I wish I had more time to prepare the perfect book, but my litigation is around the corner, and I wanted to ensure I helped the next person with some of the same concerns that I believe you or others may be facing. I referenced Supreme Court case law and Department of Justice examples every time I could because these are the laws of the land and not my words. Stand for your rights and help the next person.

I close with the following quotes to show the importance of combatting modern-day redlining. I am convinced that if underserved communities are intentionally targeted and locked out of economic opportunity to properly develop a healthy and balanced environment, the conditions in deprived communities will continue to manifest in unfortunate ways. If I and thousands and millions of other black commercial property owners can't secure financing because of fraud and unequal protection of the law, then those blighted buildings can never be developed. If those buildings can never be developed, then new businesses will not occupy them. If new businesses cannot occupy them, no jobs will be created in our underserved communities. If no new jobs are created, then a local mother or father is unemployed or underemployed. If the head of the household cannot provide, then there is an imbalance within the house with one or multiple dependents. When those dependents are in an intentionally deprived environment their entire lives, and they are the second generation of being in an intentionally deprived environment, trauma compounds among both generations. For me to invest in an intentionally deprived community and to be here as long as I have, I have started to recognize certain repetitive behaviors from this trauma-filled environment. Many talk and look down on the reality inside deprived communities like this, but so few in leadership are doing anything to improve the conditions here.

We can improve our communities if given a fair chance. I am asking you wherever you are, especially if you desire to improve the conditions of the most deprived, to use your capacity, to use the law, to use your passion, to use your resources to help the intentionally deprived as best as possible. We can create healthy and balanced communities, but it will take as much intentional positive effort as has been targeted against the same communities for just as many years and generations to improve the conditions correctly.
Call for Action:

What I see in Birmingham, AL, is too common across the U.S. in black communities that are not just faced with traditional forms of racism (discrimination, oppression, redlining, and inside deals violating their rights from others). Many black leaders are inclusive with their former oppressors and are now oppressing their own communities. Many are compliant with corruption.

1. If you can't find a lawyer and you have the capacity to research, in case you have to stand alone, never stop believing in yourself. Believe in your ability to learn so you can stand for your rights. It's scary and lonely. Your dreams, your family, your future family, your community, your legacy, your rights, and your country are all worth fighting for.
2. If you live or invest on the western side of Birmingham, you have a right to file a lawsuit against the City of Birmingham and all other entities involved with Federal Program Fraud. Please visit www.briankrice.com or look up my federal lawsuit, as the violations are very detailed so that others can decide to join or file their lawsuits. I will be listed as the Plaintiff, and Governor Kay Ivey will be the first defendant in case you need to search in federal court. I do not believe Governor Ivey was aware of the intentionally fraudulent, well concealed reports sent to her by the City of Birmingham, but the reports were used to influence legislation with her signature. This action caused a 10-year IRS tax unprecedented exclusion from 2018 – 2028 where investors have benefitted greatly in areas selected due to fraud.
3. If you know of an African American contractor who faces barriers to entry, fronts in professional services, construction

services from their local government, please share this book so that they can read the chapters on affirmative action and legal fights. If you are in Birmingham, please download the 2007 and 2022 City of Birmingham racial disparity studies posted on my website. The 2022 study has been concealed from the public because there are areas where Blacks in a nearly 70% black city receive less than 1/3 of a 1 percent out of $60 million in contracts.

4. If you work for the Department of Justice or know someone who does, please share this book, as we need federal accountability in Birmingham, AL.

5. If you know someone inside of the U.S. Attorney General's office and they are heading up the combating redlining initiative, please have them read about the $0.00 appraisal and the federal program fraud in Birmingham. Please have them read the letter I wrote to the FBI near the end of the book because we are experiencing appraisal, banking, over-taxation, federal program fraud, redlining and reverse redlining all at the same time in the Downtown Ensley business district in Birmingham, AL.

6. If you know a firm willing to take on an undeniable $600 million inside deal through federal program fraud with federal opportunity zones, please share this book and have them read the letter to the FBI near the end of the book.

7. Please share this book if you know a law firm with the legal capacity, integrity, competency, and courage to stand up for economic injustice in my hometown.

8. If you know someone or you have the resources to help pay for the multiple needed economic injustice legal fights in this book, please help.

9. If you know someone campaigning anywhere in this country and familiar with using government funds to pay for political campaigns, please have them read the section on Birmingham Promise revolving doors. We can't let this type of behavior to be common practice through a 501(c)(3). If you were a candidate in the last mayoral election in Birmingham, please visit my website, download my federal civil action, and review the pattern of racketeering #1 involving Birmingham Promise. If you

ran or voted in the election and feel the need to stand against fair campaign practices, please file a formal complaint with the Secretary of State or take legal action and file an injunction or suit for damages.

10. If you know a foundation, a non-profit entity, or someone(s) that can help me preserve and restore my buildings while I'm faced with the pending legal battle and the covered-up $0.00 appraisal from the local to the federal level, please have them visit www.briankrice.com and help.

Our communities are suffering here, and we don't know who to go to for help. I am pleading for equal rights and economic justice to matters of public concern. Details and names involving public servants and private co-conspirators are listed. Inclusive Systemic Economic Injustice is written as a plea for justice where injustice has become covert and inclusive of both black and white leaders.

## Matter of Public Concern:

I believe it critical that the reader know the importance of our 1st Amendment right when it comes to matters of public concern. Please read the federal rules and traditional doctrine on the matter as too many public servants are violating our rights. Names are specifically shared because millions of public dollars are at stake for their actions which invoke our 1st amendment rights. We must protect the government of the people.

The following code of Federal Regulations reaches our highest public leaders, and each state has similar ethic requirements per state law. The first written words "Public service is a public trust" are the words we trust, believe in and hope to be there for us when we petition the government or as government leaders perform their daily duties.:

*5 CFR § 2635.101 - Basic obligation of public service.*

*(a) **Public service is a public trust.** Each employee has a responsibility to the United States Government and its citizens to place loyalty to the Constitution, laws and ethical principles above private gain. To ensure that every citizen can have complete confidence in the integrity of the Federal Government, each employee shall respect and adhere to the principles of ethical conduct set forth in this section, as well as the implementing standards contained in this part and in supplemental agency regulations.*

## Matters of Public Concern:
https://www.lawinsider.com/dictionary/matter-of-public-concern

*Matter of public concern means a violation of state, federal, or municipal law, regulation, or ordinance; a danger to public health or safety; gross mismanagement, substantial waste of funds, or clear abuse of authority; a matter that the office of the ombudsman has accepted for investigation; or interference or failure to cooperate with the Legislative Budget and Audit Committee.*

*Matter of public concern means any matter on which it is in the interest of the public to be published, including but not limited to matters concerning all branches of government, politics, public health and safety, law enforcement, administration of justice, consumer and social interest, the environment, economic matters, the exercise of power, science, art and culture.*

Libel: https://www.law.cornell.edu/wex/libel

I intentionally cited sources next to all quotes to help the reader find the facts. I encourage you to search out the original sources to secure any additional details that the author may have quoted.

With equal rights, our communities can thrive. With equal rights, our cities can be full of healthy and balanced communities.

Brian K. Rice

Made in the USA
Columbia, SC
09 February 2024

31082433R00143